LONDON TO LADYSMITH
VIA
PRETORIA

BY
WINSTON SPENCER CHURCHILL

Scrawny Goat Books

London to Ladysmith via Pretoria

By Winston Spencer Churchill

First published 1900

This edition 2022

Scrawny Goat Books
124 City Road
London, EC1V 2NX

scrawnygoatbooks.com

ISBN 978-1-64764-512-0

Contents

Introductory Note	1
Chapter I: Steaming South	3
Chapter II: The State of the Game	11
Chapter III: Along the Southern Frontier	18
Chapter IV: In Natal	23
Chapter V: A Cruise in the Armoured Train	28
Chapter VI: Distant Guns	35
Chapter VII: The Fate of the Armoured Train	44
Chapter VIII: Prisoners of War	56
Chapter IX: Through the Dutch Camps	64
Chapter X: In Afrikander Bonds	85
Chapter XI: I Escape from the Boers	104
Chapter XII: Back to the British Lines	121
Chapter XIII: Christmas and New Year	133
Chapter XIV: A Military Demonstration and Some Good News	139
Chapter XV: The Dash for Potgieter's Ferry	146
Chapter XVI: Trichardt's Drift and the Affair of Acton Homes	157
Chapter XVII: The Battle of Spion Kop	171
Chapter XVIII: Through the Five Days' Action	182
Chapter XIX: A Fresh Effort and an Army Chaplain	195
Chapter XX: The Combat of Vaal Krantz	200

.../continued

Contents (continued)

Chapter XXI: Hussar Hill	210
Chapter XXII: The Engagement of Monte Cristo	217
Chapter XXIII: The Passage of the Tugela	227
Chapter XXIV: The Battle of Pieters: The Third Day	235
Chapter XXV: Upon Majuba Day	246
Chapter XXVI: The Relief of Ladysmith	254
Chapter XXVII: After the Siege	264
Index	281

List of Illustrations:

The author in his uniform of the South African Light Horse, Natal, 1900.	2
The armoured train which was deployed to Natal, one of four which were made in the Cape at the beginning of the war. Later models were far more substantial.	43
Winston Churchill, right front, wearing soft cap, as a prisoner of war, 1889.	57
Boer artillery and soldiers during the Siege of Ladysmith.	83
A Troop, Natal Carabineers, 1899.	83
Winston Churchill, fourth from the left (back to camera) disembarks at Pretoria train station, a prisoner of the Boers.	84
States Model Schools	105

A reward poster circulated after the author's escape. It translates as follows:

Twenty-five Pounds) REWARD is offered by the Sub-Commis-

List of Illustrations (continued)

sion of he fifth division, on behalf of the Special Constable of the said division, to anyone who brings the escaped prisoner of war CHURCHILL, dead or alive to this office. For the Sub-commission of the fifth division, Lodewyk de Haas, Sec.   119

Winston Churchill on his arrival back in Durban.   120

The Theatre of Operations in Natal   123

A Naval 4.7 inch gun in action, Natal.   132

Troops of the Dublin Fusiliers in action, Natal.   132

Pom Pom Bridge at Thukela Heights near Ladysmith.   137

British artillery in action.   138

Much to the Boers' astonishment, the British Army routinely deployed observation balloons to help determine battlefield strategy.   145

Plan of Potgieter's Ferry   153

Winston Churchill at the front.   156

General White and staff, Ladysmith.   156

Plan of position at Monte Cristo   223

Area of operations Colenso - Ladysmith.   226

Plan of the Colenso Position   230

Boer artillery outside Ladysmith.   263

General Buller enters Ladysmith.   263

DEDICATION

THIS COLLECTION OF LETTERS IS INSCRIBED TO

THE STAFF OF THE

NATAL GOVERNMENT RAILWAY

WHOSE CAREFUL AND COURAGEOUS DISCHARGE OF

THEIR EVERY-DAY DUTIES

AMID THE PERILS OF WAR

HAS MADE THEM HONOURABLY CONSPICUOUS

EVEN AMONG THEIR FELLOW COLONISTS

INTRODUCTORY NOTE

This small book is mainly a personal record of my adventures and impressions during the first five months of the African War. It may also be found to give a tolerably coherent account of the operations conducted by Sir Redvers Buller for the Relief of Ladysmith.

The correspondence of which it is mainly composed appeared in the columns of the *Morning Post* newspaper, and I propose, if I am not interrupted by the accidents of war, to continue the series of letters.

The stir and tumult of a camp do not favour calm or sustained thought, and whatever is written herein must be regarded simply as the immediate effect produced by men powerfully moved, and scenes swiftly changing upon what I hope is a truth-seeking mind.

The fact that a man's life depends upon my discretion compels me to omit an essential part of the story of my escape from the Boers; but if the book and its author survive the war, and when the British flag is firmly planted at Bloemfontein and Pretoria, I shall hasten to fill the gap in the narrative.

WINSTON S. CHURCHILL.

March 10, 1900.

The author in his uniform of the South African Light Horse, Natal, 1900.

CHAPTER I
STEAMING SOUTH

R.M.S. 'Dunottar Castle,' at sea: October 26, 1899.

The last cry of 'Any more for the shore?' had sounded, the last good-bye had been said, the latest pressman or photographer had scrambled ashore, and all Southampton was cheering wildly along a mile of pier and promontory when at 6 P.M., on October 14, the Royal Mail steamer 'Dunottar Castle' left her moorings and sailed with Sir Redvers Buller[1] for the Cape.

For a space the decks remained crowded with the passengers who, while the sound of many voices echoed in their ears, looked back towards the shores swiftly fading in the distance and the twilight, and wondered whether, and if so when, they would come safe home again; then everyone hurried to his cabin, arranged his luggage, and resigned himself to the voyage.

What an odious affair is a modern sea journey! In ancient times there were greater discomforts and perils; but they were recognised.

A man took ship prepared for the worst. Nowadays he expects the best as a matter of course, and is, therefore, disappointed.

Besides, how slowly we travel! In the sixteenth century nobody minded taking five months to get anywhere. But a fortnight is a large slice out of the nineteenth century; and the child of civilisation, long petted by Science, impatiently complains to his indulgent guardian of all delay in travel, and petulantly calls on her to complete her task and finally eliminate the factor of distance from human calculations. A fortnight is a long time in modern life. It is also a long time in modern war—especially at the beginning.

---

1 General Sir Redvers Henry Buller (1839–1908) served as Commander-in-Chief of British Forces in South Africa during the early months of the war, and then commanded the army in Natal until November 1900. He was widely blamed for the initial British setbacks in the opening stages of the war.

To be without news for a fortnight at any time is annoying. To be without news for a fortnight now is a torture. And this voyage lasts more than a fortnight! At the very outset of our enterprise we are compelled to practise Mr. Morley's[2] policy of patience.

We left London amid rumours of all kinds. The Metropolis was shrouded in a fog of credulous uncertainty, broken only by the sinister gleam of the placarded lie or the croak of the newsman. Terrible disasters had occurred and had been contradicted; great battles were raging—unconfirmed; and beneath all this froth the tide of war was really flowing, and no man could shut his eyes to grave possibilities.

Then the ship sailed, and all was silence—a heaving silence. But Madeira was scarcely four days' journey. There we should find the answers to many questions. At Madeira, however, we learned nothing, but nothing, though satisfactory, is very hard to understand. Why did they declare war if they had nothing up their sleeves? Why are they wasting time now? Such were the questions.

Then we sailed again, and again silence shut down, this time, however, on a more even keel. Speculation arises out of ignorance. Many and various are the predictions as to what will be the state of the game when we shall have come to anchor in Table Bay.

Forecasts range from the capture of Pretoria by Sir George White[3] and the confinement of President Kruger in the deepest level beneath the Johannesburg Exchange, on the one hand, to the surrender of Cape Town to the Boers, the proclamation of

---

[2] John Morley, 1st Viscount Morley of Blackburn, (1838–1923) was a British Liberal statesman, writer and newspaper editor. Elected as a Member of Parliament for the Liberal Party in 1883, he served as Chief Secretary for Ireland in 1886 and between 1892 and 1895; Secretary of State for India between 1905 and 1910 and again in 1911; and Lord President of the Council between 1910 and 1914. Morley was best known for his writings and his staunch opposition to imperialism and Britain's involvement in the Second Anglo-Boer War.

[3] Field Marshal Sir George White (1835–1912) served in India, Afghanistan and Burma before being deployed to Natal, where he commanded the besieged town of Ladysmith.

Chapter 1: Steaming South

Mr. Schreiner[4] as King of South Africa, and a fall of two points in Rand Mines on the other. Between these wild extremes all shades of opinion are represented. Only one possibility is unanimously excluded—an inconclusive peace.

There are on board officers who travelled this road eighteen years ago with Lord Roberts, and reached Cape Town only to return by the next boat. But no one anticipates such a result this time.

Monotony is the characteristic of a modern voyage, and who shall describe it? The lover of realism might suggest that writing the same paragraph over and over again would enable the reader to experience its weariness, if he were truly desirous of so doing.

But I hesitate to take such a course, and trust that some of these lines even once repeated may convey some inkling of the dullness of the days. Monotony of view—for we live at the centre of a complete circle of sea and sky; monotony of food—for all things taste the same on board ship; monotony of existence—for each day is but a barren repetition of the last; all fall to the lot of the passenger on great waters.

It was malevolent to try to bring the realisation home to others. Yet all earthly evils have their compensations, and even monotony is not without its secret joy.

For a time we drop out of the larger world, with its interests and its obligations, and become the independent citizens of a tiny State:—a Utopian State where few toil and none go hungry—bounded on all sides by the sea and vassal only to the winds and waves. Here during a period which is too long while it lasts, too short when it is over, we may placidly reflect on the busy world that lies behind and the tumult that is before us.

The journalists read books about South Africa; the politician—were the affair still in the domain of words—might examine the justice of the quarrel. The Headquarter Staff pore over maps or calculate the sizes of camps and entrenchments; and

---

4 William Philip Schreiner (1857–1919) was a barrister, politician, statesman and Prime Minister of the Cape Colony in 1898.

in the meantime, the great ship lurches steadily forward on her course, carrying to the south at seventeen miles an hour schemes and intentions of war.

But let me record the incidents rather than their absence.

One day the first shoal of flying fish is seen—a flight of glittering birds that, flushed by the sudden approach of the vessel, skim away over the waters and turn in the cover of a white-topped wave.

On another we crossed the Equator. Neptune and his consort boarded us near the forecastle and paraded round the ship in state. Never have I seen such a draggle-tailed divinity. An important feature in the ritual which he prescribes is the shaving and ducking of all who have not passed the line before.

But our attitude was strictly Erastian, and the demigod retired discomfited to the second class, where from the sounds which arose, he seemed to find more punctilious votaries.

On the 23rd we sighted a sail—or rather the smoke of another steamer. As the comparatively speedy 'Dunottar Castle' overtook the stranger everybody's interest was aroused.

Under the scrutiny of many brand-new telescopes and field glasses—for all want to see as much of a war as possible—she developed into the 'Nineveh,' hired transport carrying the Australian Lancers to the Cape.

Signals were exchanged. The vessels drew together, and after an hour's steaming we passed her almost within speaking distance. The General went up to the bridge. The Lancers crowded the bulwarks and rigging of the 'Nineveh' and one of them waggled a flag violently.

An officer on our ship replied with a pocket-handkerchief.

The Australians asked questions: 'Is Sir Redvers Buller on board?' The answer 'Yes' was signalled back, and immediately the Lancers gave three tremendous cheers, waving their broad-brimmed hats and gesticulating with energy while the steam siren emitted a frantic whoop of salutation.

Chapter 1: Steaming South

Then the speed of the larger vessel told, and we drew ahead of the transport until her continued cheers died away.

She signalled again: 'What won the Cesarewitch?' But the distance was now too great for us to learn whether the answer gave satisfaction or not.

We have a party of cinematographers on board, and when they found that we were going to speak the 'Nineveh' they bustled about preparing their apparatus. But the cumbrous appliances took too long to set up, and, to the bitter disappointment of the artists, the chance of making a moving picture was lost for ever; and indeed it was a great pity, because the long green transport, pitching in the sea, now burying her bows in foam, now showing the red paint of her bottom, her decks crowded with the active brown figures of the soldiers, her halyards bright with signal flags, was a scene well worth recording even if it had not been the greeting given in mid-ocean to the commander of the army by the warlike contingent which the need or convenience of the Empire had drawn from the Antipodes.

South of the line the weather cools rapidly, and various theories are advanced to explain the swift change. According to some, it is due to the masses of ice at the Antarctic Pole; others contend that it is because we are further from the land.

But whatever the cause may be, the fall in temperature produces a rise in spirits, and under greyer skies everyone develops activity. The consequence of this is the organisation of athletic sports. A committee is appointed. Sir Redvers Buller becomes President.

A two days' meeting is arranged, and on successive afternoons the more energetic passengers race violently to and fro on the decks, belabour each other with bolsters, or tumble into unforeseen troughs of water to their huge contentment and the diversion of the rest.

Occasionally there are light gusts of controversy.

It is Sunday. The parson proposes to read the service. The captain objects. He insists on the maintenance of naval supremacy.

On board ship, 'or at any rate on board this ship,' no one but the captain reads the service.

The minister, a worthy Irishman, abandons the dispute—not without regret.

'Any other clergyman of the Church of England,' he observes with warmth, 'would have told the captain to go to Hell.'

Then there is to be a fancy-dress ball. Opinions are divided. On the one part it is urged that fancy dress balls are healthy and amusing. On the other, that they are exceedingly tiresome. The discussion is prolonged. In the end the objectors are overruled—still objecting. Such are the politics of the State.

Inoculation against enteric fever proceeds daily. The doctors lecture in the saloon.

One injection of serum protects; a second secures the subject against attacks. Wonderful statistics are quoted in support of the experiment. Nearly everyone is convinced.

The operations take place forthwith, and the next day sees haggard forms crawling about the deck in extreme discomfort and high fever. The day after, however, all have recovered and rise gloriously immune.

Others, like myself, remembering that we still stand only on the threshold of pathology, remain unconvinced, resolved to trust to 'health and the laws of health.' But if they will, invent a system of inoculation against bullet wounds I will hasten to submit myself.

Yesterday we passed a homeward-bound liner, who made great efforts to signal to us, but as she was a Union boat, the captain refused to go near enough to read the flags, and we still remain ignorant of the state of the war.

If the great lines of steamships to the Cape were to compete against each other, as do those of the Atlantic, by increasing their speeds, by lowering their rates, by improving the food and accommodation, no one would complain, but it is difficult to see how the public can be the gainers by the silly antagonism I have described. However, the end is drawing very near, and since we have had a safe and prosperous journey criticism may well waive the opportunity. Yet there are few among the travellers who will not experience a keen feeling of relief in exchanging the pettiness, the monotony, and the isolation of the voyage for the activity of great enterprise and the interest of real affairs: a relief which may, perhaps, be shared by the reader of these letters.

Yet if he has found the account of a dull voyage dull, he should not complain; for is not that successful realism?

October 29.

News at last! This morning we sighted a sail—a large homeward-bound steamer, spreading her canvas to catch the trades, and with who should say what tidings on board.

We crowded the decks, and from every point of view telescopes, field glasses, and cameras were directed towards the stranger.

She passed us at scarcely two hundred yards, and as she did so her crew and company, giving three hearty cheers, displayed a long black board, on which was written in white paint: 'Boers defeated; three battles; Penn Symons killed.' There was a little gasp of excitement.

Everyone stepped back from the bulwarks. Those who had not seen ran eagerly up to ask what had happened.

A dozen groups were formed, a hum of conversation arose, and meanwhile the vessels separated—for the pace of each was swift—and in a few moments the homeward bound lay far in our wake.

What does it mean—this scrap of intelligence which tells so much and leaves so much untold? To-morrow night we shall know all. This at least is certain: there has been fierce fighting in Natal, and, under Heaven, we have held our own: perhaps more.

'Boers defeated.' Let us thank God for that. The brave garrisons have repelled the invaders. The luck has turned at last.

The crisis is over, and the army now on the seas may move with measured strides to effect a final settlement that is both wise and just. In that short message eighteen years of heartburnings are healed.

The abandoned colonist, the shamed soldier, the 'cowardly Englishman,' the white flag, the 'How about Majuba?'—all gone for ever.

At last— 'the Boers defeated.' Hurrah! Hurrah! Hurrah!

So, Sir Penn Symons is killed! Well, no one would have laid down his life more gladly in such a cause. Twenty years ago the merest chance saved him from the massacre at Isandhlwana, and Death promoted him in an afternoon from subaltern to senior captain. Thenceforward his rise was rapid. He commanded the First Division of the Tirah Expeditionary Force among the mountains with prudent skill. His brigades had no misfortunes: his rearguards came safely into camp. In the spring of 1898, when the army lay around Fort Jumrood, looking forward to a fresh campaign, I used often to meet him.

Everyone talked of Symons, of his energy, of his jokes, of his enthusiasm. It was Symons who had built a racecourse on the stony plain; who had organised the Jumrood Spring Meeting; who won the principal event himself, to the delight of the private soldiers, with whom he was intensely popular; who, moreover, was to be first and foremost if the war with the tribes broke out again; and who was entrusted with much of the negotiations with their *jirgas*.

Dinner with Symons in the mud tower of Jumrood Fort was an experience. The memory of many tales of sport and war remains. At the end, the General would drink the old Peninsular toasts: 'Our Men,' 'Our Women,' 'Our Religion,' 'Our Swords,' 'Ourselves,' 'Sweethearts and Wives,' and 'Absent Friends'—one for every night in the week.

The night when I dined the toast was 'Our Men.' May the State in her necessities find others like him!

CHAPTER II
THE STATE OF THE GAME

Cape Town: November 1, 1899.

The long-drawn voyage came to an end at last.

On the afternoon of October 30, we sighted land, and looking westward I perceived what looked like a dark wave of water breaking the smooth rim of the horizon.

A short time developed the wave into the rocks and slopes of Robben Island—a barren spot inhabited by lepers, poisonous serpents, and dogs undergoing quarantine.

Then with the darkness we entered Table Bay, and, steaming slowly, reached the anchorage at ten o'clock.

Another hour of waiting followed until the tugboat obeyed the signal; but at last, she ran alongside, and there stepped on board a Man Who Knew.

Others with despatches pushed roughly through the crowd of soldiers, officers, passengers, and war correspondents to the General's cabin.

We caught the Man Who Knew, however, and, setting him half way up the ladder to the hurricane deck, required him forthwith to tell us of the war. Doubtless you have been well informed of all, or at any rate of much, that has passed.

The man told his story quickly, with an odd quiver of excitement in his voice, and the audience—perhaps we were 300—listened breathless.

Then for the first time we heard of Elandslaagte, of Glencoe, of Rietfontein, a tale of stubborn, well-fought fights with honour for both sides, triumph for neither.

'Tell us about the losses—who are killed and wounded?' we asked this wonderful man. I think he was a passage agent or something like that.

So he told us—and among the group of officers gathered above him on the hurricane deck I saw now one, now another, turn away, and hurry out of the throng.

A gentleman I had met on the voyage—Captain Weldon—asked questions. 'Do you know any names of killed in the Leicesters?'

The man reflected. He could not be sure: he thought there was an officer named Weldon killed—oh, yes! he remembered there were two Weldons—one killed, one wounded, but he did not know which was in the Leicesters.

'Tell us about Mafeking,' said someone else. Then we heard about Mafeking—the armoured trains, the bombardment, the sorties, the dynamite wagons—all, in fact, that is yet known of what may become an historic defence.

'And how many Boers are killed?' cried a private soldier from the back.

The man hesitated, but the desire to please was strong within him. 'More than two thousand,' he said, and a fierce shout of joy answered him.

The crowd of brown uniforms under the electric clusters broke up into loud-voiced groups; some hastened to search for newspapers, some to repeat what they had heard to others; only a few leaned against the bulwarks and looked long and silently towards the land, where the lights of Cape Town, its streets, its quays, and its houses gleamed from the night like diamonds on black velvet.

It is along casualty list of officers—of the best officers in the world. The brave and accomplished General of Glencoe; Colonel Chisholme, who brought the 9th Lancers out of action in Afghanistan; Sherston, who managed the Indian Polo Association; Haldane, Sir William Lockhart's brilliant aide-de-camp; Barnes, adjutant of the 4th Hussars, who played back of our team and went with me to Cuba; Brooke, who had tempted fortune more often than anyone else in the last four years—Chitral, Matabeleland, Samana, Tira, Atbara, and Omdurman—and fifty others who are only names to me, but are dear and precious to many, all

Chapter II: The State of the Game

lying under the stony soil or filling the hospitals at Pietermaritzburg and Durban.

Two thousand Boers killed! I wish I could believe there were.

Next morning Sir Redvers Buller landed in state. Sir F. Forestier-Walker and his staff came to meet him. The ship was decked out in bunting from end to end.

A guard of honour of the Duke of Edinburgh's Volunteers lined the quay; a mounted escort attended the carriage; an enormous crowd gathered outside the docks.

At nine o'clock precisely the General stepped on to the gangway. The crew and stokers of the 'Dunottar Castle' gave three hearty cheers; the cinematograph buzzed loudly; forty cameras clicked; the guard presented arms, and the harbour batteries thundered the salute.

Then the carriage drove briskly off into the town through streets bright with waving flags and black with cheering people.

So Sir Redvers Buller came back again to South Africa, the land where his first military reputation was made, where he won his Victoria Cross, the land which—let us pray—he will leave having successfully discharged the heavy task confided to him by the Imperial Government.

Now, what is the situation which confronts the General and the army? I will adventure an explanation, though the picture of war moves very swiftly. In their dealing with the military republics which had become so formidable a power throughout the Cape, the Ministers who were responsible for the security of our South African possessions were compelled to reckon with two volumes of public opinion—British and colonial.

The colonial opinion was at its best (from our point of view) about three months ago. But the British opinion was still unformed. The delays and diplomatic disputes which have gradually roused the nation to a sense of its responsibilities and perils, and which were absolutely necessary if we were to embark on the struggle united, have had an opposite effect out here.

The attempts to satisfy the conscientious public by giving the republics every possible opportunity to accept our terms and the delays in the despatch of troops which were an expensive tribute to the argument 'Do not seek peace with a sword,' have been misinterpreted in South Africa.

The situation in the Cape Colony has become much graver. We have always been told of the wonderful loyalty of the Dutch. It is possible that had war broken out three months ago that loyalty would have been demonstrated for all time.

War after three months of hesitation—for such it was considered—has proved too severe a test, and it is no exaggeration to say that a considerable part of the Colony trembles on the verge of rebellion.

On such a state of public opinion the effect of any important military reverse would be lamentable. Nor is the military position such as to exclude anxiety.

The swift flame of war ran in a few days around the whole circle of the republican frontiers.

Far away to the north there was a skirmish at Tuli. On the west, Khama's[1] territories are threatened with invasion. Mafeking is surrounded, isolated, and manfully defending itself against continual attack.

Vryburg has been treacherously surrendered by its rebel inhabitants to the enemy.

Kimberley offers a serene front to a hesitating attack, and even retaliates with armoured trains and other enterprises. The southern frontier is armed, and menaced, and the expectation of collision is strong.

But it is on the eastern side that the Boers have concentrated their greatest energies. They have gone Nap on Natal. The configuration of the country favours an invader. The reader has scarcely to look at the map, with which he is already familiar, to realise

---

1 The leader of the Tswana tribe, Khama III (1837?–1923), whose people occupied (and still occupy) the territory known in the present day as Botswana, and previously as Bechuanaland.

Chapter II: The State of the Game

how strategically powerful the Boer position was and is. The long tongue of plain running up into the mountains could be entered from both sides. The communications of the advanced garrisons would be assailed: their retreat imperilled.

The Boers seemed bound to clear northern Natal of the troops.

If, on the other hand, they were, or should now be, suddenly driven back on their own country, they have only to retire up the tongue of plain, with their exposed front narrowing every mile between the mountains, and await their pursuers on the almost inexpugnable position of Laing's Nek.

Appreciating all this, their leaders have wisely resolved to put forth their main strength against the force in Natal, and by crushing it to rouse their sympathisers within the Cape Colony.

Should they succeed either on this front or on any other to a serious extent, though the disaffection would not take a very violent form, for all the bravoes have already joined the enemy, the general insecurity would demand the employment of an army corps in addition to that already on the seas.

A democratic Government cannot go to war unless the country is behind it, and until it has general support must not place itself in a position whence, without fighting, there is no retreat.

The difficulty of rallying public opinion in the face of the efforts of Mr. Morley, Mr. Courtney,[2] Sir William Harcourt,[3] and others have caused a most dangerous delay in the despatch of reinforcements.

War has been aggravated by the Peace Party; and thus these humanitarian gentlemen are personally—for they occupy no official position—responsible for the great loss of life. They will find their several consolations: Mr. Morley will rejoice that he

---

2 Leonard Henry Courtney, 1st Baron Courtney of Penwith (1832–1918) was elected to Parliament as a liberal, and was one of the foremost opponents of imperialism and militarism. He was forced to resign in 1900 because of his antiwar activities.
3 Sir William Harcourt (1827–1904), a liberal politician and leader of the opposition. Well-known for his absolute opposition to the war in South Africa.

London to Ladysmith via Pretoria

has faithfully pursued Mr. Gladstone's policy in South Africa; Mr. Courtney that he has been consistent at all costs; Sir William Harcourt that he has hampered the Government.

But for those who lose their sons and brothers in a quarrel thus unnecessarily extended, there will only remain vain regrets, and to the eyewitness only a bitter anger. For the last three months the Imperial Government has been in the unpleasant position of watching its adversaries grow continually stronger without being able to make adequate counter-preparations. But when once this initial disability has been stated, it must also be admitted that the course of the military operations has been—apart from their success or failure—very lucky.

The Boers had the advantage of drawing first blood, and the destruction of the armoured train near Mafeking was magnified by them, as by the sensational Press in Great Britain, into a serious disaster.

A very bad effect was produced in the undecided districts—it is perhaps wiser not to specify them at this moment. But a few days later another armoured train ran out from Kimberley, and its Maxim guns killed five Boers without any loss to the troops. The magnifying process was also applied to this incident with equal though opposite results.

Then came the news of the battle of Glencoe. The first accounts, which were very properly controlled—for we are at war with the pen as well as the sword—told only of the bravery of the troops, of the storming of the Boer position, and of the capture of prisoners.

That the troops had suffered the heavier loss, that the Boers had retired to further positions in rear of the first, drawing their artillery with them, and that General Yule[4] had retreated by forced marches to Ladysmith after the victory—for tactical victory it undoubtedly was—leaked into Cape Colony very gradually; nor was it until a week later that it was known that the wounded

---

4 Brigadier-General James Yule (1847–1920) briefly acted as General Officer Commanding the 4th Division after the dearm of General Symons.

Chapter II: The State of the Game

had been left behind, and that the camp with all stores and baggage, except ammunition, had fallen into the enemy's hands.

Before that happened the news of Elandslaagte had arrived, and this brilliant action, which reflects no less credit on Generals French[5] and Hamilton[6] who fought it than on Sir George White who ordered it, dazzled all eyes, so that the sequel to Glencoe was unnoticed, or at any rate produced little effect on public opinion.

The Natal Field Force is now concentrated at Ladysmith, and confronts in daily opposition the bulk of the Boer Army.

Though the numbers of the enemy are superior, and their courage claims the respect of their professional antagonists, it is difficult to believe that any serious reverse can take place in that quarter, and meanwhile many thousand soldiers are on the seas.

But the fact is now abundantly plain to those who are acquainted with the local conditions and with the Boer character, that a fierce, certainly bloody, possibly prolonged struggle lies before the army of South Africa.

The telegrams, however, which we receive from Great Britain of the national feeling, of the bye-election, of Lord Rosebery's speech,[7] are full of encouragement and confidence.

'At last,' says the British colonist, as he shoulders his rifle and marches out to fight, no less bravely than any soldier (witness the casualty lists), for the ties which bind South Africa to the Empire—'at last they have made up their minds at home.'

---

5 Field Marshal John French (1852-1925) became, like like this book's author, a national hero at home in Britain during the war.
6 Sir Ian Hamilton (1853–1947) was a long-serving office who was wounded during the Battle of Majuba during the First Anglo-Boer War.
7 Archibald Primrose, 5th Earl of Rosebery (1847–1929), was a leading Liberal politician and former Prime Minister who supported the war in South Africa during a speech delivered in the House of Commons on October 11, 1899.

CHAPTER III
ALONG THE SOUTHERN FRONTIER

East London: November 5, 1899.

We have left Headquarters busy with matters that as yet concern no one but themselves in the Mount Nelson Hotel at Cape Town—a most excellent and well-appointed establishment, which may be thoroughly appreciated after a sea voyage, and which, since many of the leading *Uitlanders*[1] have taken up their abode there during the war, is nicknamed 'The Helot's Rest.' Last night I started by rail for East London, whence a small ship carries the weekly English mail to Natal, and so by this circuitous route I hope to reach Ladysmith on Sunday morning.

We have thus gained three days on our friends who proceed by the 'Dunottar Castle,' and who were mightily concerned when they heard—too late to follow—of our intentions.

But though it is true in this case that the longest way round is the shortest way, there were possibilities of our journey being interrupted, because the line from De Aar Junction to Naauwpoort runs parallel to the southern frontier of the Free State, and though hostile enterprises have not yet been attempted against this section of the railways they must always be expected.

Railway travelling in South Africa is more expensive but just as comfortable as in India. Lying-down accommodation is provided for all, and meals can be obtained at convenient stopping places. The train, which is built on the corridor system, runs smoothly over the rails—so smoothly, indeed, that I found no difficulty in writing.

The sun is warm, and the air keen and delicious. But the scenery would depress the most buoyant spirits. We climbed up the mountains during the night, and with the daylight the train was in the middle of the Great Karroo. Wherefore was this misera-

---
1 Literally, "foreigners." The English-speakers who swarmed to the Witwatersrand in the Boer Republic of the Transvaal

Chapter III: Along the Southern Frontier

ble land of stone and scrub created? Huge mounds of crumbling rock, fashioned by the rains into the most curious and unexpected shapes, rise from the gloomy desert of the plain.

Yet, though the Karroo looks a hopeless wilderness, flocks of sheep at distant intervals—one sheep requires six hundred acres of this scrappy pasture for nourishment—manage to subsist; and in consequence, now and again the traveller sees some far-off farm.

We look about eagerly for signs of war. Little is as yet to be seen, and the Karroo remains unsympathetic. But all along the southern frontier of the Free State the expectation of early collision grows.

The first sign after leaving Cape Town is the Proclamation against treason published by Sir Alfred Milner. The notice-boards of the railway stations are freely placarded with the full text in English and Dutch, beginning with 'Whereas a state of war exists between the Government of her Majesty and the Governments of the South African Republic and of the Orange Free State. . ." continuing to enjoin good and loyal behaviour on all, detailing the pains and penalties for disobedience, and ending with 'God save the Queen.' Both races have recorded their opinions on their respective versions: the British by underlining the penalties, the Dutch by crossing out the first word of 'God Save the Queen.' It is signed 'A. Milner,' and below, in bitter irony, 'W.P. Schreiner.'

Beyond Matjesfontein every bridge, and even every culvert, is watched by a Kaffir[2] with a flag, so that the train runs no risk of coming on unexpected demolitions.

---

[2] The term "kaffir"—widely used at the time this book was originally written, by both Europeans and Africans, was not intended in a racially-derogatory manner, but merely as a classification. The word originally merely meant "unbeliever," or "infidel," and was used to refer to the fact that the Africans were not Christians at the time of the first contact between the races. It originated in the Arabic word "kufur," which was, *and still is*, used to refer to non-Muslims and was originally applied to Christians. In the present day, however, the word "kaffir" has become racially charged, is widely regarded as derogatory, and its use is discouraged.

On the road to De Aar, we passed the second half of the Brigade Division of Artillery, which sailed so long ago from the Mersey in the notorious transports 'Zibengla' and 'Zayathla.' The gunners were hurrying to the front in three long trains, each taking half a battery complete with guns, horses, and men.

All were light-hearted and confident, as soldiers going off to the wars always are, and in this case their, satisfaction at being on land after five weeks of uncomfortable voyage in antiquated ships was easily to be understood. But this is no time for reproaches.

At Beaufort West grave news awaited the mail, and we learned of the capitulation of twelve hundred soldiers near Ladysmith. It is generally believed that this will precipitate a rising of the Dutch throughout this part of the colony and an invasion by the commandos now gathered along the Orange River.

The Dutch farmers talk loudly and confidently of 'our victories,' meaning those of the Boers, and the racial feeling runs high.

But the British colonists have an implicit faith—marvellous when the past is remembered—in the resolve of the Imperial Government and of the nation never to abandon them again.

At De Aar, the stage of our journey which may be said to have been uncertain began. Armoured trains patrol the line; small parties of armed police guard the bridges; infantry and artillery detachments occupy the towns.

De Aar, Colesberg, and Stormberg are garrisoned as strongly as the present limited means allow, and all the forces, regulars and volunteers alike, are full of enthusiasm. But, on the other hand, the reports of Boer movements seem to indicate that a hostile advance is imminent.

The Colesberg bridge across the Orange River has been seized by the enemy, the line between Bethulie and Colesberg has just been cut, and each train from De Aar to Stormberg is expected to be the last to pass unassailed. We, however, slept peacefully through the night, and, passing Colesberg safely, arrived at Stormberg, beyond which all is again secure.

Chapter III: Along the Southern Frontier

Stormberg Junction stands at the southern end of a wide expanse of rolling grass country, and though the numerous rocky hills, or kopjes as they are called, which rise inconveniently on all sides, make its defence by a small force difficult, a large force occupying an extended position would be secure. Here we found the confirmation of many rumours.

The news of a Boer advance on Burghersdorp, twenty-five miles away, is, it seems, well founded, and when our train arrived the evacuation of Stormberg by its garrison, of a half-battalion of the Berkshire Regiment, 350 men of the Naval Brigade, a company of mounted infantry, and a few guns, was busily proceeding.

The sailors were already in their train, and only prevented from starting by the want of an engine. The infantry and artillery were to start in a few hours. It is rather an unsatisfactory business, though the arrival of more powerful forces will soon restore the situation.

Stormberg is itself an important railway junction. For more than a week, the troops have been working night and day to put it in a state of defence. Little redoubts have been built on the kopjes,[3] entrenchments have been dug, and the few houses near the station are already strongly fortified.

I was shown one of these by the young officer in charge. The approaches were, cleared of everything except wire fences and entanglements; the massive walls were loopholed, the windows barricaded with sandbags, and the rooms inside broken one into the other for convenience in moving about. Its garrison of twenty-five men and its youthful commander surveyed the work with pride. They had laid in stores of all kinds for ten days, and none doubted that Fort Chabrol, as they called it, would stand a gallant siege. Then suddenly had come the message to evacuate and retreat. So it was with the others. The train with the naval detachment and its guns steamed off, and we gave it a feeble cheer. Another train awaited the Berkshires.

The mounted infantry were already on the march.

---

3 Small hills, from the Dutch word for "little heads".

'Mayn't we even blow up this lot?' said a soldier, pointing to the house he had helped to fortify. But there was no such order, only this one which seemed to pervade the air: 'The enemy are coming. Retreat—retreat—retreat!'

The stationmaster—one of the best types of Englishmen to be found on a long journey—was calm and cheerful. 'No more traffic north of this,' he said. 'Yours was the last train through from De Aar. I shall send away all my men by the special to-night. And that's the end as far as Stormberg goes.'

'And you?'

'Oh, I shall stay. I have lived here for twelve years, and am well known. Perhaps I may be able to protect the company's property.'

While we waited the armoured train returned from patrolling—an engine between two carriages cloaked from end to end with thick plates and slabs of blue-grey iron. It had seen nothing of the advancing Boers, but, like us and like the troops, it had to retire southwards.

There were fifty Uitlanders from Johannesburg on the platform. They had been employed entrenching; now they were bundled back again towards East London.

So we left Stormberg in much anger and some humiliation, and jolted away towards the open sea, where British supremacy is not yet contested by the Boer. At Molteno we picked up a hundred volunteers—fine-looking fellows all eager to encounter the enemy, but much surprised at the turn events had taken. They, too, were ordered to fall back. The Boers were advancing, and to despondent minds even the rattle of the train seemed to urge 'Retreat, retreat, retreat.'

I do not desire to invest this wise and prudent though discouraging move with more than its proper importance. Anything is better than to leave small garrisons to be overwhelmed. Until the Army Corps comes, the situation will continue to be unsatisfactory, and the ground to be recovered afterwards will increase in extent. But with the arrival of powerful and well-equipped forces the tide of war will surely turn.

CHAPTER IV
IN NATAL

Estcourt: November 6, 1899.

The reader may remember that we started post haste from Cape Town, and, having the good fortune to pass along the southern frontier from De Aar to Stormberg by the last train before the interruption of traffic, had every hope of reaching Ladysmith while its investment was incomplete.

I had looked forward to writing an account of our voyage from East London to Durban while on board the vessel; but the weather was so tempestuous, and the little steamer of scarcely 100 tons burthen so buffeted by the waves, that I lay prostrate in all the anguish of sea-sickness, and had no thought for anything else.

Moreover, we were delayed some twenty hours by contrary winds; nor was it until we had passed St. John's that the gale, as if repenting, veered suddenly to the south-west and added as much to our speed as it had formerly delayed us.

With the change of the wind, the violence of the waves to some degree abated, and, though unable to then record them on paper, I had an opportunity of gaining some impressions of the general aspect of the coasts of Pondoland and Natal.

These beautiful countries stretch down to the ocean in smooth slopes of the richest verdure, broken only at intervals by lofty bluffs crowned with forests.

The many rivulets to which the pasture owes its life and the land its richness glide to the shore through deep-set creeks and chines, or plunge over the cliffs in cascades which the strong winds scatter into clouds of spray.

These are regions of possibility, and as we drove along before our now friendly wind I could not but speculate on the future. Here are wide tracts of fertile soil watered by abundant rains. The temperate sun warms the life within the soil. The cooling breeze refreshes the inhabitant. The delicious climate stimulates the vigour of the European. The highway of the sea awaits the produce of his labour.

All Nature smiles, and here at last is a land where white men may rule and prosper. As yet only the indolent Kaffir enjoys its bounty, and, according to the antiquated philosophy of Liberalism, it is to such that it should for ever belong.

But while Englishmen choke and fester in crowded cities, while thousands of babies are born every month who are never to have a fair chance in life, there will be those who will dream another dream of a brave system of State-aided—almost State-compelled—emigration, a scheme of old age pensions that shall anticipate old age, and by preventing paupers terminate itself; a system that shall remove the excess of the old land to provide the deficiency of the new, and shall offer even to the most unfortunate citizen of the Empire fresh air and open opportunity.

And as I pondered on all these things, the face of the country seemed changed.

Thriving ports and townships rose up along the shore, and, upon the hillsides, inland towers, spires, and tall chimneys attested the wealth and industry of men.

Here in front of us was New Brighton; the long shelving ledge of rock was a seawall already made, rows of stately buildings covered the grassy slopes; the shipping of many nations lay in the roadstead; above the whole scene waved *The Flag*, and in the foreground on the sandy beach the great-grandchildren of the crossing-sweeper and the sandwich-man sported by the waves that beat by the Southern Pole, or sang aloud for joy in the beauty of their home and the pride of their race.

And then with a lurch—for the motion was still considerable—I came back from the land of dreams to reality and the hideous fact that Natal is invaded and assailed by the Boer.

The little steamer reached Durban safely at midnight on November 4, and we passed an impatient six hours in a sleeping town waiting for daylight and news. Both came in their turn.

Chapter IV: In Natal

The sun rose, and we learned that Ladysmith was cut off. Still, 'As far as you can as quickly as you can' must be the motto of the war correspondent, and seven o'clock found us speeding inland in the extra coach of a special train carrying the mails.

The hours I passed in Durban were not without occupation. The hospital ship 'Sumatra' lay close to our moorings, and as soon as it was light I visited her to look for friends, and found, alas! several in a sorry plight.

All seemed to be as well as the tenderest care and the most lavish expenditure of money could make them.

All told much the same tale—the pluck and spirit of the troops, the stubborn unpretentious valour of the Boer, the searching musketry. Everyone predicted a prolonged struggle.

'All these colonials tell you,' said an officer severely wounded at Elandslaagte, 'that the Boers only want one good thrashing to satisfy them. Don't you believe it. They mean going through with this to the end. What about our Government?'

And the answer that all were united at home, and that Boer constancy would be met with equal perseverance and greater resources, lighted the pain-drawn features with a hopeful smile.

'Well, I never felt quite safe with those politicians. I can't get about for two months' (he was shot through the thigh), 'but I hope to be in at the death. It's our blood against theirs.'

Pietermaritzburg is sixty miles from Durban, but as the railway zigzags up and down hill and contorts itself into curves that would horrify the domestic engineer, the journey occupies four hours.

The town looks more like Ootacamund[1] than any place I have seen. To those who do not know the delightful hill station of Southern India let me explain that Pietermaritzburg stands in a basin of smooth rolling downs, broken frequently by forests of fir and blue gum trees. It is a sleepy, dead-alive place.

---

1 Ootacamund (now known as Ooty) is located in India, a town surrounded by the Nilgiri Hills founded by a British administrator in 1819.

Even the fact that Colonel Knowle, the military engineer, was busily putting it into a state of defence, digging up its hills, piercing its walls, and encircling it with wire obstructions did not break its apathy.

The 'Times of Natal' struggled to rouse excitement, and placarded its office with the latest telegrams from the front, some of which had reached Pietermaritzburg *via* London.

But the composure of the civil population is a useful factor in war, and I wish it were within the power of my poor pen to bring home to the people of England how excellently the colonists of Natal have deserved of the State.

There are several points to be remembered in this connection. First, the colonists have had many dealings with the Boers. They knew their strength, they feared their animosity. But they have never for one moment lost sight of their obligations as a British colony. Their loyalty has been splendid.

From the very beginning they warned the Imperial Government that their territories would be invaded. Throughout the course of the long negotiations they knew that if war should come, on them would fall the first fury of the storm. Nevertheless, they courageously supported and acclaimed the action of the Ministry.

Now at last there is war. It means a good deal to all of us, but more than to any it comes home to the Natalian. He is invaded; his cattle have been seized by the Boer; his towns are shelled or captured; the most powerful force on which he relies for protection is isolated in Ladysmith; his capital is being loopholed and entrenched; Newcastle has been abandoned, Colenso has fallen, Estcourt is threatened; the possibility that the whole province will be overrun stares him in the face.

From the beginning he asked for protection. From the beginning he was promised complete protection; but scarcely a word of complaint is heard.

The townsfolk are calm and orderly, the Press dignified and sober. The men capable of bearing arms have responded nobly.

Chapter IV: In Natal

Boys of sixteen march with men of fifty to war—to no light easy war.

All the volunteers are in the field bearing their full share of the fighting like men. Nor are the Outlanders backward in their own quarrel. The Imperial Light Infantry is eagerly filled. The Imperial Light Horse can find no more vacancies, not even for those who will serve without pay.

I talked with a wounded Gordon Highlander—one of those who dashed across the famous causeway of Dargai and breasted the still more glorious slope of Elandslaagte.

'We had the Imperial Horse with us,' he said. 'They're the best I've ever seen.'

The casualty lists tell the same tale. To storm the hill, the regiment dismounted less than two hundred men. They reached the top unchecked, their Colonel, their Adjutant, Lieutenant Barnes, seven other officers, and upwards of sixty men killed or wounded—nearly 30 per cent.

Many of this corps came from Johannesburg. After this who will dare call Outlanders cowards? Not that it will ever matter again.

Viewed in quieter days, the patient, trustful attitude of this colony of Natal will impress the historian.

The devotion of its people to their Sovereign and to their motherland should endear them to all good Englishmen, and win them general respect and sympathy; and full indemnity to all individual colonists who have suffered loss must stand as an Imperial debt of honour.

CHAPTER V
A CRUISE IN THE ARMOURED TRAIN

Estcourt: November 9, 1899.

How many more letters shall I write you from an unsatisfactory address? Sir George White's Headquarters are scarcely forty miles away, but between them and Estcourt stretches the hostile army.

Whether it may be possible or wise to try to pass the lines of investment is a question which I cannot yet decide; and meanwhile I wait here at the nearest post collecting such information as dribbles through native channels, and hoping that early events may clear the road.

To wait is often weary work—but even at this exciting time I come to a standstill at length with a distinct feeling of relief.

The last month has been passed in continual travel. The fading, confused faces at Waterloo as the train swept along the platform; the cheering crowds at Southampton; the rolling decks of the 'Dunottar Castle;' the suspense, the excitement of first news; a brief day's scurry at Cape Town; the journey to East London by the last train to pass along the frontier; the tumultuous voyage in the 'Umzimvubu' amid so great a gale that but for the Royal Mail the skipper would have put back to port; on without a check to Pietermaritzburg, and thence, since the need seemed urgent and the traffic slow, by special train here—all moving, restless pictures—and here at last—a pause.

Let us review the situation.

On Wednesday last, on November 1, the Boer lines of investment drew round Ladysmith.

On Thursday the last train passed down the railway under the fire of artillery. That night the line was cut about four miles north of Colenso. Telegraphic communication also ceased.

Chapter V: A Cruise in the Armoured Train

On Friday Colenso was itself attacked. A heavy gun came into action from the hills which dominate the town, and the slender garrison of infantry volunteers and naval brigade evacuated in a hurry, and, covered to some extent by the armoured train, fell back on Estcourt.

Estcourt is a South African town—that is to say, it is a collection of about three hundred detached stone or corrugated iron houses, nearly all one-storied, arranged along two broad streets—for space is plentiful—or straggling away towards the country.

The little place lies in a cup of the hills, which rise in green undulations on all sides. For this reason, it will be a very difficult place to defend if the invaders should come upon it.

It is, besides, of mean and insignificant aspect; but, like all these towns in Natal, it is the centre of a large agricultural district, at once the market and the storehouse of dozens of prosperous farms scattered about the country, and consequently it possesses more importance than the passing stranger would imagine.

Indeed, it was a surprise to find on entering the shops how great a variety and quantity of goods these unpretentious shanties contained.

Estcourt now calls itself 'The Front.' There is another front forty miles away, but that is ringed about by the enemy, and since we live in expectation of attack, with no one but the Boers beyond the outpost line, Estcourt considers that its claim is just, Colonel Wolfe Murray, the officer who commands the lines of communication of the Natal Field Force, hastened up as soon as the news of the attack on Colenso was received to make preparation to check the enemy's advance.

The force at his disposal is not, however, large—two British battalions—the Dublin Fusiliers, who fought at Glencoe, and were hurried out of Ladysmith to strengthen the communications when it became evident that a blockade impended, and the Border Regiment from Malta, a squadron of the Imperial Light Horse, 300 Natal volunteers with 25 cyclists, and a volunteer battery of nine-pounder guns—perhaps 2,000 men in all.

With so few it would be quite impossible to hold the long line of hills necessary for the protection of the town, but a position has been selected and fortified, where the troops can maintain themselves—at any rate for several days.

But the confidence of the military authorities in the strength of Estcourt may be gauged by the frantic efforts they are making to strengthen Pietermaritzburg, seventy-six miles, and even Durban, one hundred and thirty miles further back, by earthworks and naval guns.

'The Boers invade Natal!' exclaims Mr. Labouchere in the number of 'Truth' current out here. 'As likely that the Chinese army should invade London.' But he is not the only false prophet.

It seems, however, certain that a considerable force will be moved here soon to restore the situation and to relieve Ladysmith.

Meanwhile we wait, not without anxiety or impatience.

The Imperial Horse, a few mounted infantry, the volunteer cyclists, and the armoured train, patrol daily towards Colenso and the north, always expecting to see the approaching Boer commandos.

Yesterday I travelled with the armoured train. This armoured train is a very puny specimen, having neither gun nor Maxims, with no roof to its trucks and no shutters to its loopholes, and being in every way inferior to the powerful machines I saw working along the southern frontier. Nevertheless, it is a useful means of reconnaissance, nor is a journey in it devoid of interest.

An armoured train! The very name sounds strange; a locomotive disguised as a knight-errant; the agent of civilisation in the habiliments of chivalry. Mr. Morley attired as Sir Lancelot would seem scarcely more incongruous. The possibilities of attack added to the keenness of the experience.

We started at one o'clock. A company of the Dublin Fusiliers formed the garrison. Half were in the car in front of the engine, half in that behind. Three empty trucks, with a platelaying gang and spare rails to mend the line, followed.

Chapter V: A Cruise in the Armoured Train

The country between Estcourt and Colenso is open, undulating, and grassy. The stations, which occur every four or five miles, are hamlets consisting of half a dozen corrugated iron houses, and perhaps a score of blue gum trees.

These little specks of habitation are almost the only marked feature of the landscape, which on all sides spreads in pleasant but monotonous slopes of green.

The train maintained a good speed; and, though it stopped repeatedly to question Kaffirs or country folk, and to communicate with the cyclists and other patrols who were scouring the country on the flanks, reached Chieveley, five miles from Colenso, by about three o'clock; and from here the Ladysmith balloon, a brown speck floating above and beyond the distant hills, was plainly visible.

Beyond Chieveley it was necessary to observe more caution. The speed was reduced—the engine walked warily. The railway officials scanned the track, and often before a culvert or bridge was traversed we disembarked and examined it from the ground.

At other times long halts were made while the officers swept the horizon and the distant hills with field glasses and telescopes. But the country was clear and the line undamaged, and we continued our slow advance.

Presently Colenso came into view—a hundred tin-pot houses under the high hills to the northward. We inspected it deliberately. On a mound beyond the village rose the outline of the sandbag fort constructed by the Naval Brigade. The flagstaff, without the flag, still stood up boldly.

But, so far as we could tell, the whole place was deserted. There followed a discussion. Perhaps the Boers were lying in wait for the armoured train; perhaps they had trained a gun on some telegraph post, and would fire the moment the engine passed it; or perhaps, again, they were even now breaking the line behind us.

Some Kaffirs approached respectfully, saluting. A Natal Volunteer—one of the cyclists—came forward to interrogate. He was an intelligent little man, with a Martini-Metford rifle, a large pair of field glasses, a dainty pair of grey skin cycling shoes, and a slouch hat. He questioned the natives, and reported their answers. The Kaffirs said that the Dutchmen were assuredly in the neighbourhood. They had been seen only that morning.

'How many?' The reply was vague—twelve, or seventeen, or one thousand; also they had a gun—or five guns—mounted in the old fort, or on the platform of the station, or on the hill behind the town.

At daylight they had shelled Colenso. 'But why,' we asked, 'should they shell Colenso?' Evidently to make sure of the range of some telegraph post.

'It only takes one shell to do the trick with the engine,' said the captain who commanded. 'Got to hit us first, though,' he added.

'Well, let's get a little bit nearer.'

The electric bell rang three times, and we crept forward—halted—looked around, forward again—halt again—another look round; and so, yard by yard, we approached Colenso. Half a mile away we stopped finally.

The officer, taking a sergeant with him, went on towards the village on foot. I followed. We soon reached the trenches that had been made by the British troops before they evacuated the place.

'Awful rot giving this place up,' said the officer.

'These lines took us a week to dig.' From here Colenso lay exposed about two hundred yards away—a silent, desolate village. The streets were littered with the belongings of the inhabitants. Two or three houses had been burned.

A dead horse lay in the road, his four legs sticking stiffly up in the air, his belly swollen. The whole place had evidently been ransacked and plundered by the Boers and the Kaffirs.

A few natives loitered near the far end of the street, and one, alarmed at the aspect of the train, waved a white rag on a stick steadily to and fro. But no Dutchmen were to be seen.

We made our way back to the railway line and struck it at the spot where it was cut. Two lengths of rails had been lifted up, and,

Chapter V: A Cruise in the Armoured Train

with the sleepers attached to them, flung over the embankment. The broken telegraph wires trailed untidily on the ground. Several of the posts were twisted. But the bridge across the Tugela was uninjured, and the damage to the lines was such as could be easily repaired. The Boers realise the advantage of the railway.

At this moment, with their trains all labelled 'To Durban,' they are drawing supplies along it from Pretoria to within six miles of Ladysmith. They had resolved to use it in their further advance, and their confidence in the ultimate issue is shown by the care with which they avoid seriously damaging the permanent way.

We had learned all that there was to learn—where the line was broken, that the village was deserted, that the bridge was safe, and we made haste to rejoin the train. Then the engine was reversed, and we withdrew out of range of the hills beyond Colenso at full speed—and some said that the Boers did not fire because they hoped to draw us nearer, and others that there were no Boers within ten miles.

On the way back I talked with the volunteer. He was friendly and communicative.

'Durban Light Infantry,' he said; 'that's my corps. I'm a builder myself by trade—nine men under me. But I had to send them all away when I was called out. I don't know how I'm going on when I get back after it's over. Oh, I'm glad to come. I wish I was in Ladysmith. You see these Dutchmen have come quite far enough into our country.

'The Imperial Government promised us protection. You've seen what protection Colenso got; Dundee and Newcastle, just the same; I don't doubt they've tried their best, and I don't blame them; but we want help here badly. I don't hold with a man crying out for help unless he makes a start himself, so I came out. I'm a cyclist. I've got eight medals at home for cycling.'

'How will you like a new one—with the Queen's head on it?'

His eye brightened. 'Ah,' he said, 'I should treasure that more than all the other eight—even more than the twenty-mile championship one.'

So we rattled back to Estcourt through the twilight; and the long car, crowded with brown-clad soldiers who sprawled smoking on the floor or lounged against the sides, the rows of loopholes along the iron walls, the black smoke of the engine bulging overhead, the sense of headlong motion, and the atmosphere of war made the volunteer seem perhaps more than he was; and I thought him a true and valiant man, who had come forward in time of trouble quietly and soberly to bear his part in warfare, and who was ready, if necessary, to surrender his humble life in honourably sustaining the quarrel of the State.

Nor do I care to correct the impression now.

CHAPTER VI
DISTANT GUNS

Estcourt: November 10, 1899.

When I awoke yesterday morning there was a strange tremor in the air. A gang of platelayers and navvies were making a new siding by the station, and sounds of hammering also came from the engine shed.

But this tremor made itself felt above these and all the other noises of a waking camp, a silent thudding, a vibration which scarcely seemed to constitute what is called sound, yet which left an intense impression on the ear. I went outside the tent to listen.

Morning had just broken, and the air was still and clear. What little wind there was came from the northwards, from the direction of Ladysmith, and I knew that it carried to Estcourt the sound of distant cannon.

When once the sounds had been localised, it was possible to examine them more carefully. There were two kinds of reports: one almost a boom, the explosion evidently of some very heavy piece of ordnance; the other only a penetrating whisper, that of ordinary field guns.

A heavy cannonade was proceeding. The smaller pieces fired at brief intervals, sometimes three or four shots followed in quick succession. Every few minutes the heavier gun or guns intervened. What was happening? We could only try to guess, nor do we yet know whether our guesses were right.

It seems to me, however, that Sir George White must have made an attack at dawn on some persecuting Boer battery, and so brought on a general action.

Later in the day we rode out to find some nearer listening point. The whole force was making a reconnaissance towards Colenso, partly for reasons of security, partly to exercise the horses and men.

Galloping over the beautiful grassy hills to the north of the town, I soon reached a spot whence the column could be seen. First of all came a cyclist—a Natal volunteer pedalling leisurely along with his rifle slung across his back—then two more, then about twenty.

Next, after an interval of a quarter of a mile, rode the cavalry—the squadron of the Imperial Light Horse, sixty Natal Carabineers, a company of mounted infantry, and about forty of the Natal mounted police.

That is the total cavalry force in Natal, all the rest is bottled up in Ladysmith, and scarcely three hundred horsemen are available for the defence of the colony against a hostile army entirely composed of mounted men.

Small were their numbers, but the quality was good. The Imperial Light Horse have shown their courage, and have only to display their discipline to equal advantage to be considered first-class soldiers.

The Natal Carabineers are excellent volunteer cavalry: the police an alert and reliable troop.

After the horse the foot: the Dublin Fusiliers wound up the hill like a long brown snake. This is a fine regiment, which distinguished itself at Glencoe, and have since impressed all who have been brought in contact with it.

The cheery faces of the Irishmen wore a proud and confident expression. They had seen war.

The other battalion—the Border Regiment—had yet their spurs to win. The volunteer battery was sandwiched between the two British battalions, and the rear of the column was brought up by the Durban volunteers.

The force, when it had thus passed in review, looked painfully small, and this impression was aggravated by the knowledge of all that depended on it.

A high, flat-topped hill to the north-west promised a wide field of vision and a nearer listening point for the Ladysmith can-

Chapter VI: Distant Guns

nonade, which still throbbed and thudded dully. With my two companions I rode towards it, and after an hour's climb reached the summit. The land lay spread before us like a map.

Estcourt, indeed, was hidden by its engulfing hills, but Colenso was plainly visible, and the tin roofs of the houses showed in squares and oblongs of pale blue against the brown background of the mountain.

Far away to the east the dark serrated range of the Drakensberg rose in a mighty wall. But it was not on these features that we turned our glasses. To the right of Colenso the hills were lower and more broken, and the country behind, though misty and indistinct, was exposed to view.

First there was a region of low rocky hills rising in strange confusion and falling away on the further side to a hollow. Above this extensive depression clouds of smoke from grass and other fires hung and drifted, like steam over a cauldron.

At the bottom—invisible in spite of our great elevation—stood the town and camp of Ladysmith. Westward rose the long, black, hog-backed outline of Bulwana Hill, and while we watched intently the ghost of a flash stabbed its side and a white patch sprang into existence, spread thinner, and vanished away.

'Long Tom'[1] was at his business.

The owner of the nearest farm joined us while we were thus engaged—a tall, red-bearded man of grave and intelligent mien. 'They've had heavy fighting this morning,' he said. 'Not since Monday week' (the Black Monday of the war) 'has there been such firing. But they are nearly finished now for the day.'

Absorbed by the distant drama, all the more thrilling since its meaning was doubtful and mysterious, we had shown ourselves against the sky-line, and our conversation was now suddenly interrupted. Over the crest of the hill to the rear, two horsemen trotted swiftly into view. A hundred yards away to the left three or four more were dismounting among the rocks. Three other

---

1 A 155mm Creusot cannon belonging to the Transvaal Republic's State Artillery.

figures appeared on the other side. We were surrounded—but by the Natal Carabineers.

'Got you, I think,' said the sergeant, who now arrived.

'Will you kindly tell us all about who you are?' We introduced ourselves as President Kruger and General Joubert,[2] and presented the farmer as Mr. Schreiner, who had come to a secret conference, and having produced our passes, satisfied the patrol that we were not eligible for capture.

The sergeant looked disappointed. 'It took us half an hour to stalk you, but if you had only been Dutchmen we'd have had you fixed up properly.'

Indeed, the whole manoeuvre had been neatly and cleverly executed, and showed the smartness and efficiency of these irregular forces in all matters of scouting and reconnaissance.

The patrol was then appeased by being photographed 'for the London papers,' and we hastened to accept the farmer's invitation to lunch.

'Only plain fare,' said he, 'but perhaps you are used to roughing it.'

The farm stood in a sheltered angle of the hill at no great distance from its summit. It was a good-sized house, with stone walls and a corrugated iron roof. A few sheds and outhouses surrounded it, four or five blue gums afforded a little shade from the sun and a little relief to the grassy smoothness of the landscape.

Two women met us at the door, one the wife, the other, I think, the sister of our host. Neither was young, but their smiling faces showed the invigorating effects of this delicious air.

'These are anxious times,' said the older; 'we hear the cannonading every morning at breakfast. What will come of it all?'

Over a most excellent luncheon we discussed many things with these kind people, and spoke of how the nation was this time resolved to make an end of the long quarrel with the Boers,

---

2 Petrus "Piet" Joubert (1831–1900), Commandant-General of the South African Republic from 1880 to his death in 1900.

Chapter VI: Distant Guns

so that there should be no more uncertainty and alarm among loyal subjects of the Queen.

'We have always known,' said the farmer, 'that it must end in war, and I cannot say I am sorry it has come at last. But it falls heavily on us. I am the only man for twenty miles who has not left his farm. Of course we are defenceless here. Any day the Dutchmen may come. They wouldn't kill us, but they would burn or plunder everything, and it's all I've got in the world. Fifteen years have I worked at this place, and I said to myself we may as well stay and face it out, whatever happens.'

Indeed, it was an anxious time for such a man. He had bought the ground, built the house, reclaimed waste tracts, enriched the land with corn and cattle, sunk all his capital in the enterprise, and backed it with the best energies of his life. Now everything might be wrecked in an hour by a wandering Boer patrol.

And this was happening to a loyal and law-abiding British subject more than a hundred miles within the frontiers of her Majesty's dominions! Now I felt the bitter need for soldiers—thousands of soldiers—so that such a man as this might be assured.

With what pride and joy could one have said: 'Work on, the fruits of your industry are safe. Under the strong arm of the Imperial Government your home shall be secure, and if perchance you suffer in the disputes of the Empire the public wealth shall restore your private losses.'

But when I recalled the scanty force which alone kept the field, and stood between the enemy and the rest of Natal, I knew the first would be an empty boast, and, remembering what had happened on other occasions, I thought the second might prove a barren promise.

We started on our long ride home, for the afternoon was wearing away and picket lines are dangerous at dusk. The military situation is without doubt at this moment most grave and critical. We have been at war three weeks. The army that was to have defended Natal, and was indeed expected to repulse the invaders with terrible loss, is blockaded and bombarded in its fortified camp. At nearly every point along the circle of the frontiers the Boers have advanced and the British retreated. Wherever we have stood we have been surrounded.

The losses in the fighting have not been unequal—nor, considering the numbers engaged and the weapons employed, have they been very severe. But the Boers hold more than 1,200 unwounded British prisoners, a number that bears a disgraceful proportion to the casualty lists, and a very unsatisfactory relation to the number of Dutchmen that we have taken.

All this is mainly the result of being unready. That we are unready is largely due to those in England who have endeavoured by every means in their power to hamper and obstruct the Government, who have scoffed at the possibility of the Boers becoming the aggressors, and who have represented every precaution for the defence of the colonies as a deliberate provocation to the Transvaal State.

It is also due to an extraordinary under-estimation of the strength of the Boers. These military republics have been for ten years cherishing vast ambitions, and for five years, enriched by the gold mines, they have been arming and preparing for the struggle.

They have neglected nothing, and it is a very remarkable fact that these ignorant peasant communities have had the wisdom and the enterprise to possess themselves of good advisers, and to utilise the best expert opinion in all matters of armament and war. Their artillery is inferior in numbers, but in nothing else, to ours.

Yesterday I visited Colenso in the armoured train. In one of the deserted British-built redoubts I found two boxes of shrapnel shells and charges. The Boers had not troubled to touch them.

Their guns were of a later pattern, and fired powder and shell made up together like a great rifle cartridge. The combination, made for the first time in the history of war, of heavy artillery and swarms of mounted infantry is formidable and effective. The enduring courage and confident spirit of the enemy must also ex-

Chapter VI: Distant Guns

cite surprise. In short, we have grossly underrated their fighting powers. Most people in England—I, among them—thought that the Boer ultimatum was an act of despair, that the Dutch would make one fight for their honour, and, once defeated, would accept the inevitable.

All I have heard and whatever I have seen out here contradict these false ideas. Anger, hatred, and the consciousness of military power impelled, the Boers to war. They would rather have fought at their own time—a year or two later—when their preparations were still further advanced, and when the British were, perhaps, involved in other quarters.

But, after all, the moment was ripe. Nearly everything was ready, and the whole people sprang to arms with alacrity, firmly believing that they would drive the British into the sea.

To that opinion they still adhere. I do not myself share it; but it cannot be denied that it seems less absurd to-day than it did before a shot had been fired.

To return to Estcourt. Here we are passing through a most dangerous period. The garrison is utterly insufficient to resist the Boers; the position wholly indefensible. Indeed, we exist here on sufferance. If the enemy attack, the troops must fall back on Pietermaritzburg, if for no other reason because they are the only force available for the defence of the strong lines now being formed around the chief town.

There are so few cavalry outside Ladysmith that the Boers could raid in all directions. All this will have been changed long before this letter reaches you, or I should not send it, but as I write the situation is saved only by what seems to me the over-confidence of the enemy.

They are concentrating all their efforts on Ladysmith, and evidently hope to compel its surrender. It may, however, be said with absolute certainty that the place can hold out for a month at the least.

How, then, could the Boers obtain the necessary time to reduce it? The reinforcements are on the seas. The railway works regularly with the coast. Even now sidings are being constructed and troop trains prepared.

It is with all this that they should interfere, and they are perfectly competent to do so. They could compel us to retreat on Pietermaritzburg, they could tear up the railway, they could blow up the bridges; and by all these means they could delay the arrival of a relieving army, and so have a longer time to worry Ladysmith, and a better chance of making it a second Saratoga.

Since Saturday last that has been our fear. Nearly a week has passed and nothing has happened.

The chance of the Boers is fleeting; the transports approach the land; scarcely forty-eight hours remain. Yet, as I write, they have done nothing. Why? To some extent I think they have been influenced by the fear of the Tugela River rising behind their raiding parties, and cutting their line of retreat; to some extent by the serene and confident way in which General Wolfe Murray, placed in a most trying position, has handled his force and maintained by frequent reconnaissance and a determined attitude the appearance of actual strength; but when all has been said on these grounds, the fact will remain that the enemy have not destroyed the railway because they do not fear the reinforcements that are coming, because they do not believe that many will come, and because they are sure that, however many may come, they will defeat them.

To this end they preserve the line, and watch the bridges as carefully as we do. It is by the railway that they are to be supplied in their march through Natal to the sea.

After what they have accomplished it would be foolish to laugh at any of their ambitions, however wicked and extravagant these may be; but it appears to most military critics at this moment that they have committed a serious strategic error, and have thrown away the chance they had almost won.

How much that error will cost them will depend on the operations of the relieving force, which I shall hope to chronicle as fully as possible in future letters.

Chapter VI: Distant Guns

The armoured train which was deployed to Natal, one of four which were made in the Cape at the beginning of the war. Later models were far more substantial.

CHAPTER VII
THE FATE OF THE ARMOURED TRAIN

Pretoria: November 20, 1899.

Now I perceive that I was foolish to choose in advance a definite title for these letters and to think that it could continue to be appropriate for any length of time.

In the strong stream of war, the swimmer is swirled helplessly about hither and thither by the waves, and he can by no means tell where he will come to land, or, indeed, that he may not be overwhelmed in the flood.

A week ago, I described to you a reconnoitring expedition in the Estcourt armoured train, and I pointed out the many defects in the construction and the great dangers in the employment of that forlorn military machine.

So patent were these to all who concerned themselves in the matter that the train was nicknamed in the camp 'Wilson's death trap.'

On Tuesday, the 14th, the mounted infantry patrols reported that the Boers in small parties were approaching Estcourt from the directions of Weenen and Colenso, and Colonel Long made a reconnaissance in force to ascertain what strength lay behind the advanced scouts.

The reconnaissance, which was marked only by an exchange of shots between the patrols, revealed little, but it was generally believed that a considerable portion of the army investing Ladysmith was moving, or was about to move, southwards to attack Estcourt, and endeavour to strike Pietermaritzburg.

The movement that we had awaited for ten days impended. Accordingly certain military preparations, which I need not now specify, were made to guard against all contingencies, and at daylight on Wednesday morning, another spray of patrols was

Chapter VII: The Fate of the Armoured Train

flung out towards the north and north-west, and the Estcourt armoured train was ordered to reconnoitre towards Chieveley.

The train was composed as follows: an ordinary truck, in which was a 7-pounder muzzle-loading gun, served by four sailors from the 'Tartar;' an armoured car fitted with loopholes and held by three sections of a company of the Dublin Fusiliers; the engine and tender, two more armoured cars containing the fourth section of the Fusilier company, one company of the Durban Light Infantry (volunteers), and a small civilian breakdown gang; lastly, another ordinary truck with the tools and materials for repairing the road; in all five wagons, the locomotive, one small gun, and 120 men.

Captain Haldane, D.S.O., whom I had formerly known on Sir William Lockhart's staff in the Tirah Expedition, and who was lately recovered from his wound at Elandslaagte, commanded.

We started at half-past five and, observing all the usual precautions, reached Frere Station in about an hour. Here a small patrol of the Natal police reported that there were no enemy within the next few miles, and that all seemed quiet in the neighbourhood. It was the silence before the storm.

Captain Haldane decided to push on cautiously as far as Chieveley, near which place an extensive view of the country could be obtained.

Not a sign of the Boers could be seen. The rolling grassy country looked as peaceful and deserted as on former occasions, and we little thought that behind the green undulations scarcely three miles away the leading commandos of a powerful force were riding swiftly forward on their invading path.

All was clear as far as Chieveley, but as the train reached the station I saw about a hundred Boer horsemen cantering southwards about a mile from the railway. Beyond Chieveley a long hill was lined with a row of black spots, showing that our further advance would be disputed.

The telegraphist who accompanied the train wired back to Estcourt reporting our safe arrival, and that parties of Boers were to be seen at no great distance, and Colonel Long replied by ordering the train to return to Frere and remain there in observation during the day, watching its safe retreat at nightfall.

We proceeded to obey, and were about a mile and three-quarters from Frere when on rounding a corner we saw that a hill which commanded the line at a distance of 600 yards was occupied by the enemy.

So after all there would be a fight, for we could not pass this point without coming under fire. The four sailors loaded their gun—an antiquated toy—the soldiers charged their magazines, and the train, which was now in the reverse of the order in which it had started moved, slowly towards the hill.

The moment approached: but no one was much concerned, for the cars were proof against rifle fire, and this ridge could at the worst be occupied only by some daring patrol of perhaps a score of men.

'Besides,' we said to ourselves, 'they little think we have a gun on board. That will be a nice surprise.'

The Boers held their fire until the train reached that part of the track nearest to their position.

Standing on a box in the rear armoured truck I had an excellent view-through my glasses. The long brown rattling serpent with the rifles bristling from its spotted sides crawled closer to the rocky hillock on which the scattered black figures of the enemy showed clearly.

Suddenly three wheeled things appeared on the crest, and within a second a bright flash of light—like a heliograph, but much yellower—opened and shut ten or twelve times. Then two much larger flashes; no smoke nor yet any sound, and a bustle and stir among the little figures. So much for the hill.

Immediately over the rear truck of the train a huge white ball of smoke sprang into being and tore out into a cone like a comet. Then came, the explosions of the near guns and the nearer shell. The iron sides of the truck tanged with a patter of bullets. There

Chapter VII: The Fate of the Armoured Train

was a crash from the front of the train and half a dozen sharp reports.

The Boers had opened fire on us at 600 yards with two large field guns, a Maxim firing small shells in a stream, and from riflemen lying on the ridge. I got down from my box into the cover of the armoured sides of the car without forming any clear thought.

Equally involuntarily, it seems that the driver put on full steam, as the enemy had intended. The train leapt forward, ran the gauntlet of the guns, which now filled the air with explosions, swung round the curve of the hill, ran down a steep gradient, and dashed into a huge stone which awaited it on the line at a convenient spot.

To those who were in the rear truck there was only a tremendous shock, a tremendous crash, and a sudden full stop.

What happened to the trucks in front of the engine is more interesting. The first, which contained the materials and tools of the breakdown gang and the guard who was watching the line, was flung into the air and fell bottom upwards on the embankment. (I do not know what befell the guard, but it seems probable that he was killed.)

The next, an armoured car crowded with the Durban Light Infantry, was carried on twenty yards and thrown over on its side, scattering its occupants in a shower on the ground. The third wedged itself across the track, half on and half off the rails. The rest of the train kept to the metals.

We were not long left in the comparative peace and safety of a railway accident. The Boer guns, swiftly changing their position, re-opened from a distance of 1,300 yards before anyone had got out of the stage of exclamations.

The tapping rifle fire spread along the hillside, until it encircled the wreckage on three sides, and a third field gun came into action from some high ground on the opposite side of the line.

To all of this our own poor little gun endeavoured to reply, and the sailors, though exposed in an open truck, succeeded in letting off three rounds before the barrel was struck by a shell, and the trunnions, being smashed, fell altogether out of the carriage.

The armoured truck gave some protection from the bullets, but since any direct shell must pierce it like paper and kill everyone, it seemed almost safer outside, and, wishing to see the extent and nature of the damage, I clambered over the iron shield, and, dropping to the ground, ran along the line to the front of the train.

As I passed the engine another shrapnel shell burst immediately, as it seemed, overhead, hurling its contents with a rasping rush through the air.

The driver at once sprang out of the cab and ran to the shelter of the overturned trucks. His face was cut open by a splinter, and he complained in bitter futile indignation. He was a civilian. What did they think he was paid for? To be killed by bombshells? Not he. He would not stay another minute.

It looked as if his excitement and misery—he was dazed by the blow on his head—would prevent him from working the engine further, and as only he understood the machinery all chances of escape seemed to be cut off.

Yet when I told this man that if he continued to stay at his post he would be mentioned for distinguished gallantry in action, he pulled himself together, wiped the blood off his face, climbed back into the cab of his engine, and thereafter during the one-sided combat did his duty bravely and faithfully—so strong is the desire for honour and repute in the human breast.

I reached the overturned portion of the train uninjured. The volunteers who, though severely shaken, were mostly unhurt, were lying down under such cover as the damaged cars and the gutters of the railway line afforded.

It was a very grievous sight to see these citizen soldiers, most of whom were the fathers of families, in such a perilous position. They bore themselves well, though greatly troubled, and their major, whose name I have not learned, directed their fire on the enemy; but since these, lying behind the crests of the surround-

Chapter VII: The Fate of the Armoured Train

ing hills, were almost invisible I did not expect that it would be very effective.

Having seen this much, I ran along the train to the rear armoured truck and told Captain Haldane that in my opinion the line might be cleared. We then agreed that he with musketry should keep the enemy's artillery from destroying us, and that I should try to throw the wreckage off the line, so that the engine and the two cars which still remained on the rails might escape.

I am convinced that this arrangement gave us the best possible chance of safety, though at the time it was made the position appeared quite hopeless.

Accordingly, Haldane and his Fusiliers began to fire through their loopholes at the Boer artillery, and, as the enemy afterwards admitted, actually disturbed their aim considerably.

During the time that these men were firing from the truck four shells passed through the armour, but luckily not one exploded until it had passed out on the further side.

Many shells also struck and burst on the outside of their shields, and these knocked all the soldiers on their backs with the concussion. Nevertheless a well-directed fire was maintained without cessation.

The task of clearing the line would not, perhaps, in ordinary circumstances have been a very difficult one. But the breakdown gang and their tools were scattered to the winds, and several had fled along the track or across the fields.

Moreover, the enemy's artillery fire was pitiless, continuous, and distracting.

The affair had, however, to be carried through. The first thing to be done was to detach the truck half off the rails from the one completely so. To do this the engine had to be moved to slacken the strain on the twisted couplings.

When these had been released, the next step was to drag the partly derailed truck backwards along the line until it was clear of the other wreckage, and then to throw it bodily off the rails.

This may seem very simple, but the dead weight of the iron truck half on the sleepers was enormous, and the engine wheels skidded vainly several times before any hauling power was obtained.

At last, the truck was drawn sufficiently far back, and I called for volunteers to overturn it from the side while the engine pushed it from the end. It was very evident that these men would be exposed to considerable danger.

Twenty were called for, and there was an immediate response. But only nine, including the major of volunteers and four or five of the Dublin Fusiliers, actually stepped out into the open.

The attempt was nevertheless successful. The truck heeled further over under their pushing, and, the engine giving a shove at the right moment, it fell off the line and the track was clear.

Safety and success appeared in sight together, but disappointment overtook them. The engine was about six inches wider than the tender, and the corner of its footplate would not pass the corner of the newly overturned truck.

It did not seem safe to push very hard, lest the engine should itself be derailed. So time after time the engine moved back a yard or two and shoved forward at the obstruction, and each time moved it a little. But soon it was evident that complications had set in.

The newly derailed truck became jammed with that originally off the line, and the more the engine pushed the greater became the block.

Volunteers were again called on to assist, but though seven men, two of whom, I think, were wounded, did their best, the attempt was a failure.

Perseverance, however, is a virtue. If the trucks only jammed the tighter for the forward pushing they might be loosened by pulling backwards. Now, however, a new difficulty arose. The coupling chains of the engine would not reach by five or six inches those of the overturned truck. Search was made for a spare

Chapter VII: The Fate of the Armoured Train

link. By a solitary gleam of good luck one was found. The engine hauled at the wreckage, and before the chains parted pulled it about a yard backwards. Now, certainly, the line was clear at last. But again the corner of the footplate jammed with the corner of the truck, and again we came to a jarring halt.

I have had, in the last four years, the advantage, if it be an advantage, of many strange and varied experiences, from which the student of realities might draw profit and instruction.

But nothing was so thrilling as this: to wait and struggle among these clanging, rending iron boxes, with the repeated explosions of the shells and the artillery, the noise of the projectiles striking the cars, the hiss as they passed in the air, the grunting and puffing of the engine—poor, tortured thing, hammered by at least a dozen shells, any one of which, by penetrating the boiler, might have made an end of all—the expectation of destruction as a matter of course, the realization of powerlessness, and the alternations of hope and despair—all this for seventy minutes by the clock with only four inches of twisted iron work to make the difference between danger, captivity, and shame on the one hand—safety, freedom, and triumph on the other.

Nothing remained but to continue pounding at the obstructing corner in the hopes that the iron work would gradually be twisted and torn, and thus give free passage.

As we pounded so did the enemy.

I adjured the driver to be patient and to push gently, for it did not seem right to imperil the slender chance of escape by running the risk of throwing the engine off the line.

But after a dozen pushes had been given with apparently little result, a shell struck the front of the engine, setting fire to the woodwork, and he thereupon turned on more steam, and with considerable momentum we struck the obstacle once more.

There was a grinding crash; the engine staggered, checked, shore forward again, until with a clanging, tearing sound it broke past the point of interception, and nothing but the smooth line lay between us and home.

Brilliant success now seemed won, for I thought that the rear and gun trucks were following the locomotive, and that all might squeeze into them, and so make an honourable escape. But the longed-for cup was dashed aside.

Looking backward, I saw that the couplings had parted or had been severed by a shell, and that the trucks still lay on the wrong side of the obstruction, separated by it from the engine.

No one dared to risk imprisoning the engine again by making it go back for the trucks, so an attempt was made to drag the trucks up to the engine.

Owing chiefly to the fire of the enemy this failed completely, and Captain Haldane determined to be content with saving the locomotive. He accordingly permitted the driver to retire along the line slowly, so that the infantry might get as much shelter from the ironwork of the engine as possible, and the further idea was to get into some houses near the station, about 800 yards away, and there hold out while the engine went for assistance.

As many wounded as possible were piled on to the engine, standing in the cab, lying on the tender, or clinging to the cow-catcher.

And all this time the shells fell into the wet earth throwing up white clouds, burst with terrifying detonations overhead, or actually struck the engine and the iron wreckage.

Besides the three field-guns, which proved to be 15-pounders, the shell-firing Maxim continued its work, and its little shells, discharged with an ugly thud, thud, thud, exploded with startling bangs on all sides.

One I remember struck the footplate of the engine scarcely a yard from my face, lit up into a bright yellow flash, and left me wondering why I was still alive. Another hit the coals in the tender, hurling a black shower into the air. A third—this also I saw—struck the arm of a private in the Dublin Fusiliers. The whole arm was smashed to a horrid pulp—bones, muscle, blood, and uniform all mixed together. At the bottom hung the hand, unhurt, but swelled instantly to three times its ordinary size.

Chapter VII: The Fate of the Armoured Train

The engine was soon crowded and began to steam homewards—a mournful, sorely battered locomotive—with the woodwork of the firebox in flames and the water spouting from its pierced tanks. The infantrymen straggled along beside it at the double.

Seeing the engine escaping the Boers increased their fire, and the troops, hitherto somewhat protected by the iron trucks, began to suffer.

The major of volunteers fell, shot through the thigh. Here and there men dropped on the ground, several screamed—this is very rare in war—and cried for help. About a quarter of the force was very soon killed or wounded.

The shells which pursued the retreating soldiers scattered them all along the track. Order and control vanished.

The engine, increasing its pace, drew out from the thin crowd of fugitives and was soon in safety. The infantry continued to run down the line in the direction of the houses, and, in spite of their disorder, I honestly consider that they were capable of making a further resistance when some shelter should be reached.

But at this moment one of those miserable incidents—much too frequent in this war—occurred. A private soldier who was wounded, in direct disobedience of the positive orders that no surrender was to be made, took it on himself to wave a pocket-handkerchief.

The Boers immediately ceased firing, and with equal daring and humanity a dozen horsemen galloped from the hills into the scattered fugitives, scarcely any of whom had seen the white flag, and several of whom were still firing, and called loudly on them to surrender.

Most of the soldiers, uncertain what to do, then halted, gave up their arms, and became prisoners of war.

Those further away from the horsemen continued to run and were shot or hunted down in twos and threes, and some made good their escape.

For my part, I found myself on the engine when the obstruction was at last passed and remained there jammed in the cab next to the man with the shattered arm.

In this way I travelled some 500 yards, and passed through the fugitives, noticing particularly a young officer, Lieutenant Frankland, who with a happy, confident smile on his face was endeavouring to rally his men.

When I approached the houses where we had resolved to make a stand, I jumped on to the line, in order to collect the men as they arrived, and hence the address from which this letter is written, for scarcely had the locomotive left me than I found myself alone in a shallow cutting and none of our soldiers, who had all surrendered on the way, to be seen.

Then suddenly there appeared on the line at the end of the cutting two men not in uniform.

'Platelayers,' I said to myself, and then, with a surge of realisation, 'Boers.'

My mind retains a momentary impression of these tall figures, full of animated movement, clad in dark flapping clothes, with slouch, storm-driven hats poising on their rifles hardly a hundred yards away.

I turned and ran between the rails of the track, and the only thought I achieved was this, 'Boer marksmanship.'

Two bullets passed, both within a foot, one on either side. I flung myself against the banks of the cutting. But they gave no cover.

Another glance at the figures; one was now kneeling to aim. Again I darted forward. Movement seemed the only chance. Again two soft kisses sucked in the air, but nothing struck me.

This could not endure. I must get out of the cutting—that damnable corridor. I scrambled up the bank. The earth sprang up beside me, and something touched my hand, but outside the cutting was a tiny depression. I crouched in this, struggling to get my wind.

Chapter VII: The Fate of the Armoured Train

On the other side of the railway a horseman galloped up, shouting to me and waving his hand. He was scarcely forty yards off. With a rifle I could have killed him easily. I knew nothing of white flags, and the bullets had made me savage.

I reached down for my Mauser pistol. 'This one at least,' I said, and indeed it was a certainty; but alas! I had left the weapon in the cab of the engine in order to be free to work at the wreckage.

What then? There was a wire fence between me and the horseman. Should I continue to fly? The idea of another shot at such a short range decided me.

Death stood before me, grim sullen Death without his light-hearted companion, Chance. So I held up my hand, and like Mr. Jorrocks's foxes,[1] cried 'Capivy.'

Then I was herded with the other prisoners in a miserable group, and about the same time I noticed that my hand was bleeding, and it began to pour with rain.

Two days before I had written to an officer in high command at home, whose friendship I have the honour to enjoy: 'There has been a great deal too much surrendering in this war, and I hope people who do so will not be encouraged.'

Fate had intervened, yet though her tone was full of irony she seemed to say, as I think Ruskin once said, 'It matters very little whether your judgments of people are true or untrue, and very much whether they are kind or unkind,' and repeating that I will make an end.

---

1 A reference to the Victorian novel *Jorrocks's Jaunts and Jollities*, a series of comic tales by Robert Smith Surtees, featuring the adventures of a Cockney grocer.

CHAPTER VIII
PRISONERS OF WAR

Pretoria: November 24, 1899.

The position of a prisoner of war is painful and humiliating. A man tries his best to kill another, and finding that he cannot succeed asks his enemy for mercy.

The laws of war demand that this should be accorded, but it is impossible not to feel a sense of humbling obligation to the captor from whose hand we take our lives.

All military pride, all independence of spirit must be put aside. These may be carried to the grave, but not into captivity. We must prepare ourselves to submit, to obey, to endure.

Certain things—sufficient food and water and protection during good behaviour—the victor must supply or be a savage, but beyond these all else is favour.

Favours must be accepted from those with whom we have a long and bitter quarrel, from those who feel fiercely that we seek to do them cruel injustice. The dog who has been whipped must be thankful for the bone that is flung to him.

When the prisoners captured after the destruction of the armoured train had been disarmed and collected in a group, we found that there were fifty-six unwounded or slightly wounded men, besides the more serious cases lying on the scene of the fight. The Boers crowded round, looking curiously at their prize, and we ate a little chocolate that by good fortune—for we had had no breakfast—was in our pockets, and sat down on the muddy ground to think. The rain streamed down from a dark leaden sky, and the coats of the horses steamed in the damp.

'Voorwärts,'[1] said a voice, and, forming in a miserable procession, two wretched officers, a bare-headed, tattered Correspond-

---

1 "Forward." The author incorrectly spells this the German way in his account. The correct Dutch/Afrikaans spelling is "voorwaarts."

Chapter VIII: Prisoners of War

Winston Churchill, right front, wearing soft cap, as a prisoner of war, 1889.

ent, four sailors with straw hats and 'H.M.S. Tartar' in gold letters on the ribbons—ill-timed jauntiness—some fifty soldiers and volunteers, and two or three railwaymen, we started, surrounded by the active Boer horsemen.

Yet, as we climbed the low hills that surrounded the place of combat I looked back and saw the engine steaming swiftly away beyond Frere Station.

Something at least was saved from the ruin; information would be carried to the troops at Estcourt, a good many of the troops and some of the wounded would escape, the locomotive was itself of value, and perhaps in saving all these things some little honour had been saved as well.

'You need not walk fast,' said a Boer in excellent English; 'take your time.'

Then another, seeing me hatless in the downpour, threw me a soldier's cap—one of the Irish Fusilier caps, taken, probably, near Ladysmith. So they were not cruel men, these enemy. That was a great surprise to me, for I had read much of the literature of this land of lies, and fully expected every hardship and indignity.

At length we reached the guns which had played on us for so many minutes—two strangely long barrels sitting very low on carriages of four wheels, like a break in which horses are exercised.

They looked offensively modern,[2] and I wondered why our Army had not got field artillery with fixed ammunition and 8,000 yards range. Some officers and men of the Staats Artillerie,[3] dressed in a drab uniform with blue facings, approached us. The commander, Adjutant Roos—as he introduced himself—made a polite salute.

---

2 These weapons were in fact of British design. Maxim-Nordfelts, 37 mm one pound guns which had originally been rejected for use by the British Army, and which had been snapped up by the Transvaal Republic in the 1890s. The "pom pom" guns, so named after the noise they made when firing, quickly proved their worth, and by mid 1900 the British Army had acquired their own and had deployed them against the Boers.
3 State Artillery.

Chapter VIII: Prisoners of War

He regretted the unfortunate circumstances of our meeting; he complimented the officers on their defence—of course, it was hopeless from the first; he trusted his fire had not annoyed us; we should, he thought, understand the necessity for them to continue; above all he wanted to know how the engine had been able to get away, and how the line could have been cleared of wreckage under his guns. In fact, he behaved as a good professional soldier should, and his manner impressed me.

We waited here near the guns for half an hour, and meanwhile the Boers searched amid the wreckage for dead and wounded.

A few of the wounded were brought to where we were, and laid on the ground, but most of them were placed in the shelter of one of the overturned trucks.

As I write I do not know with any certainty what the total losses were, but the Boers say that they buried five dead, sent ten seriously wounded into Ladysmith, and kept three severely wounded in their field ambulances.

Besides this, we are told that sixteen severely wounded escaped on the engine, and we have with the prisoners seven men, including myself, slightly wounded by splinters or injured in the derailment. If this be approximately correct, it seems that the casualties in the hour and a half of fighting were between thirty-five and forty: not many, perhaps, considering the fire, but out of 120 enough at least.

After a while we were ordered to march on, and looking over the crest of the hill a strange and impressive sight met the eye. Only about 300 men had attacked the train, and I had thought that this was the enterprise of a separate detachment, but as the view extended I saw that this was only a small part of a large, powerful force marching south, under the personal direction of General Joubert, to attack Estcourt.

Behind every hill, thinly veiled by the driving rain, masses of mounted men, arranged in an orderly disorder, were halted, and from the rear long columns of horsemen rode steadily forward. Certainly I did not see less than 3,000, and I did not see nearly all.

Evidently an important operation was in progress, and a collision either at Estcourt or Mooi River impended. This was the long expected advance: worse late than never.

Our captors conducted us to a rough tent which had been set up in a hollow in one of the hills, and which we concluded was General Joubert's headquarters. Here we were formed in a line, and soon surrounded by a bearded crowd of Boers cloaked in mackintosh.

I explained that I was a Special Correspondent, and asked to see General Joubert. But in the throng it was impossible to tell who were the superiors.

My credentials were taken from me by a man who said he was a Field Cornet, and who promised that they should be laid before the General forthwith.

Meanwhile we waited in the rain, and the Boers questioned us. My certificate as a correspondent bore a name better known than liked in the Transvaal. Moreover, some of the private soldiers had been talking.

'You are the son of Lord Randolph Churchill?' said a Scottish Boer, abruptly. I did not deny the fact.

Immediately there was much talking, and all crowded round me, looking and pointing, while I heard my name repeated on every side.

'I am a newspaper correspondent,' I said, 'and you ought not to hold me prisoner.'

The Scottish Boer laughed. 'Oh,' he said, 'we do not catch lords' sons every day.'

Whereat they all chuckled, and began to explain that I should be allowed to play football at Pretoria.

All this time I was expecting to be brought before General Joubert, from whom I had some hopes I should obtain assurances that my character as a press correspondent would be respected. But suddenly a mounted man rode up and ordered the prisoners to march away towards Colenso.

Chapter VIII: Prisoners of War

The escort, twenty horsemen, closed round us. I addressed their leader, and demanded either that I should be taken before the General, or that my credentials should be given back. But the so-called Field Cornet was not to be seen.

The only response was, 'Voorwärts,' and as it seemed useless, undignified, and even dangerous to discuss the matter further with these people, I turned and marched off with the rest.

We tramped for six hours across sloppy fields and along tracks deep and slippery with mud, while the rain fell in a steady downpour and soaked everyone to the skin. The Boer escort told us several times not to hurry and to go our own pace, and once they allowed us to halt for a few moments. But we had had neither food nor water, and it was with a feeling of utter weariness that I saw the tin roofs of Colenso rise in the distance.

We were put into a corrugated iron shed near the station, the floors of which were four inches deep with torn railway forms and account books.

Here we flung ourselves down exhausted, and what with the shame, the disappointment, the excitement of the morning, the misery of the present, and physical weakness, it seemed that love of life was gone, and I thought almost with envy of a soldier I had seen during the fight lying quite still on the embankment, secure in the calm philosophy of death from 'the slings and arrows of outrageous fortune.'[4]

After the Boers had lit two fires they opened one of the doors of the shed and told us we might come forth and dry ourselves. A newly slaughtered ox lay on the ground, and strips of his flesh were given to us. These we toasted on sticks over the fire and ate greedily, though since the animal had been alive five minutes before one felt a kind of cannibal.

Other Boers not of our escort who were occupying Colenso came to look at us. With two of these who were brothers, English by race, Afrikanders by birth, Boers by choice, I had some conversation.

---

4 From Shakespeare's *Hamlet,* 1602.

The war, they said, was going well. Of course, it was a great matter to face the power and might of the British Empire, still they were resolved. They would drive the English out of South Africa for ever, or else fight to the last man.

I said: 'You attempt the impossible. Pretoria will be taken by the middle of March. What hope have you of withstanding a hundred thousand soldiers?'

'If I thought,' said the younger of the two brothers vehemently, 'that the Dutchmen would give in because Pretoria was taken, I would smash my rifle on those metals this very moment. We will fight for ever.'

I could only reply: 'Wait and see how you feel when the tide is running the other way. It does not seem so easy to die when death is near.'

The man said, 'I will wait.'

Then we made friends.

I told him that I hoped he would come safely through the war, and live to see a happier and a nobler South Africa under the flag which had been good enough for his forefathers; and he took off his blanket—which he was wearing with a hole in the middle like a cloak—and gave it to me to sleep in.

So we parted, and presently, as night fell, the Field Cornet who had us in charge bade us carry a little forage into the shed to sleep on, and then locked us up in the dark, soldiers, sailors, officers, and Correspondent—a broken-spirited jumble.

I could not sleep. Vexation of spirit, a cold night, and wet clothes withheld sweet oblivion. The rights and wrongs of the quarrel, the fortunes and chances of the war, forced themselves on the mind.

What men they were, these Boers! I thought of them as I had seen them in the morning riding forward through the rain—thousands of independent riflemen, thinking for themselves, possessed of beautiful weapons, led with skill, living as they rode, without commissariat or transport or ammunition column,

Chapter VIII: Prisoners of War

moving like the wind, and supported by iron constitutions and a stern, hard Old Testament God who should surely smite the Amalekites hip and thigh.

And then, above the rain storm that beat loudly on the corrugated iron, I heard the sound of a chaunt.

The Boers were singing their evening psalm, and the menacing notes—more full of indignant war than love and mercy—struck a chill into my heart, so that I thought after all that the war was unjust, that the Boers were better men than we, that Heaven was against us, that Ladysmith, Mafeking, and Kimberley would fall, that the Estcourt garrison would perish, that foreign Powers would intervene, that we should lose South Africa, and that would be the beginning of the end.

So for the time I despaired of the Empire, nor was it till the morning sun—all the brighter after the rain storms, all the warmer after the chills—struck in through the windows that things reassumed their true colours and proportions.

CHAPTER IX
THROUGH THE DUTCH CAMPS

Pretoria: November 30, 1899.

The bitter wind of disappointment pierces even the cloak of sleep. Moreover, the night was cold and the wet clothes chilled and stiffened my limbs, provoking restless and satisfactory dreams. I was breakfasting with President Kruger and General Joubert.

'Have some jam,' said the President.

'Thanks,' I replied, 'I would rather have marmalade.'

But there was none. Their evident embarrassment communicated itself to me.

'Never mind,' I said, 'I'd just as soon have jam.'

But the President was deeply moved.

'No, no,' he cried; 'we are not barbarians. Whatever you are entitled to you shall have, if I have to send to Johannesburg for it.' So he got up to ring the bell, and with the clang I woke.

The first light of dawn was just peering in through the skylight of the corrugated iron shed.

The soldiers lay in a brown litter about the floor, several snoring horribly.

The meaning of it came home with a slap. Imprisoned; not able to come and go at will; about to be dragged off and put in some secluded place while others fought the great quarrel to the end; out of it all—like a pawn taken early in the game and flung aside into the box.

I groaned with vexation, and, sitting up, aroused Frankland, who shared my blanket. Then the Boers unlocked the doors and ordered us to get ready to march at once.

The forage which we had spread on the floor rustled, and the first idea of escape crossed my mind. Why not lie buried under-

Chapter IX: Through the Dutch Camps

neath this litter until prisoners and escort had marched away together? Would they count? Would they notice? I did not think so.

They would reason—we know they all went in; it is certain none could have escaped during the night: therefore all must be here this morning.

Suppose they missed me? 'Where is the "reporter," with whom we talked last evening?' Haldane would reply that he must have slipped out of the door before it was shut.

They might scour the country; but would they search the shed? It seemed most unlikely.

The scheme pleased my fancy exceedingly, and I was just resolving to conceal myself, when one of the guards entered and ordered everyone to file out forthwith.

We chewed a little more of the ox, slain and toasted the night before, and drank some rainwater from a large puddle, and, after this frugal breakfast, intimated that we were ready.

Then we set out—a sorry gang of dirty, tramping prisoners, but yesterday the soldiers of the Queen; while the fierce old farmers cantered their ponies about the veldt or closed around the column, looking at us from time to time with irritating disdain and still more irritating pity.

We marched across the waggon bridge of the Tugela, and following the road, soon entered the hills.

Among these we journeyed for several hours, wading across the gullies which the heavy rains had turned into considerable streams and persecuted by the slanting rays of the sun.

Here and there parties of Boers met us, and much handshaking and patting on the back ensued between the newcomers and our escort.

Once we halted at a little field hospital—a dozen tents and waggons with enormous red-cross flags, tucked away in a deep hollow.

We passed through Pieters without a check at the same toilsome plod and on to Nelthorpe. Here we began to approach the

Dutch lines of investment round Ladysmith, and the advance of half an hour brought us to a very strong picket, where we were ordered to halt and rest.

Nearly two hundred Boers swarmed round in a circle and began at once—for they are all keen politicians and as curious as children—to ask questions of every sort.

What did we think of South Africa? Would we like to go in an armoured train again? How long would the English go on fighting? When would the war end? and the reply, 'When you are beaten,' was received with shouts of laughter.

'Oh no, old chappie, you can never beat us. Look at Mafeking. We have taken Mafeking. You will find Baden Powell waiting for you at Pretoria. Kimberley, too, will fall this week. Rhodes is trying to escape in a balloon, disguised as a woman—a fine woman.'

Great merriment at this.

'What about Ladysmith?'

'Ten days. Ten days more and then we shall have some whisky.'

Listen. There was the boom of a heavy gun, and, turning, I saw the white cloud of smoke hanging on the crest of Bulwana.

'That goes on always,' said the Boer. 'Can any soldiers bear that long? Oh, you will find all the English army at Pretoria. Indeed, if it were not for the sea-sickness we would take England. Besides, do you think the European Powers will allow you to bully us?'

I said, 'Why bully if you are so strong?'

'Well, why should you come and invade our country?'

'Your country? I thought this was Natal.'

'So it is: but Natal is ours. You stole it from us. Now we take it back again. That's all.'[1]

A hum of approval ran round the grinning circle.

An old Boer came up. He did not understand what induced the soldiers to go in the armoured train.

---

1 In fact Natal had been the very first Boer Republic, and had been annexed by Britain in 1843.

Chapter IX: Through the Dutch Camps

Frankland replied, 'Ordered to. Don't you have to obey your orders?'

The old man shook his head in bewilderment, then he observed, 'I fight to kill: I do not fight to be killed. If the Field Cornet was to order me to go in an armoured train, I would say to him, "Field Cornet, go to hell."'

'Ah, you are not soldiers.'

'But we catch soldiers and kill soldiers and make soldiers run away.' There was a general chorus of 'Yaw, yaw, yaw,'[2] and grunts of amusement.

'You English,' said a well-dressed man, 'die for your country: we Afrikanders live for ours.'

I said, 'Surely you don't think you will win this war?'

'Oh, yes; we will win all right this time, just the same as before.'[3]

'But it is not the same as before. Gladstone is dead, they are determined at home. If necessary they will send three hundred thousand men and spend a hundred millions.'

'We are not afraid; no matter how many thousand penny soldiers you send,' and an English Boer added, 'Let 'em all come.'

But there was one discordant note in the full chorus of confidence. It recurred again and again.

'Where is Buller?' 'When is Buller coming?' These merry fellows were not without their doubts.

'He will come when the army is ready.'

'But we have beaten the army.'

'No, the war has not begun yet.'

'It's all over for you, old chappie, anyway.'

It was a fair hit. I joined the general laughter, and, reviewing the incident by the light of subsequent events, feel I had some

---

2. What the Dutch/Afrikaans word "Ja" (meaning "yes") sounds like to English-speakers.
3 The Boers had won the First Anglo-Boer War, fought 1880 to 1881.

right to. Very soon after this, we were ordered to march again, and we began to move to the eastward in the direction of the Bulwana Hill, descending as we did so into the valley of the Klip River.

The report of the intermittent guns engaged in the bombardment of Ladysmith seemed very loud and near, and the sound of the British artillery making occasional reply could be plainly distinguished.

After we had crossed the railway line beyond Nelthorpe, I caught sight of another evidence of the proximity of friends.

High above the hills, to the left of the path, hung a speck of gold-beater's skin. It was the Ladysmith balloon. There, scarcely two miles away, were safety and honour.

The soldiers noticed the balloon too. 'Those are our blokes,' they said.

'We ain't all finished yet,' and so they comforted themselves, and a young sergeant advanced a theory that the garrison would send out cavalry to rescue us.

We kept our eyes on the balloon till it was hidden by the hills, and I thought of all that lay at the bottom of its rope. Beleaguered Ladysmith, with its shells, its flies, its fever, and its filth seemed a glorious paradise to me.

We forded the Klip River breast high, and, still surrounded by our escort, trudged on towards the laagers behind Bulwana. But it was just three o'clock, after about ten hours' marching, that we reached the camp where we were to remain for the night.

Having had no food—except the toasted ox, a disgusting form of nourishment—and being besides unused to walking far, I was so utterly worn out on arrival that at first, I cared for nothing but to lie down under the shade of a bush.

But after the Field-Cornet had given us some tea and bully beef, and courteously bidden us to share the shelter of his tent, I felt equal to further argument.

The Boers were delighted and crowded into the small tent.

Chapter IX: Through the Dutch Camps

'Will you tell us why there is this war?'

I said that it was because they wanted to beat us out of South Africa and we did not like the idea.

'Oh no, that is not the reason.'

Now that the war had begun, they would drive the British into the sea; but if we had been content with what we had they would not have interfered with us—except to get a port and have their full independence recognised.

'I will tell you what is the real cause of this war. It's all those damned capitalists. They want to steal our country, and they have bought Chamberlain,[4] and now these three, Rhodes, Beit,[5] and Chamberlain, think they will have the Rand to divide between them afterwards.'

'Don't you know that the gold mines are the property of the shareholders, many of whom are foreigners—Frenchman and Germans and others? After the war, whatever government rules, they will still belong to these people.'

'What are we fighting for then?'

'Because you hate us bitterly, and have armed yourselves in order to attack us, and we naturally chose to fight when we are not occupied elsewhere. "Agree with thine adversary whiles thou art in the way with him."'

'Don't you think it wicked to try to steal our country?'

'We only want to protect ourselves and our own interests. We didn't want your country.'

'No, but the damned capitalists do.'

'If you had tried to keep on friendly terms with us there would have been no war. But you want to drive us out of South Africa.

---

4 Joseph Chamberlain (1836–1914), the British Secretary of State for the Colonies.

5 Alfred Beit (1853–1906), the German-Jewish "Randlord" who was life-governor of the De Beers diamond company and also a director of numerous other companies such as Rand Mines, Rhodesia Railways and the Beira Railway Company. His South-African assets formed the basis for the Corner House Group, and Cecil Rhodes was initially his employee.

Think of a great Afrikander Republic—all South Africa speaking Dutch—a United States under your President and your Flag, sovereign and international.'

Their eyes glittered.

'That's what we want,' said one.

'Yaw, yaw,' said the others, 'and that's what we're going to have.'

'Well, that's the reason of the war.'

'No, no. You know it's those damned capitalists and Jews who have caused the war.'

And the argument recommenced its orbit.

So the afternoon wore away. As the evening fell the Commandant required us to withdraw to some tents which had been pitched at the corner of the laager.

A special tent was provided for the officers, and now, for the first time, they found themselves separated from their men. I had a moment in which to decide whether I would rank as officer or private, and chose the former, a choice I was soon to regret.

Gradually it became night. The scene as the daylight faded was striking and the circumstances were impressive.

The dark shadow of Bulwana mountain flung back over the Dutch camp, and the rugged, rock-strewn hills rose about it on all sides. The great waggons were arranged to enclose a square, in the midst of which stood clusters of variously shaped tents and lines of munching oxen.

Within the laager and around it little fires began to glow, and by their light the figures of the Boers could be seen busy cooking and eating their suppers, or smoking in moody, muttering groups.

All was framed by the triangular doorway of the tent, in which two ragged, bearded men sat nursing their rifles and gazing at their captives in silence.

Nor was it till my companions prepared to sleep that the stolid guards summoned the energy and wit to ask, in struggling Eng-

Chapter IX: Through the Dutch Camps

lish (for these were real veldt Boers), the inevitable question, 'And after all, what are we fighting for? Why is there this war?' But I was tired of arguing, so I said, 'It is the will of God,' and turned to rest with a more confident feeling than the night before, for I felt that these men were wearying of the struggle.

To rest but not to sleep, for the knowledge that the British lines at Ladysmith lay only five miles away filled my brain with hopes and plans of escape. I had heard it said that all Dutchmen slept between 12 and 2 o'clock, and I waited, trusting that our sentries would observe the national custom. But I soon saw that I should have been better situated with the soldiers.

We three officers were twenty yards from the laager, and around our little tent, as I learned by peering through a rent in the canvas, no less than four men were posted.

At intervals they were visited or relieved, at times they chatted together; but never for a minute was their vigilance relaxed, and the continual clicking of the Mauser breech bolts, as they played with their rifles, unpleasantly proclaimed their attention.

The moon was full and bright, and it was obvious that no possible chance of success awaited an attempt.

With the soldiers the circumstances were more favourable. Their tent stood against the angle of the laager, and although the sentries watched the front and sides it seemed to me that a man might crawl through the back, and by walking boldly across the laager itself pass safely out into the night.

It was certainly a road none would expect a fugitive to take; but whatever its chances it was closed to me, for the guard was changed at midnight and a new sentry stationed between our tent and those near the laager. I examined him through the torn tent. He was quite a child—a boy of about fourteen—and needless to say appreciated the importance of his duties. He played this terrible game of soldiers with all his heart and soul; so at last I abandoned the idea of flight and fell asleep.

In the morning, before the sun was up, the Commandant Davel came to rouse us. The prisoners were to march at once to

Elandslaagte Station. 'How far?' we asked, anxiously, for all were very footsore.

'Only a very little way—five hours' slow walking.'

We stood up—for we had slept in our clothes and cared nothing for washing—and said that we were ready. The Commandant then departed, to return in a few minutes bringing some tea and bully beef, which he presented to us with an apology for the plainness of the fare. He asked an English-speaking Boer to explain that they had nothing better themselves.

After we had eaten and were about to set forth, Davel said, through his interpreter, that he would like to know from us that we were satisfied with the treatment we met with at his laager.

We gladly gave him the assurance, and with much respect bade good-bye to this dignified and honourable enemy. Then we were marched away over the hills towards the north, skirting the picket line round Ladysmith to the left.

Every half-mile or so the road led through or by some Boer laager, and the occupants—for it was a quiet day in the batteries—turned out in hundreds to look at us. I do not know how many men I saw, but certainly during this one march not less than 5,000.

Of this great number two only offered insults to the gang of prisoners.

One was a dirty, mean-looking little Hollander. He said, 'Well, Tommy, you've got your franchise, anyhow.'

The other was an Irishman. He addressed himself to Frankland, whose badges proclaimed his regiment. What he said when disentangled from obscenity amounted to this: 'I am glad to see you Dublin fellows in trouble.'

The Boers silenced him at once and we passed on. But that was all the taunting we received during the whole journey from Frere Station to Pretoria, and when one remembers that the Burghers are only common men with hardly any real discipline, the fact seems very remarkable.

Chapter IX: Through the Dutch Camps

But little and petty as it was it galled horribly. The soldiers felt the sting and scowled back; the officers looked straight before them. Yet it was a valuable lesson. Only a few days before I had read in the newspapers of how the Kaffirs had jeered at the Boer prisoners when they were marched into Pietermaritzburg, saying, 'Where are your passes?' It had seemed a very harmless joke then, but now I understood how a prisoner feels these things.

It was about eleven o'clock when we reached Elandslaagte Station. A train awaited the prisoners. There were six or seven closed vans for the men and a first-class carriage for the officers. Into a compartment of this we were speedily bundled.

Two Boers with rifles sat themselves between us, and the doors were locked. I was desperately hungry, and asked for both food and water.

'Plenty is coming,' they said, so we waited patiently, and sure enough, in a few minutes a railway official came along the platform, opened the door, and thrust before us in generous profusion two tins of preserved mutton, two tins of preserved fish, four or five loaves, half a dozen pots of jam, and a large can of tea. As far as I could see the soldiers fared no worse.

The reader will believe that we did not stand on ceremony, but fell to at once and made the first satisfying meal for three days.

While we ate a great crowd of Boers gathered around the train and peered curiously in at the windows. One of them was a doctor, who, noticing that my hand was bound up, inquired whether I were wounded.

The cut caused by the splinter of bullet was insignificant, but since it was ragged and had received no attention for two days it had begun to fester. I therefore showed him my hand, and he immediately bustled off to get bandages and hot water and what not, with which, amid the approving grins of the rough fellows who thronged the platform, he soon bound me up very correctly.

The train whereby we were to travel was required for other business besides; and I noticed about a hundred Boers embarking with their horses in a dozen large cattle trucks behind the engine. At or about noon, we steamed off, moving slowly along the line, and Captain Haldane pointed out to me the ridge of Elandslaagte, and gave me some further account of that successful action and of the great skill with which Hamilton had directed the infantry attack.

The two Boers who were guarding us listened with great interest, but the single observation they made was that we had only to fight Germans and Hollanders at Elandslaagte.

'If these had been veldt Boers in front of you——' My companion replied that even then the Gordon Highlanders might have made some progress.

Whereat both Boers laughed softly and shook their heads with the air of a wiseacre, saying, 'You will know better when you're as old as me,' a remark I constantly endure from very worthy people.

Two stations beyond Elandslaagte the Boer commando, or portion of commando, left the train, and the care and thought that had been lavished on the military arrangements were very evident.

All the stations on the line were fitted with special platforms three or four hundred yards long, consisting of earth embankments revetted with wood towards the line and sloping to the ground on the other side.

The horsemen were thereby enabled to ride their horses out of the trucks, and in a few minutes, all were cantering away across the plain.

One of the Boer guards noticed the attention I paid to these arrangements. 'It is in case we have to go back quickly to the Biggarsberg or Laing's Nek,' he explained.

As we travelled on I gradually fell into conversation with this man. His name, he told me, was Spaarwater, which he pronounced *Spare*-water. He was a farmer from the Ermelo district. In times of peace he paid little or no taxes. For the last four years he had escaped altogether. The Field Cornet, he remarked, was a friend of his.

Chapter IX: Through the Dutch Camps

But for such advantages he lay under the obligation to serve without pay in war-time, providing horse, forage, and provisions. He was a polite, meek-mannered little man, very anxious in all the discussion to say nothing that could hurt the feelings of his prisoners, and I took a great liking to him.

He had fought at Dundee. 'That,' he said, 'was a terrible battle. Your artillery? *Bang! bang! bang*! came the shells all round us. And the bullets! *Whew*, don't tell me the soldiers can't shoot. They shoot jolly well, old chappie. I, too, can shoot. I can hit a bottle six times out of seven at a hundred yards, but when there is a battle then I do not shoot so well.'

The other man, who understood a little English, grinned at this, and muttered something in Dutch.

'What does he say?' I inquired.

'He says "He too,"' replied Spaarwater. 'Besides, we cannot see your soldiers. At Dundee I was looking down the hill and saw nothing except rows of black boots marching and the black belts of one of the regiments.'

'But,' I said, 'you managed to hit some of them after all.'

He smiled, 'Ah, yes, we are lucky, and God is on our side. Why, after Dundee, when we were retiring, we had to cross a great open plain, never even an ant-hill, and you had put twelve great cannons—I counted them—and Maxims as well, to shoot us as we went; but not one fired a shot. Was it not God's hand that stopped them? After that we knew.'

I said: 'Of course the guns did not fire, because you had raised the white flag.'

'Yes,' he answered, 'to ask for armistice, but not to give in. We are not going to give in yet. Besides, we have heard that your Lancers speared our wounded at Elandslaagte.'

We were getting on dangerous ground.

He hastened to turn the subject. 'It's all those lying newspapers that spread these reports on both sides, just like the capitalists made the war by lying.'

A little further on the ticket collector came to join in the conversation. He was a Hollander, and very eloquent.

'Why should you English take this country away from us?' he asked, and the silent Boer chimed in broken English.

'Are not our farms our own? Why must we fight for them?'

I endeavoured to explain the ground of our quarrel.

'After all British government is not a tyranny.'

'It's no good for a working-man,' said the ticket collector; 'look at Kimberley. Kimberley was a good place to live in before the capitalists collared it. Look at it now. Look at me. What are my wages?'

I forget what he said they were, but they were extraordinary wages for a ticket collector.

'Do you suppose I should get such wages under the English Government?'

I said 'No.'

'There you are,' he said.

'No English Government for me,' and added inconsequently, 'We fight for our freedom.'

Now I thought I had an argument that would tell. I turned to the farmer, who had been listening approvingly:

'Those are very good wages.'

'Ah, yes.'

'Where does the money come from?'

'Oh, from the taxes . . . and from the railroad.'

'Well, now, you send a good deal of your produce by rail, I suppose?'

'Ya' (an occasional lapse into Dutch).

'Don't you find the rates very high?'

'Ya, ya,' said both the Boers together; 'very high.'

'That is because he' (pointing to the ticket collector) 'is getting such good wages. You are paying them.'

Chapter IX: Through the Dutch Camps

At this they both laughed heartily, and Spaarwater said that that was quite true, and that the rates were too high.

'Under the English Government,' I said, 'he will not get such high wages; you will not have to pay such high rates.'

They received the conclusion in silence. Then Spaarwater said, 'Yes, but we shall have to pay a tribute to your Queen.'

'Does Cape Colony?' I asked.

'Well, what about that ironclad?'[6]

'A present, a free-will offering because they are contented—as you will be some day—under our flag.'

'No, no, old chappie, we don't want your flag; we want to be left alone. We are free, you are not free.'

'How do you mean "not free"?'

'Well, is it right that a dirty Kaffir should walk on the pavement—without a pass too? That's what they do in your British Colonies. Brother! Equal! Ugh! Free! Not a bit. We know how to treat Kaffirs.'

Probing at random I had touched a very sensitive nerve. We had got down from underneath the political and reached the social.

What is the true and original root of Dutch aversion to British rule? It is not Slagters Nek,[7] nor Boomplatz,[8] nor Majuba,[9] nor

---

6 In 1897, the parliament of the Cape Colony offered to pay for an ironclad warship to be purchased as a gift to the Royal Navy. Although given much publicity, the offer was never enacted and no ironclad was ever actually acquired with Cape Colony funds.

7 An uprising by Boers in 1815 against British rule on the eastern border of the Cape Colony following what the frontiersmen perceived to be a bias by the authorities against the white farmers in favour of the natives..

8 The Battle of Boomplaats (29 August 1848) was fought between the British and the Trek Boers trying to establish an independent state north of the Orange River. The British were victorious, but the conflict eventually led to the signing of the Sand River Convention. This was the first move by the British to fonally recognize Boer independence.

9 The Battle of Majuba Hill (27 February 1881) was the final victorious battle which saw the British defeated in the First Anglo Boer War.

the Jameson Raid.[10] Those incidents only fostered its growth. It is the abiding fear and hatred of the movement that seeks to place the native on a level with the white man.

British government is associated in the Boer farmer's mind with violent social revolution. Black is to be proclaimed the same as white. The servant is to be raised against the master; the Kaffir is to be declared the brother of the European, to be constituted his legal equal, to be armed with political rights.

The dominant race is to be deprived of their superiority; nor is a tigress robbed of her cubs more furious than is the Boer at this prospect.

I mused on the tangled skein of politics and party principles. This Boer farmer was a very typical character, and represented to my mind all that was best and noblest in the African Dutch character.

Supposing he had been conducting Mr. Morley to Pretoria, not as a prisoner of war, but as an honoured guest, instead of me, what would their conversation have been? How excellently they would have agreed on the general question of the war! I could imagine the farmer purring with delight as his distinguished charge dilated in polished sentences upon liberty and the rights of nationalities.

Both would together have bewailed the horrors of war and the crime of aggression; both would have condemned the tendencies of modern Imperialism and Capitalism; both would have been in complete accord whenever the names of Rhodes, Chamberlain, or Milner were mentioned.

And the spectacle of this citizen soldier, called reluctant, yet not unwilling, from the quiet life of his farm to fight bravely in defence of the soil on which he lived, which his fathers had won by all manner of suffering and peril, and to preserve the inde-

---

10 The Jameson Raid (29 December 1895–2 January 1896) was an unsuccessful attempt by a group of privateers financed by Cecil Rhodes and led by his colleague Leander Starr Jameson to invade the Transvaal Republic and spark off an armed uprising by the Uitlanders in Johannesburg against Boer rule.

Chapter IX: Through the Dutch Camps

pendence which was his pride and joy, against great enemies of regulars—surely that would have drawn the most earnest sympathy of the eminent idealist.

And then suddenly a change, a jarring note in the duet of agreement.

'*We* know how to treat Kaffirs in *this* country. Fancy letting the black filth walk on the pavement!'

And after that no more agreement: but argument growing keener and keener; gulf widening every moment.

'Educate a Kaffir! Ah, that's you English all over. No, no, old chappie. We educate 'em with a stick. Treat 'em with humanity and consideration—I like that. They were put here by the God Almighty to work for us. We'll stand no damned nonsense from them. We'll keep them in their proper places. What do you think? Insist on their proper treatment will you? Ah, that's what we're going to see about now. We'll settle whether you English are to interfere with us before this war is over.'[11]

The afternoon dragged away before the train passed near Dundee.

Lieutenant Frankland had helped to storm Talana Hill, and was much excited to see the field of battle again under these new circumstances.

'It would all have been different if Symons had lived. We should never have let them escape from under our guns. That commando would have been smashed up altogether.'

'But what about the other commando that came up the next day?'

'Oh, the General would have managed them all right. He'd have, soon found some way of turning them out.'

Nor do I doubt he would, if the fearless confidence with which he inspired his troops could have protected his life. But the bullet

---

11 Doubtless the author did meet individuals like this, but it remains a fact that the British victors in the Second Anglo-Boer War also refused to grant Africans the franchise in the post-war Union of South Africa.

is brutally indiscriminating, and before it the brain of a hero or the quarters of a horse stand exactly the same chance to the vertical square inch.

After Talana Hill was lost to view, we began to search for Majuba, and saw it just as night closed in—a great dark mountain with memories as sad and gloomy as its appearance.

The Boer guards pointed out to us where they had mounted their big cannons to defend Laing's Nek, and remarked that the pass was now impregnable.

I could not resist saying, 'This is not the only road into the Transvaal.'

'Ah, but you English always come where we want you to come.'

We now approached the frontier.

I had indulged in hopes of leaving the train while in the Volksrust Tunnel by climbing out of the window. The possibility had, however, presented itself to Spaarwater, for he shut both windows, and just before we reached the entrance opened the breech of his Mauser to show me that it was fully loaded.

So prudence again imposed patience.

It was quite dark when the train reached Volksrust, and we knew ourselves actually in the enemy's country.

The platform was densely crowded with armed Boers. It appeared that two new commandos had been called out, and were waiting for trains to take them to the front. Moreover, a strong raiding party had just come back from British Swaziland. The windows were soon blocked with the bearded faces of men who gazed stolidly and commented freely to each other on our appearance. It was like being a wild beast in a cage.

After some time, a young woman pushed her way to the window and had a prolonged stare, at the end of which she observed in a loud voice (I must record it)— 'Why, they're not so bad looking after all.'

At this there was general laughter, and Spaarwater, who was much concerned, said that they meant no harm, and that if we

Chapter IX: Through the Dutch Camps

were annoyed, he would have everyone cleared away. But I said: 'Certainly not; let them feast their eyes.'

So they did, for forty minutes by the clock. Their faces were plain and rough, but not unkindly. The little narrow-set pig-eyes were the most displeasing feature. For the rest they looked what they were, honest ignorant peasants with wits sharpened by military training and the conditions of a new country.

Presently I noticed at the window furthest from the platform one of quite a different type. A handsome boyish face without beard or moustache, and a very amiable expression. We looked at each other. There was no one else at that side of the carriage.

'Will you have some cigarettes?' he said, holding me out a packet. I took one, and we began to talk.

'Is there going to be much more war?' he inquired anxiously.

'Yes, very much more; we have scarcely begun.' He looked quite miserable.

I said, 'You have not been at the front yet?'

'No, I am only just commandeered.'

'How old are you?'

'Sixteen.'

'That's very young to go and fight.' He shook his head sadly.

'What's your name?'

'Cameron.'

'That's not a Dutch name?'

'No, I'm not a Dutchman. My father came from Scotland.'

'Then why do you go and fight against the British?'

'How can I help it? I live here. You must go when you're commandeered. They wouldn't let me off. Mother tried her best. But it's "come out and fight or leave the country" here, and we've got nothing but the farm.'

'The Government would have paid you compensation afterwards.'

'Ah! that's what they told father last time. He was loyal, and helped to defend the Pretoria laager. He lost everything, and he had to begin all over again.'

'So now you fight against your country?'

'I can't help it,' he repeated sullenly, 'you must go when you're commandeered.'

And then he climbed down off the footboard, and I did not see him again—one piteous item of Gladstone's legacy—the ruined and abandoned loyalist in the second generation.

Before the train left Volksrust, we changed our guards. The honest burghers who had captured us had to return to the front, and we were to be handed over to the police.

The leader of the escort—a dear old gentleman—I am ignorant of his official rank—approached and explained through Spaarwater that it was he who had placed the stone and so caused our misfortunes. He said he hoped we bore no malice.

We replied by no means, and that we would do the same for him with pleasure any day.

Frankland asked him what rewards he would get for such distinguished service. In truth he might easily have been shot, had we turned the corner a minute earlier. The subaltern apparently contemplated some Republican V.C. or D.S.O.

But the farmer was much puzzled by his question. After some explaining we learnt that he had been given fourteen days' furlough to go home to his farm and see his wife. His evident joy and delight were touching.

I said 'Surely this is a very critical time to leave the front. You may miss an important battle.'

'Yes,' he replied simply, 'I hope so.'

Then we said 'good-bye,' and I gave him, and also Spaarwater, a little slip of paper setting forth that they had shown kindness and courtesy to British prisoners of war, and personally requesting anyone into whose hands the papers might come to treat them well, should they themselves be taken by the Imperial forces.

Chapter IX: Through the Dutch Camps

We were then handed to a rather dilapidated policeman of a gendarme type, who spat copiously on the floor of the carriage and informed us that we should be shot if we attempted to escape.

Having no desire to speak to this fellow, we let down the sleeping shelves of the compartment and, as the train steamed out of Volksrust, turned to sleep.

Boer artillery and soldiers during the Siege of Ladysmith.

A Troop, Natal Carbineers, 1899.

Winston Churchill, fourth from the left (back to camera) disembarks at Pretoria train station, a prisoner of the Boers.

CHAPTER X
IN AFRIKANDER BONDS

Pretoria: December 3rd, 1899.

It was, as nearly as I can remember, midday when the train-load of prisoners reached Pretoria. We pulled up in a sort of siding with an earth platform on the right side which opened into the streets of the town.

The day was fine, and the sun shone brightly. There was a considerable crowd of people to receive us; ugly women with bright parasols, loafers and ragamuffins, fat burghers too heavy to ride at the front, and a long line of untidy, white-helmeted policemen— 'zarps'[1] as they were called—who looked like broken-down constabulary.

Someone opened—unlocked, that is, the point—the door of the railway carriage and told us to come out; and out we came—a very ragged and tattered group of officers—and waited under the sun blaze and the gloating of many eyes.

About a dozen cameras were clicking busily, establishing an imperishable record of our shame. Then they loosed the men and bade them form in rank. The soldiers came out of the dark vans, in which they had been confined, with some eagerness, and began at once to chirp and joke, which seemed to me most ill-timed good humour.

We waited altogether for about twenty minutes. Now for the first time since my capture I hated the enemy. The simple, valiant burghers at the front, fighting bravely as they had been told 'for their farms,' claimed respect, if not sympathy.

But here in Pretoria all was petty and contemptible. Slimy, sleek officials of all nationalities—the red-faced, snub-nosed Hollander, the oily Portuguese half-caste—thrust or wormed their

---

1 The "Zuid-Afrikaansche Republiek Politie" (South African Republic Police), ZARP for short.

way through the crowd to look. I seemed to smell corruption in the air. Here were the creatures who had fattened on the spoils. There in the field were the heroes who won them. Tammany Hall was defended by the Ironsides.

From these reflections I was recalled by a hand on my shoulder. A lanky, unshaven police sergeant grasped my arm.

'You are not an officer,' he said; 'you go this way with the common soldiers,' and he led me across the open space to where the men were formed in a column of fours. The crowd grinned: the cameras clicked again.

I fell in with the soldiers and seized the opportunity to tell them not to laugh or smile, but to appear serious men who cared for the cause they fought for; and when I saw how readily they took the hint, and what influence I possessed with them, it seemed to me that perhaps with two thousand prisoners something some day might be done. But presently a superior official—superior in rank alone, for in other respects he looked a miserable creature—came up and led me back to the officers.

At last, when the crowd had thoroughly satisfied their patriotic curiosity, we were marched off; the soldiers to the enclosed camp on the racecourse, the officers to the States Model Schools prison.

The distance was short, so far as we were concerned, and surrounded by an escort of three armed policemen to each officer, we swiftly traversed two sandy avenues with detached houses on either hand, and reached our destination.

We turned a corner; on the other side of the road stood a long, low, red brick building with a slated verandah and a row of iron railings before it. The verandah was crowded with bearded men in *khaki* uniforms or brown suits of flannel—smoking, reading, or talking. They looked up as we arrived.

The iron gate was opened, and passing in we joined sixty British officers 'held by the enemy;' and the iron gate was then shut again.

Chapter X: In Afrikander Bonds

'Hullo! How are you? Where did they catch you? What's the latest news of Buller's advance? Are we going to be exchanged?' and a dozen other questions were asked.

It was the sort of reception accorded to a new boy at a private school, or, as it seemed to me, to a new arrival in hell. But after we had satisfied our friends in as much as we could, suggestions of baths, clothes, and luncheon were made which were very welcome.

So we settled down to what promised to be a long and weary waiting.

The States Model Schools is a one-storied building of considerable size and solid structure, which occupies a corner formed by two roads through Pretoria. It consists of twelve large classrooms, seven or eight of which were used by the British officers as dormitories and one as a dining-room; a large lecture-hall, which served as an improvised fives-court; and a well-fitted gymnasium.

It stood in a quadrangular playground about one hundred and twenty yards square, in which were a dozen tents for the police guards, a cookhouse, two tents for the soldier servants, and a newly set-up bath-shed.

I do not know how the arrival of other prisoners may have modified these arrangements, but at the time of my coming into the prison, there was room enough for everyone.

The Transvaal Government provided a daily ration of bully beef and groceries, and the prisoners were allowed to purchase from the local storekeeper, a Mr. Boshof, practically everything they cared to order, except alcoholic liquors.

During the first week of my detention, we requested that this last prohibition might be withdrawn, and after profound reflection and much doubtings, the President consented to countenance the buying of bottled beer.

Until this concession was obtained, our liquid refreshment would have satisfied the most immoderate advocate of temperance, and the only relief was found when the Secretary of State for War, a kind-hearted Portuguese,[2] would smuggle in a bottle of whiskey hidden in his tail-coat pocket or amid a basket of fruit.

A very energetic and clever young officer of the Dublin Fusiliers, Lieutenant Grimshaw, undertook the task of managing the mess, and when he was assisted by another subaltern—Lieutenant Southey, of the Royal Irish Fusiliers—this became an exceedingly well-conducted concern.

In spite of the high prices prevailing in Pretoria—prices which were certainly not lowered for our benefit—the somewhat meagre rations which the Government allowed were supplemented, until we lived, for three shillings a day, quite as well as any regiment on service.

On arrival, every officer was given a new suit of clothes, bedding, towels, and toilet necessaries, and the indispensable Mr, Boshof was prepared to add to this wardrobe whatever might be required on payment either in money or by a cheque on Messrs. Cox & Co.,[3] whose accommodating fame had spread even to this distant hostile town.

I took an early opportunity to buy a suit of tweeds of a dark neutral colour, and as unlike the suits of clothes issued by the Government as possible. I would also have purchased a hat, but another officer told me that he had asked for one and had been refused. After all, what use could I find for a hat, when there were plenty of helmets to spare if I wanted to walk in the courtyard? And yet my taste ran towards a slouch hat.

The case of the soldiers was less comfortable than ours. Their rations were very scanty: only one pound of bully beef once a week and two pounds of bread; the rest was made up with mealies,[4] potatoes, and such-like—and not very much of them. Moreover, since they had no money of their own, and since prisoners of

---

2 Louis Francisco de Souza, (1865-1900). the Portuguese-origin Boer Under-Secretary for War.
3 Cox & Co. was a famous British bank, founded in 1758, and eventually acquired by Lloyds Bank Limited in 1923.
4 Maize.

Chapter X: In Afrikander Bonds

war received no pay, they were unable to buy even so much as a pound of tobacco. In consequence they complained a good deal, and were, I think, sufficiently discontented to require nothing but leading to make them rise against their guards.

The custody and regulating of the officers were entrusted to a board of management, four of whose members visited us frequently and listened to any complaints or requests. M. de Souza, the Secretary of War, was perhaps the most friendly and obliging of these, and I think we owed most of the indulgences to his representations.

He was a far-seeing little man who had travelled to Europe, and had a very clear conception of the relative strengths of Britain and the Transvaal. He enjoyed a lucrative and influential position under the Government, and was therefore devoted to its interests, but he was nevertheless suspected by the Inner Ring of Hollanders and the Relations of the President of having some sympathy for the British. He had therefore to be very careful.

Commandant Opperman, who was directly responsible for our safe custody, was in times of peace a Landrost or Justice. He was too fat to go and fight, but he was an honest and patriotic Boer, who would have gladly taken an active part in the war.

He firmly believed that the Republics would win, and when, as sometimes happened, bad news reached Pretoria, Opperman looked a picture of misery, and would come to us and speak of his resolve to shoot his wife and children and perish in the defence of the capital.

Dr. Gunning was an amiable little Hollander, fat, rubicund, and well educated. He was a keen politician, and much attached to the Boer Government, which paid him an excellent salary for looking after the State Museum. He had a wonderful collection of postage stamps, and was also engaged in forming a Zoological Garden.

This last ambition had just before the war led him into most serious trouble, for he was unable to resist the lion which Mr. Rhodes had offered him. He confided to me that the President had spoken 'most harshly' to him in consequence, and had peremptorily ordered the immediate return of the beast under threats of instant dismissal.

Gunning said that he could not have borne such treatment, but that after all a man must live. My private impression is that he will acquiesce in any political settlement which leaves him to enlarge his museum undisturbed. But whether the Transvaal will be able to indulge in such luxuries, after blowing up many of other people's railway bridges, is a question which I cannot answer.

The fourth member of the Board, Mr. Malan, was a foul and objectionable brute. His personal courage was better suited to insulting the prisoners in Pretoria than to fighting the enemy at the front.

He was closely related to the President, but not even this advantage could altogether protect him from taunts of cowardice, which were made even in the Executive Council, and somehow filtered down to us.

On one occasion, he favoured me with some of his impertinence; but I reminded him that in war either side may win, and asked whether he was wise to place himself in a separate category as regards behaviour to the prisoners.

'Because,' quoth I, 'it might be so convenient to the British Government to be able to make one or two examples.'

He was a great gross man, and his colour came and went on a large over-fed face; so that his uneasiness was obvious. He never came near me again, but some days later the news of a Boer success arrived, and on the strength of this he came to the prison and abused a subaltern in the Dublin Fusiliers, telling him that he was no gentleman, and other things which it is not right to say to a prisoner.

The subaltern happens to be exceedingly handy with his fists, so that after the war is over Mr.

Malan is going to get his head punched quite independently of the general settlement. Although, as I have frequently stated,

Chapter X: In Afrikander Bonds

there were no legitimate grounds of complaint against the treatment of British regular officers while prisoners of war, the days I passed at Pretoria were the most monotonous and among the most miserable of my life.

Early in the sultry mornings, for the heat at this season of the year was great, the soldier servants—prisoners like ourselves—would bring us a cup of coffee, and sitting up in bed we began to smoke the cigarettes and cigars of another idle, aimless day.

Breakfast was at nine: a nasty uncomfortable meal.

The room was stuffy, and there are more enlivening spectacles than seventy British officers caught by Dutch farmers and penned together in confinement.

Then came the long morning, to be killed somehow by reading, chess, or cards—and perpetual cigarettes. Luncheon at one: the same as breakfast, only more so; and then a longer afternoon to follow a long morning.

Often some of the officers used to play rounders in the small yard which we had for exercise. But the rest walked moodily up and down, or lounged over the railings and returned the stares of the occasional passers-by.

Later would come the 'Volksstem'[5]—permitted by special indulgence—with its budget of lies. Sometimes we get a little fillip of excitement.

One evening, as I was leaning over the railings, more than forty yards from the nearest sentry, a short man with a red moustache walked quickly down the street, followed by two colley dogs.

As he passed, but without altering his pace in the slightest, or even looking towards me, he said quite distinctly 'Methuen beat the Boers to hell at Belmont.'

That night the air seemed cooler and the courtyard larger. Already we imagined the Republics collapsing and the bayonets of the Queen's Guards in the streets of Pretoria.

---

[5] One of the very first newspapers to appear in the Boer Republics, dating from 1873.

Next day I talked to the War Secretary. I had made a large map upon the wall and followed the course of the war as far as possible by making squares of red and green paper to represent the various columns.

I said: 'What about Methuen? He has beaten you at Belmont. Now he should be across the Modder. In a few days he will relieve Kimberley.'

De Souza shrugged his shoulders. 'Who can tell?' he replied; 'but,' he put his finger on the map, 'there stands old Piet Cronje in a position called Scholz Nek, and we don't think Methuen will ever get past him.'

The event justified his words, and the battle which we call Magersfontein (and ought to call 'Maasfontayne') the Boers call Scholz Nek.

Long, dull, and profitless were the days. I could not write, for the ink seemed to dry upon the pen. I could not read with any perseverance, and during the whole month I was locked up, I only completed Carlyle's 'History of Frederick the Great' and Mill's 'Essay on Liberty,' neither of which satisfied my peevish expectations.

When at last the sun sank behind the fort upon the hill and twilight marked the end of another wretched day, I used to walk up and down the courtyard looking reflectively at the dirty, unkempt 'zarps' who stood on guard, racking my brains to find some way, by force or fraud, by steel or gold, of regaining my freedom.

Little did these Transvaal Policemen think, as they leaned on their rifles, smoking and watching the 'tame officers,' of the dark schemes of which they were the object, or of the peril in which they would stand but for the difficulties that lay *beyond* the wall.

For we would have made short work of them and their weapons any misty night could we but have seen our way clear after that. As the darkness thickened, the electric lamps were switched on and the whole courtyard turned blue-white with black velvet shadows.

Chapter X: In Afrikander Bonds

Then the bell clanged, and we crowded again into the stifling dining hall for the last tasteless meal of the barren day.

The same miserable stories were told again and again—Colonel Moller's surrender after Talana Hill, and the white flag at Nicholson's Nek—until I knew how the others came to Pretoria as well as I knew my own story.

'We never realised what had happened until we were actually prisoners,' said the officers of the Dublin Fusiliers Mounted Infantry, who had been captured with Colonel Moller on October 20.

'The "cease fire" sounded: no one knew what had happened. Then we were ordered to form up at the farmhouse, and there we found Boers, who told us to lay down our arms: we were delivered into their hands and never even allowed to have a gallop for freedom. But wait for the Court of Inquiry.'

I used always to sit next to Colonel Carleton at dinner, and from him and from the others learned the story of Nicholson's Nek, which it is not necessary to repeat here, but which filled me with sympathy for the gallant commander and soldiers who were betrayed by the act of an irresponsible subordinate.

The officers of the Irish Fusiliers told me of the amazement with which they had seen the white flag flying.

'We had still some ammunition,' they said; 'it is true the position was indefensible—but we only wanted to fight it out.'

'My company was scarcely engaged,' said one poor captain, with tears of vexation in his eyes at the memory; and the Gloucesters told the same tale.

'We saw the hateful thing flying. The firing stopped. No one knew by whose orders the flag had been hoisted. While we doubted, the Boers were all among us disarming the men.'

I will write no more upon these painful subjects except to say this, that the hoisting of a white flag in token of surrender is an act which can be justified only by clear proof that there was no prospect of gaining the slightest military advantage by going on fighting; and that the raising of a white flag in any case by an unauthorised person—i.e. not the officer in chief command—in such a manner as to compromise the resistance of a force, deserves sentence of death, though in view of the high standard of discipline and honour prevailing in her Majesty's army, it might not be necessary to carry the sentence into effect.

I earnestly trust that in justice to gallant officers and soldiers, who have languished these weary months in Pretoria, there will be a strict inquiry into the circumstances under which they became prisoners of war.

I have no doubt we shall be told that it is a foolish thing to wash dirty linen in public; but much better wash it in public than wear it foul.

One day shortly after I had arrived, I had an interesting visit, for de Souza, wishing to have an argument brought Mr. Grobelaar to see me. This gentleman was the Under Secretary for Foreign Affairs, and had just returned from Mafeking, whither he had been conducting a 6-inch gun. He was a very well-educated person, and so far as I could tell, honest and capable besides.

With him came Reuter's Agent, Mr. Mackay, and the odious Malan. I received them sitting on my bed in the dormitory, and when they had lighted cigars, of which I always kept a stock, we had a regular *durbar*.

I began:

'Well, Mr. Grobelaar, you see how your Government treats representatives of the Press.'

Grobelaar. 'I hope you have nothing to complain of.'

Self. 'Look at the sentries with loaded rifles on every side. I might be a wild beast instead of a special correspondent.'

Grobelaar. 'Ah, but putting aside the sentries with loaded rifles, you do not, I trust, Mr. Churchill, make any complaint.'

Self. 'My chief objection to this place is that I am in it.'

Grobelaar. 'That of course is your misfortune, and Mr. Chamberlain's fault.'

Chapter X: In Afrikander Bonds

Self. 'Not at all. We are a peace-loving people, but we had no choice but to fight or be—what was it your burghers told me in the camps?—"driven into the sea." The responsibility of the war is upon you and your President.'

Grobelaar. 'Don't you believe that. We did not want to fight. We only wanted to be left alone.'

Self. 'You never wanted war?'

de Souza. 'Ah, my God, no! Do you think we would fight Great Britain for amusement?'

Self. 'Then why did you make every preparation—turn the Republics into armed camps—prepare deep-laid plans for the invasion of our Colonies?'

Grobelaar. 'Why, what could we do after the Jameson Raid? We had to be ready to protect ourselves.'

Self. 'Surely less extensive armaments would have been sufficient to guard against another similar inroad.'

Grobelaar. 'But we knew your Government was behind the Raiders. Jameson was in front, but Rhodes and your Colonial Office were at his elbow.'

Self. 'As a matter of fact, no two people were more disconcerted by the Raid than Chamberlain and Rhodes. Besides, the British Government disavowed the Raiders' action and punished the Raiders, who, I am quite prepared to admit, got no more than they deserved.'

de Souza. 'I don't complain about the British Government's action at the time of the Raid.

Chamberlain behaved very honourably then. But it was afterwards, when Rhodes was not punished, that we knew it was all a farce, and that the British Government was bent on our destruction. When the burghers knew that Rhodes was not punished, they lost all trust in England.'

Malan. 'Ya, ya. That Rhodes, he is the ... at the bottom of it all. You wait and see what we will do to Rhodes when we take Kimberley.'

Self. 'Then you maintain, de Souza, that the distrust caused in this country by the fact that Rhodes was not punished—though how you can punish a man who breaks no law I cannot tell—was the sole cause of your Government making these gigantic military preparations, because it is certain that these preparations were the actual cause of war.'

Grobelaar. 'Why should they be a cause of war? We would never have attacked you.'

Self. 'But at this moment you are invading Cape Colony and Natal, while no British soldier has set foot on Republican soil. Moreover, it was you who declared war upon us.'

Grobelaar. 'Naturally we were not such fools as to wait till your army was here. As soon as you began to send your army, we were bound to declare war. If you had sent it earlier we should have fought earlier. Really, Mr. Churchill, you must see that is only common sense.'

Self. 'I am not criticising your policy or tactics. You hated us bitterly—I dare say you had cause to. You made tremendous preparations—I don't say you were wrong—but look at it from our point of view. We saw a declared enemy armed and arming. Against us, and against us alone, could his preparations be directed. It was time we took some precautions: indeed, we were already too late. Surely what has happened at the front proves that we had no designs against you. You were ready. We were unready. It is the wolf and lamb if you like; but the wolf was asleep and never before was a lamb with such teeth and claws.'

Grobelaar. 'Do you really mean to say that we forced this war on you, that you did not want to fight us?'

Self. 'The country did not wish for war with the Boers. Personally, I have always done so. I saw that you had six rifles to every burgher in the Republic. I knew what that meant. It meant that you were going to raise a great Afrikander revolt against us. One does not set extra places at table unless one expects company to dinner. On the other hand, we have affairs all over the world, and at any moment may become embroiled with a European power.

Chapter X: In Afrikander Bonds

At this time things are very quiet. The board is clear in other directions. We can give you our undivided attention. Armed and ambitious as you were, the war had to come sooner or later. I have always said "sooner." Therefore, I rejoiced when you sent your ultimatum and roused the whole nation.'

Malan. 'You don't rejoice quite so much now.'

Self. 'My opinion is unaltered, except that the necessity for settling the matter has become more apparent. As for the result, that, as I think Mr. Grobelaar knows, is only a question of time and money expressed in terms of blood and tears.'

Grobelaar. 'No: our opinion is quite unchanged. We prepared for the war. We have always thought we could beat you. We do not doubt our calculations now. We have done better even than we expected. The President is extremely pleased.'

Self. 'There is no good arguing on that point. We shall have to fight it out. But if you had tried to keep on friendly terms with us, the war would not have come for a long time; and the delay was all on your side.'

Grobelaar. 'We have tried till we are sick of it. This Government was badgered out of its life with Chamberlain's despatches—such despatches. And then look how we have been lied about in your papers, and called barbarians and savages.'

Self. 'I think you have certainly been abused unjustly. Indeed, when I was taken prisoner the other day, I thought it quite possible I should be put to death, although I was a correspondent' (great laughter, 'Fancy that!' etc.). 'At the best I expected to be held in prison as a kind of hostage. See how I have been mistaken.'

I pointed at the sentry who stood in the doorway, for even members of the Government could not visit us alone. Grobelaar flushed.

'Oh, well, we will hope that the captivity will not impair your spirits. Besides, it will not last long. The President expects peace before the New Year.'

'I shall hope to be free by then.'

And with this the interview came to an end, and my visitors withdrew.

The actual conversation had lasted more than an hour, but the dialogue above is not an inaccurate summary.

About ten days after my arrival at Pretoria I received a visit from the American Consul, Mr. Macrum. It seems that some uncertainty prevailed at home as to whether I was alive, wounded or unwounded, and in what light I was regarded by the Transvaal authorities.

Mr. Bourke Cockran, an American Senator who had long been a friend of mine, telegraphed from New York to the United States representative in Pretoria, hoping by this neutral channel to learn how the case stood. I had not, however, talked with Mr. Macrum for very long before I realised that neither I nor any other British prisoner was likely to be the better for any efforts which he might make on our behalf. His sympathies were plainly so much with the Transvaal Government that he even found it difficult to discharge his diplomatic duties.

However, he so far sank his political opinions as to telegraph to Mr. Bourke Cockran, and the anxiety which my relations were suffering on my account was thereby terminated.

I had one other visitor in these dull days, whom I should like to notice. During the afternoon which I spent among the Boers in their camp behind Bulwana Hill I had exchanged a few words with an Englishman whose name is of no consequence, but who was the gunner entrusted with the aiming of the big 6-inch gun.

He was a light-hearted jocular fellow outwardly, but I was not long in discovering that his anxieties among the Boers were grave and numerous. He had been drawn into the war, so far as I could make out, more by the desire of sticking to his own friends and neighbours than even of preserving his property.

But besides this local spirit, which counterbalanced the racial and patriotic feelings, there was a very strong desire to be upon

Chapter X: In Afrikander Bonds

the winning side, and I think that he regarded the Boers with an aversion which increased in proportion as their successes fell short of their early anticipations.

One afternoon he called at the States Model Schools prison and, being duly authorised to visit the prisoners, asked to see me. In the presence of Dr. Gunning, I had an interesting interview. At first our conversation was confined to generalities, but gradually, as the other officers in the room, with ready tact, drew the little Hollander Professor into an argument, my renegade and I were able to exchange confidences.

I was of course above all things anxious to get true news from the outer world, and whenever Dr. Gunning's attention was distracted by his discussion with the officers, I managed to get a little.

'Well, you know,' said the gunner, 'you English don't play fair at Ladysmith at all. We have allowed you to have a camp at Intombi Spruit for your wounded, and yet we see red cross flags flying in the town, and we have heard that in the Church there is a magazine of ammunition protected by the red cross flag. Major Erasmus, he says to me "John, you smash up that building," and so when I go back I am going to fire into the church.'

Gunning broke out into panegyrics on the virtues of the Afrikanders: my companion dropped his voice.

'The Boers have had a terrible beating at Belmont; the Free Staters have lost more than 200 killed; much discouraged; if your people keep on like this the Free State will break up.'

He raised his voice, 'Ladysmith hold out a month? Not possible; we shall give it a fortnight's more bombardment, and then you will just see how the burghers will scramble into their trenches. Plenty of whisky then, ha, ha, ha!' Then lower, 'I wish to God I could get away from this, but I don't know what to do; they are always suspecting me and watching me, and I have to keep on pretending I want them to win. This is a terrible position for a man to be in: curse the filthy Dutchmen!'

I said, 'Will Methuen get to Kimberley?'

'I don't know, but he gave them hell at Belmont and at Graspan, and they say they are fighting again to-day at Modder River. Major Erasmus is very down-hearted about it. But the ordinary burghers hear nothing but lies; all lies, I tell you. *(Crescendo)* Look at the lies that have been told about us! Barbarians! savages! every name your papers have called us, but you know better than that now; you know how well we have treated you since you have been a prisoner; and look at the way your people have treated our prisoners—put them on board ship to make them sea-sick! Don't you call that cruel?'

Here Gunning broke in that it was time for visitors to leave the prison.

And so, my strange guest, a feather blown along by the wind, without character or stability, a renegade, a traitor to his blood and birthplace, a time-server, had to hurry away. I took his measure; nor did his protestations of alarm excite my sympathy, and yet somehow I did not feel unkindly towards him; a weak man is a pitiful object in times of trouble.

Some of our countrymen who were living in the Transvaal and the Orange Free State at the outbreak of the war have been placed in such difficult positions and torn by so many conflicting emotions that they must be judged very tolerantly.

How few men are strong enough to stand against the prevailing currents of opinion! Nor, after the desertion of the British residents in the Transvaal in 1881, have we the right to judge their successors harshly if they have failed us, for it was Great and Mighty Britain who was the renegade and traitor then.

No sooner had I reached Pretoria than I demanded my release from the Government, on the grounds that I was a Press correspondent and a non-combatant.

So many people have found it difficult to reconcile this position with the accounts which have been published of what transpired during the defence of the armoured train, that I am compelled to explain. Besides the soldiers of the Dublin Fusiliers and Durban Light Infantry who had been captured, there were also

Chapter X: In Afrikander Bonds

eight or ten civilians, including a fireman, a telegraphist, and several men of the breakdown gang.

Now it seems to me that according to international practice and the customs of war, the Transvaal Government were perfectly justified in regarding all persons connected with a military train as actual combatants; indeed, the fact that they were not soldiers was, if anything, an aggravation of their case.

But the Boers were at that time overstocked with prisoners whom they had to feed and guard, and they therefore announced that the civilians would be released as soon as their identity was established, and only the military retained as prisoners.

In my case, however, an exception was to be made, and General Joubert, who had read the gushing accounts of my conduct which appeared in the Natal newspapers, directed that since I had taken part in the fighting I was to be treated as a combatant officer.

Now, as it happened, I had confined myself strictly to the business of clearing the line, which was entrusted to me, and although I do not pretend that I considered the matter in its legal aspect at the time, the fact remains that I did not give a shot, nor was I armed when captured.

I therefore claimed to be included in the same category as the civilian railway officials and men of the breakdown gang, whose declared duty it was to clear the line, pointing out that though my action might differ in degree from theirs, it was of precisely the same character, and that if they were regarded as non-combatants I had a right to be considered a non-combatant too.

To this effect I wrote two letters, one to the Secretary of War and one to General Joubert; but, needless to say, I did not indulge in much hope of the result, for I was firmly convinced that the Boer authorities regarded me as a kind of hostage, who would make a pleasing addition to the collection of prisoners they were forming against a change of fortune.

I therefore continued to search for a path of escape; and indeed, it was just as well that I did so, for I never received any answer to either of my applications while I was a prisoner, although I have since heard that one arrived by a curious coincidence the very day *after* I had departed.

While I was looking about for means, and awaiting an opportunity to break out of the Model Schools, I made every preparation to make a graceful exit when the moment should arrive.

I gave full instructions to my friends as to what was to be done with my clothes and the effects I had accumulated during my stay; I paid my account to date with the excellent Boshof; cashed a cheque on him for 20*l.*; changed some of the notes I had always concealed on my person since my capture into gold; and lastly, that there might be no unnecessary unpleasantness, I wrote the following letter to the Secretary of State:

States Model Schools Prison: December 10, 1899.

Sir,—I have the honour to inform you that as I do not consider that your Government have any right to detain me as a military prisoner, I have decided to escape from your custody. I have every confidence in the arrangements I have made with my friends outside, and I do not therefore expect to have another opportunity of seeing you. I therefore take this occasion to observe that I consider your treatment of prisoners is correct and humane, and that I see no grounds for complaint.

When I return to the British lines, I will make a public statement to this effect. I have also to thank you personally for your civility to me, and to express the hope that we may meet again at Pretoria before very long, and under different circumstances.

Regretting that I am unable to bid you a more ceremonious or a personal farewell,

I have the honour, to be, Sir,

Your most obedient servant,

WINSTON CHURCHILL.

To Mr. de Souza, Secretary of War, South African Republic.

Chapter X: In Afrikander Bonds

I arranged that this letter, which I took great pleasure in writing, should be left on my bed, and discovered so soon as my flight was known.

It only remained now to find a hat. Luckily for me Mr. Adrian Hofmeyr, a Dutch clergyman and pastor of Zeerust, had ventured before the war to express opinions contrary to those which the Boers thought befitting for a Dutchman to hold.

They had therefore seized him on the outbreak of hostilities, and after much ill-treatment and many indignities on the Western border, brought him to the States Schools. He knew most of the officials, and could, I think, easily have obtained his liberty had he pretended to be in sympathy with the Republics.

He was, however, a true man, and after the clergyman of the Church of England, who was rather a poor creature, omitted to read the prayer for the Queen one Sunday, it was to Hofmeyr's evening services alone that most of the officers would go.

I borrowed his hat.

CHAPTER XI
I ESCAPE FROM THE BOERS

Lourenço Marques: December 22, 1899,

How unhappy is that poor man who loses his liberty! What can the wide world give him in exchange? No degree of material comfort, no consciousness of correct behaviour, can balance the hateful degradation of imprisonment.

Before I had been an hour in captivity, as the previous pages evidence, I resolved to escape. Many plans suggested themselves, were examined, and rejected. For a month I thought of nothing else. But the peril and difficulty restrained action.

I think that it was the report of the British defeat at Stormberg that clinched the matter. All the news we heard in Pretoria was derived from Boer sources, and was hideously exaggerated and distorted. Every day we read in the 'Volksstem'—probably the most astounding tissue of lies ever presented to the public under the name of a newspaper—of Boer victories and of the huge slaughters and shameful flights of the British.

However much one might doubt and discount these tales, they made a deep impression. A month's feeding on such literary garbage weakens the constitution of the mind. We wretched prisoners lost heart.

Perhaps Great Britain would not persevere; perhaps Foreign Powers would intervene; perhaps there would be another disgraceful, cowardly peace. At the best the war and our confinement would be prolonged for many months.

I do not pretend that impatience at being locked up was not the foundation of my determination; but I should never have screwed up my courage to make the attempt without the earnest desire to do something, however small, to help the British cause.

Of course, I am a man of peace. I did not then contemplate becoming an officer of Irregular Horse. But swords are not the only

Chapter XI: I Escape from the Boers

weapons in the world. Something may be done with a pen. So I determined to take all hazards; and, indeed, the affair was one of very great danger and difficulty.

The States Model Schools stand in the midst of a quadrangle, and are surrounded on two sides by an iron grille and on two by a corrugated iron fence about 10 ft. high. These boundaries offered little obstacle to anyone who possessed the activity of youth, but the fact that they were guarded on the inside by sentries, fifty yards apart, armed with rifle and revolver, made them a well-nigh insuperable barrier.

No walls are so hard to pierce as living walls. I thought of the penetrating power of gold, and the sentries were sounded. They were incorruptible.

I seek not to deprive them of the credit, but the truth is that the bribery market in the Transvaal has been spoiled by the millionaires. I could not afford with my slender resources to insult them heavily enough. So nothing remained but to break out in spite of them.

With another officer who may for the present—since he is still a prisoner—remain nameless, I formed a scheme. After anxious reflection and continual watching, it was discovered that when the sentries near the offices walked about on their beats, they were at certain moments unable to see the top of a few yards of the wall.

The electric lights in the middle of the quadrangle brilliantly lighted the whole place but cut off the sentries beyond them from looking at the eastern wall, for from behind the lights all seemed darkness by contrast.

The first thing was therefore to pass the two sentries near the offices. It was necessary to hit off the exact moment when both their backs should be turned together. After the wall was scaled, we should be in the garden of the villa next door.

There our plan came to an end. Everything after this was vague and uncertain. How to get out of the garden, how to pass unnoticed through the streets, how to evade the patrols that surround-

Chapter XI: I Escape from the Boers

ed the town, and above all how to cover the two hundred and eighty miles to the Portuguese frontiers, were questions which would arise at a later stage.

All attempts to communicate with friends outside had failed. We cherished the hope that with chocolate, a little Kaffir knowledge, and a great deal of luck, we might march the distance in a fortnight, buying mealies at the native kraals and lying hidden by day. But it did not look a very promising prospect.

We determined to try on the night of the 11th of December, making up our minds quite suddenly in the morning, for these things are best done on the spur of the moment.

I passed the afternoon in positive terror. Nothing, since my schooldays, has ever disturbed me so much as this. There is something appalling in the idea of stealing secretly off in the night like a guilty thief.

The fear of detection has a pang of its own. Besides, we knew quite well that on occasion, even on excuse, the sentries would fire. Fifteen yards is a short range. And beyond the immediate danger lay a prospect of severe hardship and suffering, only faint hopes of success, and the probability at the best of five months in Pretoria Gaol.

The afternoon dragged tediously away.

I tried to read Mr. Lecky's 'History of England,' but for the first time in my life that wise writer wearied me. I played chess and was hopelessly beaten.

At last it grew dark. At seven o'clock the bell for dinner rang and the officers trooped off. Now was the time. But the sentries gave us no chance. They did not walk about. One of them stood exactly opposite the only practicable part of the wall.

We waited for two hours, but the attempt was plainly impossible, and so with a most unsatisfactory feeling of relief to bed.

Tuesday, the 12th! Another day of fear, but fear crystallising more and more into desperation.

Anything was better than further suspense.

Night came again. Again the dinner bell sounded. Choosing my opportunity, I strolled across the quadrangle and secreted myself in one of the offices. Through a chink I watched the sentries. For half an hour they remained stolid and obstructive.

Then all of a sudden, one turned and walked up to his comrade and they began to talk. Their backs were turned.

Now or never. I darted out of my hiding place and ran to the wall, seized the top with my hands and drew myself up. Twice I let myself down again in sickly hesitation, and then with a third resolve scrambled up.

The top was flat. Lying on it I had one parting glimpse of the sentries, still talking, still with their backs turned; but, I repeat, fifteen yards away.

Then I lowered myself silently down into the adjoining garden and crouched among the shrubs. I was free.

The first step had been taken, and it was irrevocable.

It now remained to await the arrival of my comrade. The bushes of the garden gave a good deal of cover, and in the moonlight their shadows lay black on the ground.

Twenty yards away was the house, and I had not been five minutes in hiding before I perceived that it was full of people; the windows revealed brightly lighted rooms, and within I could see figures moving about. This was a fresh complication. We had always thought the house unoccupied.

Presently—how long afterwards I do not know, for the ordinary measures of time, hours, minutes, and seconds are quite meaningless on such occasions—a man came out of the door and walked across the garden in my direction.

Scarcely ten yards away he stopped and stood still, looking steadily towards me. I cannot describe the surge of panic which nearly overwhelmed me. I must be discovered. I dared not stir an inch. My heart beat so violently that I felt sick.

But amid a tumult of emotion, reason, seated firmly on her throne, whispered, 'Trust to the dark background.'

Chapter XI: I Escape from the Boers

I remained absolutely motionless. For a long time the man and I remained opposite each other, and every instant I expected him to spring forward.

A vague idea crossed my mind that I might silence him.

'Hush, I am a detective. We expect that an officer will break out here to-night. I am waiting to catch him.'

Reason—scornful this time—replied: 'Surely a Transvaal detective would speak Dutch. Trust to the shadow.'

So I trusted, and after a spell another man came out of the house, lighted a cigar, and both he and the other walked off together.

No sooner had they turned than a cat pursued by a dog rushed into the bushes and collided with me. The startled animal uttered a 'miaul' of alarm and darted back again, making a horrible rustling. Both men stopped at once. But it was only the cat, as they doubtless observed, and they passed out of the garden gate into the town.

I looked at my watch. An hour had passed since I climbed the wall. Where was my comrade? Suddenly I heard a voice from within the quadrangle say, quite loud, 'All up.'

I crawled back to the wall. Two officers were walking up and down the other side jabbering Latin words, laughing and talking all manner of nonsense—amid which I caught my name. I risked a cough.

One of the officers immediately began to chatter alone.

The other said slowly and clearly, '. . . cannot get out. The sentry suspects. It's all up. Can you get back again?' But now all my fears fell from me at once.

To go back was impossible. I could not hope to climb the wall unnoticed. Fate pointed onwards. Besides, I said to myself, 'Of course, I shall be recaptured, but I will at least have a run for my money.'

I said to the officers, 'I shall go on alone.'

Now I was in the right mood for these undertakings—that is to say that, thinking failure almost certain, no odds against success affected me. All risks were less than the certainty.

A glance at the plan will show that the rate which led into the road was only a few yards from another sentry.

I said to myself, 'Toujours de l'audace'[1] put my hat on my head, strode into the middle of the garden, walked past the windows of the house without any attempt at concealment, and so went through the gate and turned to the left.

I passed the sentry at less than five yards. Most of them knew me by sight. Whether he looked at me or not I do not know, for I never turned my head. But after walking a hundred yards and hearing no challenge, I knew that the second obstacle had been surmounted.

I was at large in Pretoria. I walked on leisurely through the night humming a tune and choosing the middle of the road. The streets were full of Burghers, but they paid no attention to me.

Gradually I reached the suburbs, and on a little bridge I sat down to reflect and consider. I was in the heart of the enemy's country. I knew no one to whom I could apply for succour. Nearly three hundred miles stretched between me and Delagoa Bay.

My escape must be known at dawn. Pursuit would be immediate. Yet all exits were barred. The town was picketed, the country was patrolled, the trains were searched, the line was guarded. I had 75*l*. in my pocket and four slabs of chocolate, but the compass and the map which might have guided me, the opium tablets and meat lozenges which should have sustained me, were in my friend's pockets in the States Model Schools.

Worst of all, I could not speak a word of Dutch or Kaffir, and how was I to get food or direction? But when hope had departed, fear had gone as well.

I formed a plan. I would find the Delagoa Bay Railway. Without map or compass I must follow that in spite of the pickets.

---

1 "Always bold"

Chapter XI: I Escape from the Boers

I looked at the stars. Orion shone brightly. Scarcely a year ago he had guided me when lost in the desert to the banks of the Nile. He had given me water. Now he should lead to freedom. I could not endure the want of either.

After walking south for half a mile, I struck the railroad. Was it the line to Delagoa Bay or the Pietersburg branch? If it were the former it should run east. But so far as I could see this line ran northwards. Still, it might be only winding its way out among the hills. I resolved to follow it.

The night was delicious. A cool breeze fanned my face and a wild feeling of exhilaration took hold of me. At any rate, I was free, if only for an hour. That was something.

The fascination of the adventure grew. Unless the stars in their courses fought for me I could not escape. Where, then, was the need of caution? I marched briskly along the line.

Here and there the lights of a picket fire gleamed. Every bridge had its watchers. But I passed them all, making very short detours at the dangerous places, and really taking scarcely any precautions. Perhaps that was the reason I succeeded.

As I walked, I extended my plan. I could not march three hundred miles to the frontier. I would board a train in motion and hide under the seats, on the roof, on the couplings—anywhere.

What train should I take? The first, of course.

After walking for two hours, I perceived the signal lights of a station. I left the line, and, circling round it, hid in the ditch by the track about 200 yards beyond it.

I argued that the train would stop at the station and that it would not have got up too much speed by the time it reached me.

An hour passed. I began to grow impatient. Suddenly I heard the whistle and the approaching rattle. Then the great yellow head lights of the engine flashed into view. The train waited five minutes at the station and started again with much noise and steaming. I crouched by the track. I rehearsed the act in my mind. I must wait until the engine had passed, otherwise I should be seen. Then I must make a dash for the carriages. The train started slowly, but gathered speed sooner than I had expected. The flaring lights drew swiftly near. The rattle grew into a roar. The dark mass hung for a second above me.

The engine-driver silhouetted against his furnace glow, the black profile of the engine, the clouds of steam rushed past.

Then I hurled myself on the trucks, clutched at something, missed, clutched again, missed again, grasped some sort of handhold, was swung off my feet—my toes bumping on the line, and with a struggle seated myself on the couplings of the fifth truck from the front of the train.

It was a goods train, and the trucks were full of sacks, soft sacks covered with coal dust. I crawled on top and burrowed in among them. In five minutes I was completely buried. The sacks were warm and comfortable.

Perhaps the engine-driver had seen me rush up to the train and would give the alarm at the next station: on the other hand, perhaps not. Where was the train going to? Where would it be unloaded? Would it be searched? Was it on the Delagoa Bay line? What should I do in the morning? Ah, never mind that. Sufficient for the day was the luck thereof. Fresh plans for fresh contingencies.

I resolved to sleep, nor can I imagine a more pleasing lullaby than the clatter of the train that carries you at twenty miles an hour away from the enemy's capital.

How long I slept I do not know, but I woke up suddenly with all feelings of exhilaration gone, and only the consciousness of oppressive difficulties heavy on me. I must leave the train before daybreak, so that I could drink at a pool and find some hiding-place while it was still dark.

Another night I would board another train. I crawled from my cosy hiding-place among the sacks and sat again on the couplings. The train was running at a fair speed, but I felt it was time to leave it.

Chapter XI: I Escape from the Boers

I took hold of the iron handle at the back of the truck, pulled strongly with my left hand, and sprang. My feet struck the ground in two gigantic strides, and the next instant I was sprawling in the ditch, considerably shaken but unhurt.

The train, my faithful ally of the night, hurried on its journey.

It was still dark. I was in the middle of a wide valley, surrounded by low hills, and carpeted with high grass drenched in dew. I searched for water in the nearest gully, and soon found a clear pool. I was very thirsty, but long after I had quenched my thirst I continued to drink, that I might have sufficient for the whole day.

Presently the dawn began to break, and the sky to the east grew yellow and red, slashed across with heavy black clouds. I saw with relief that the railway ran steadily towards the sunrise. I had taken the right line, after all.

Having drunk my fill, I set out for the hills, among which I hoped to find some hiding-place, and as it became broad daylight I entered a small grove of trees which grew on the side of a deep ravine. Here I resolved to wait till dusk.

I had one consolation: no one in the world knew where I was—I did not know myself.

It was now four o'clock. Fourteen hours lay between me and the night. My impatience to proceed, while I was still strong, doubled their length. At first it was terribly cold, but by degrees the sun gained power, and by ten o'clock the heat was oppressive.

My sole companion was a gigantic vulture, who manifested an extravagant interest in my condition, and made hideous and ominous gurglings from time to time.

From my lofty position I commanded a view of the whole valley. A little tin-roofed town lay three miles to the westward. Scattered farmsteads, each with a clump of trees, relieved the monotony of the undulating ground. At the foot of the hill stood a Kaffir kraal, and the figures of its inhabitants dotted the patches of cultivation or surrounded the droves of goats and cows which fed on the pasture. The railway ran through the middle of the valley, and I could watch the passage of the various trains. I counted four passing each way, and from this I drew the conclusion that the same number would run by night.

I marked a steep gradient up which they climbed very slowly, and determined at nightfall to make another attempt to board one of these.

During the day I ate one slab of chocolate, which, with the heat, produced a violent thirst.

The pool was hardly half a mile away, but I dared not leave the shelter of the little wood, for I could see the figures of white men riding or walking occasionally across the valley, and once a Boer came and fired two shots at birds close to my hiding-place. But no one discovered me.

The elation and the excitement of the previous night had burnt away, and a chilling reaction followed. I was very hungry, for I had had no dinner before starting, and chocolate, though it sustains, does not satisfy.

I had scarcely slept, but yet my heart beat so fiercely and I was so nervous and perplexed about the future that I could not rest. I thought of all the chances that lay against me; I dreaded and detested more than words can express the prospect of being caught and dragged back to Pretoria. I do not mean that I would rather have died than have been retaken, but I have often feared death for much less.

I found no comfort in any of the philosophical ideas which some men parade in their hours of ease and strength and safety. They seemed only fair-weather friends. I realised with awful force that no exercise of my own feeble wit and strength could save me from my enemies, and that without the assistance of that High Power which interferes in the eternal sequence of causes and effects more often than we are always prone to admit, I could never succeed.

I prayed long and earnestly for help and guidance. My prayer, as it seems to me, was swiftly and wonderfully answered, I cannot now relate the strange circumstances which followed, and

Chapter XI: I Escape from the Boers

which changed my nearly hopeless position into one of superior advantage. But after the war is over ,I shall hope to lengthen this account, and so remarkable will the addition be that I cannot believe the reader will complain.

The long day reached its close at last. The western clouds flushed into fire; the shadows of the hills stretched out across the valley. A ponderous Boer waggon, with its long team, crawled slowly along the track towards the town. The Kaffirs collected their herds and drew around their kraal. The daylight died, and soon it was quite dark.

Then, and not till then, I set forth, I hurried to the railway line, pausing on my way to drink at a stream of sweet, cold water. I waited for some time at the top of the steep gradient in the hope of catching a train. But none came, and I gradually guessed, and I have since found that I guessed right, that the train I had already travelled in was the only one that ran at night.

At last I resolved to walk on, and make, at any rate, twenty miles of my journey. I walked for about six hours. How far I travelled I do not know, but I do not think that it was very many miles in the direct line.

Every bridge was guarded by armed men; every few miles were gangers' huts; at intervals there were stations with villages clustering round them. All the veldt was bathed in the bright rays of the full moon, and to avoid these dangerous places I had to make wide circuits and often to creep along the ground.

Leaving the railroad, I fell into bogs and swamps, and brushed through high grass dripping with dew, so that I was drenched to the waist. I had been able to take little exercise during my month's imprisonment, and I was soon tired out with walking, as well as from want of food and sleep. I felt very miserable when I looked around and saw here and there the lights of houses, and thought of the warmth and comfort within them, but knew that they only meant danger to me.

After six or seven hours of walking I thought it unwise to go further lest I should exhaust myself, so I lay down in a ditch to sleep. I was nearly at the end of my tether. Nevertheless, by the will of God, I was enabled to sustain myself during the next few days, obtaining food at great risk here and there, resting in concealment by day and walking only at night.

On the fifth day I was beyond Middelburg, so far as I could tell, for I dared not inquire nor as yet approach the stations near enough to read the names. In a secure hiding-place I waited for a suitable train, knowing that there is a through service between Middelburg and Lourenço Marques.

Meanwhile, there had been excitement in the States Model Schools, temporarily converted into a military prison. Early on Wednesday morning—barely twelve hours after I had escaped—my absence was discovered—I think by Dr. Gunning.

The alarm was given. Telegrams with my description at great length were despatched along all the railways. Three thousand photographs were printed. A warrant was issued for my immediate arrest. Every train was strictly searched. Everyone was on the watch.

The worthy Boshof, who knew my face well, was hurried off to Komati Poort to examine all and sundry people "with red hair" travelling towards the frontier.

The newspapers made so much of the affair that my humble fortunes and my whereabouts were discussed in long columns of print, and even in the crash of the war I became to the Boers a topic all to myself. The rumours in part amused me. It was certain, said the "Standard and Diggers' News," that I had escaped disguised as a woman. The next day I was reported captured at Komati Poort dressed as a Transvaal policeman.

There was great delight at this, which was only changed to doubt when other telegrams said that I had been arrested at Brugsbank, at Middelburg, and at Bronkerspruit. But the captives proved to be harmless people after all.

Finally it was agreed that I had never left Pretoria. I had—it appeared—changed clothes with a waiter, and was now in hiding at the house of some British sympathiser in the capital. On the

Chapter XI: I Escape from the Boers

strength of this all the houses of suspected persons were searched from top to bottom, and these unfortunate people were, I fear, put to a great deal of inconvenience. A special commission was also appointed to investigate 'stringently' (a most hateful adjective in such a connection) the causes 'which had rendered it possible for the War Correspondent of the "Morning Post" to escape.'

The 'Volksstem' noticed as a significant fact that I had recently become a subscriber to the State Library, and had selected Mill's essay 'On Liberty.' It apparently desired to gravely deprecate prisoners having access to such inflammatory literature. The idea will, perhaps, amuse those who have read the work in question.

I find it very difficult in the face of the extraordinary efforts which were made to recapture me, to believe that the Transvaal Government seriously contemplated my release *before* they knew I had escaped them.

Yet a telegram was swiftly despatched from Pretoria to all the newspapers, setting forth the terms of a most admirable letter, in which General Joubert explained the grounds which prompted him generously to restore my liberty.

I am inclined to think that the Boers hate being beaten even in the smallest things, and always fight on the win, tie, or wrangle principle; but in my case I rejoice I am not beholden to them, and have not thus been disqualified from fighting. All these things may provoke a smile of indifference, perhaps even of triumph, after the danger is past; but during the days when I was lying up in holes and corners, waiting for a good chance to board a train, the causes that had led to them preyed more than I knew on my nerves.

To be an outcast, to be hunted, to lie under a warrant for arrest, to fear every man, to have imprisonment—not necessarily military confinement either—hanging overhead, to fly the light, to doubt the shadows—all these things ate into my soul and have left an impression that will not perhaps be easily effaced.

On the sixth day the chance I had patiently waited for came. I found a convenient train duly labelled to Lourenço Marques standing in a siding. I withdrew to a suitable spot for boarding it—for I dared not make the attempt in the station—and, filling a bottle with water to drink on the way, I prepared for the last stage of my journey.

The truck in which I ensconced myself was laden with great sacks of some soft merchandise, and I found among them holes and crevices by means of which I managed to work my way to the inmost recess. The hard floor was littered with gritty coal dust, and made a most uncomfortable bed. The heat was almost stifling. I was resolved, however, that nothing should lure or compel me from my hiding-place until I reached Portuguese territory.

I expected the journey to take thirty-six hours; it dragged out into two and a half days. I hardly dared sleep for fear of snoring. I dreaded lest the trucks should be searched at Komati Poort, and my anxiety as the train approached this neighbourhood was very great.

To prolong it we were shunted on to a siding for eighteen hours either at Komati Poort or the station beyond it.

Once indeed they began to search my truck, and I heard the tarpaulin rustle as they pulled at it, but luckily they did not search deep enough, so that, providentially protected, I reached Delagoa Bay at last, and crawled forth from my place of refuge and of punishment, weary, dirty, hungry, but free once more.

Thereafter everything smiled. I found my way to the British Consul, Mr. Ross, who at first mistook me for a fireman off one of the ships in the harbour, but soon welcomed me with enthusiasm.

I bought clothes, I washed, I sat down to dinner with a real tablecloth and real glasses; and fortune, determined not to overlook the smallest detail, had arranged that the steamer 'Induna' should leave that very night for Durban.

As soon as the news of my arrival spread about the town, I received many offers of assistance from the English residents, and lest any of the Boer agents with whom Lourenço Marques is infested should attempt to recapture me in neutral territory,

Chapter XI: I Escape from the Boers

nearly a dozen gentlemen escorted me to the steamer armed with revolvers.

It is from the cabin of this little vessel, as she coasts along the sandy shores of Africa, that I write the concluding lines of this letter, and the reader who may persevere through this hurried account will perhaps understand why I write them with a feeling of triumph, and better than triumph, a feeling of pure joy.

A reward poster circulated after the author's escape. It translates as follows: Twenty-five Pounds) REWARD is offered by the Sub-Commission of he fifth division, on behalf of the Special Constable of the said division, to anyone who brings the escaped prisoner of war CHURCHILL, dead or alive to this office. For the Sub-commission of the fifth division, Lodewyk de Haas, Sec.

London to Ladysmith via Pretoria

Winston Churchill on his arrival back in Durban.

CHAPTER XII
BACK TO THE BRITISH LINES

Frere: December 24, 1899.

The voyage of the "Induna" from Delagoa Bay to Durban was speedy and prosperous, and on the afternoon of the 23rd, we approached our port, and saw the bold headland that shields it rising above the horizon to the southward.

An hour's steaming brought us to the roads. More than twenty great transports and supply vessels lay at anchor, while three others, crowded from end to end with soldiery, circled impatiently as they waited for pilots to take them into the harbour.

Our small vessel was not long in reaching the jetty, and I perceived that a very considerable crowd had gathered to receive us. But it was not until I stepped on shore that I realised that I was myself the object of this honourable welcome.

I will not chronicle the details of what followed. It is sufficient to say that many hundreds of the people of Durban took occasion to express their joy at my tiny pinch of triumph over the Boers, and that their enthusiasm was another sincere demonstration of their devotion to the Imperial cause, and their resolve to carry the war to an indisputable conclusion.

After an hour of turmoil, which I frankly admit I enjoyed extremely, I escaped to the train, and the journey to Pietermaritzburg passed very quickly in the absorbing occupation of devouring a month's newspapers and clearing my palate from the evil taste of the exaggerations of Pretoria by a liberal antidote of our own versions.

I rested a day at Government House, and enjoyed long conversations with Sir Walter Hely-Hutchinson—the Governor under whose wise administration Natal has become the most patriotic province of the Empire. Moreover, I was fortunate in meeting Colonel Hime, the Prime Minister of the Colony, a tall, grey, keen-eyed man, who talked only of the importance of fighting this quarrel out to the end, and of the obstinate determination of the people he represented to stand by the Queen's Government through all the changing moods of fortune.

I received then and have since been receiving a great number of telegrams and messages from all kinds of people and from all countries of the earth.

One gentleman invited me to shoot with him in Central Asia. Another favoured me with a poem which he had written in my honour, and desired me to have it set to music and published.

A third—an American—wanted me to plan a raid into Transvaal territory along the Delagoa Bay line to arm the prisoners and seize the President.

Five Liberal Electors of the borough of Oldham wrote to say that they would give me their votes on a future occasion 'irrespective of politics.'

Young ladies sent me woollen comforters. Old ladies forwarded their photographs; and hundreds of people wrote kind letters, many of which in the stir of events I have not yet been able to answer.

The correspondence varied vastly in tone as well as in character, and I cannot help quoting a couple of telegrams as specimens.

The first was from a worthy gentleman who, besides being a substantial farmer, is also a member of the Natal Parliament.

He wrote: 'My heartiest congratulations on your wonderful and glorious deeds, which will send such a thrill of pride and enthusiasm through Great Britain and the United States of America, that the Anglo-Saxon race will be irresistible.'

The intention of the other, although his message was shorter, was equally plain.

'London, December 30th.—Best friends here hope you won't go making further ass of yourself.—M'NEILL.'

This shows, I think, how widely human judgment may differ even in regard to ascertained facts.

Chapter XII: Back to the British Lines

THE THEATRE OF OPERATIONS IN NATAL

I found time to visit the hospitals—long barracks which before the war were full of healthy men, and are now crammed with sick and wounded.

Everything seemed beautifully arranged, and what money could buy and care provide was at the service of those who had sustained hurt in the public contention. But for all that I left with a feeling of relief.

Grim sights and grimmer suggestions were at every corner. Beneath a verandah a dozen wounded officers, profusely swathed in bandages, clustered in a silent brooding group. Nurses waited quietly by shut doors that none might disturb more serious cases. Doctors hurried with solemn faces from one building to another.

Here and there men pushed stretchers on rubber-tyred wheels about the paths, stretchers on which motionless forms lay shrouded in blankets. One, concerning whom I asked, had just had part of his skull trepanned: another had suffered amputation.

And all this pruning and patching up of broken men to win them a few more years of crippled life caught one's throat like the penetrating smell of the iodoform. Nor was I sorry to hasten away by the night mail northwards to the camps.

It was still dark as we passed Estcourt, but morning had broken when the train reached Frere, and I got out and walked along the line inquiring for my tent, and found it pitched by the side of the very same cutting down which I had fled for my life from the Boer marksmen, and only fifty yards from the spot on which I had surrendered myself prisoner.

So after much trouble and adventure I came safely home again to the wars. Six weeks had passed since the armoured train had been destroyed. Many changes had taken place. The hills which I had last seen black with the figures of the Boer riflemen were crowned with British pickets.

The valley in which we had lain exposed to their artillery fire was crowded with the white tents of a numerous army. In the hollows and on the middle slopes canvas villages gleamed like patches of snowdrops.

Chapter XII: Back to the British Lines

The iron bridge across the Blue Krantz River lay in a tangle of crimson-painted wreckage across the bottom of the ravine, and the railway ran over an unpretentious but substantial wooden structure.

All along the line near the station fresh sidings had been built, and many trains concerned in the business of supply occupied them.

When I had last looked on the landscape it meant fierce and overpowering danger, with the enemy on all sides. Now I was in the midst of a friendly host.

But though much was altered some things remained the same. The Boers still held Colenso. Their forces still occupied the free soil of Natal.

It was true that thousands of troops had arrived to make all efforts to change the situation. It was true that the British Army had even advanced ten miles. But Ladysmith was still locked in the strong grip of the invader, and as I listened I heard the distant booming of the same bombardment which I had heard two months before, and which all the time I was wandering had been remorselessly maintained and patiently borne.

Looking backward over the events of the last two months, it is impossible not to admire the Boer strategy. From the beginning they have aimed at two main objects: to exclude the war from their own territories, and to confine it to rocky and broken regions suited to their tactics. Up to the present time they have been entirely successful.

Though the line of advance northwards through the Free State lay through flat open country, and they could spare few men to guard it, no British force has assailed this weak point. The 'farmers' have selected their own ground and compelled the generals to fight them on it.

No part of the earth's surface is better adapted to Boer tactics than Northern Natal, yet observe how we have been gradually but steadily drawn into it, until the mountains have swallowed up the greater part of the whole Army Corps.

By degrees we have learned the power of our adversary. Before the war began men said: 'Let them come into Natal and attack us if they dare. They would go back quicker than they would come.'

So the Boers came and fierce fighting took place, but it was the British who retired.

Then it was said: 'Never mind. The forces were not concentrated. Now that all the Natal Field Force is massed at Ladysmith, there will be no mistake.'

But still, in spite of Elandslaagte, concerning which the President remarked: 'The foolhardy shall be punished,' the Dutch advance continued.

The concentrated Ladysmith force, twenty squadrons, six batteries, and eleven battalions, sallied out to meet them.

The Staff said: 'By to-morrow night there will not be a Boer within twenty miles of Ladysmith.'

But by the evening of October 30 the whole of Sir George White's command had been flung back into the town with three hundred men killed and wounded, and nearly a thousand prisoners.

Then every one said: 'But now we have touched bottom. The Ladysmith position is the *ne plus ultra*. So far they have gone; but no further!' Then it appeared that the Boers were reaching out round the flanks.

What was their design? To blockade Ladysmith? Ridiculous and impossible! However, send a battalion to Colenso to keep the communications open, and make assurance doubly sure.

So the Dublin Fusiliers were railed southwards, and entrenched themselves at Colenso.

Two days later, the Boers cut the railway south of Ladysmith at Pieters, shelled the small garrison out of Colenso, shut and locked the gate on the Ladysmith force, and established themselves in the almost impregnable positions north of the Tugela.

Still there was no realisation of the meaning of the investment. It would last a week, they said, and all the clever correspondents

Chapter XII: Back to the British Lines

laughed at the veteran Bennet Burleigh[1] for his hurry to get south before the door was shut.

Only a week of isolation! Two months have passed. But all the time we have said: 'Never mind; wait till our army comes. We will soon put a stop to the siege—for it soon became more than a blockade—of Ladysmith.'

Then the army began to come. Its commander, knowing the disadvantageous nature of the country, would have preferred to strike northwards through the Free State and relieve Ladysmith at Bloemfontein. But the pressure from home was strong.

First two brigades, then four, the artillery of two divisions, and a large mounted force were diverted from the Cape Colony and drawn into Natal.

Finally, Sir Redvers Buller had to follow the bulk of his army. Then the action of Colenso was fought, and in that unsatisfactory engagement, the British leaders learned that the blockade of Ladysmith was no unstable curtain that could be brushed aside, but a solid wall.

Another division is hurried to the mountains, battery follows battery, until at the present moment, the South Natal Field Force numbers two cavalry and six infantry brigades, and nearly sixty guns. It is with this force that we hope to break through the lines of Boers who surround Ladysmith.

The army is numerous, powerful, and high-spirited. But the task before it is one which no man can regard without serious misgivings.

Whoever selected Ladysmith as a military centre must sleep uneasily at nights. I remember hearing the question of a possible war with the Boers discussed by several officers of high rank.

---

1 Bennet Burley (1840–1914). Born in Scotland, he served during the American Civil War on the Confederate side as a naval privateer, disrupting Union shipping. Arrested, he escaped to Canada, changing his last name to Burleigh to avoid further detection. After that war, he was employed by British newspapers to cover foreign wars, and worked in South Africa for the *Daily Telegraph*. His book, *The Natal Campaign*, (1900) is being referred to here.

The general impression was that Ladysmith was a tremendous strategic position, which dominated the lines of approach both into the Transvaal and the Orange Free State, whereas of course it does nothing of the sort.

The fact that it stands at the junction of the railways may have encouraged the belief, but both lines of advance are barred by a broken and tangled country abounding in positions of extraordinary strength.

Tactically Ladysmith may be strongly defensible, politically it has become invested with much importance, but for strategic purposes it is absolutely worthless. It is worse. It is a regular trap. The town and cantonment stand in a huge circle of hills which enclasp it on all sides like the arms of a giant, and though so great is the circle that only guns of the heavier class can reach the town from the heights, once an enemy has established himself on these heights it is beyond the power of the garrison to dislodge him, or perhaps even to break out.

Not only do the surrounding hills keep the garrison in, but they also form a formidable barrier to the advance of a relieving force. Thus it is that the ten thousand troops in Ladysmith are at this moment actually an encumbrance.

To extricate them—I write advisedly, to endeavour to extricate them—brigades and divisions must be diverted from all the other easy lines of advance, and Sir Redvers Buller, who had always deprecated any attempt to hold Natal north of the Tugela, is compelled to attack the enemy on their own terms and their own ground.

What are those terms? The northern side of the Tugela River at nearly every point commands the southern bank. Ranges of high hills strewn with boulders and dotted with trees rise abruptly from the water, forming a mighty rampart for the enemy.

Before this the river, a broad torrent with few and narrow fords and often precipitous banks, flows rapidly—a great moat. And before the river again, on our side stretches a smooth, undulating, grassy country—a regular glacis. To defend the rampart and

Chapter XII: Back to the British Lines

sweep the glacis are gathered, according to my information derived in Pretoria, twelve thousand, according to the Intelligence Branch, fifteen thousand, of the best riflemen in the world armed with beautiful magazine rifles, supplied with an inexhaustible store of ammunition, and supported by fifteen or twenty excellent quick-firing guns, all artfully entrenched and concealed.

The drifts of the river across which our columns must force their way are all surrounded with trenches and rifle pits, from which a converging fire may be directed, and the actual bottom of the river is doubtless obstructed by entanglements of barbed wire and other devices.

But when all these difficulties have been overcome the task is by no means finished. Nearly twenty miles of broken country, ridge rising beyond ridge, kopje above kopje, all probably already prepared for defence, intervene between the relieving army and the besieged garrison.

Such is the situation, and so serious are the dangers and difficulties that I have heard it said in the camp that on strict military grounds Ladysmith should be left to its fate; that a division should remain to hold this fine open country south of the Tugela and protect Natal; and that the rest should be hurried off to the true line of advance into the Free State from the south.

Though I recognise all this, and do not deny its force, I rejoice that what is perhaps a strategically unwise decision has been taken. It is not possible to abandon a brave garrison without striking a blow to rescue them.

The attempt will cost several thousand lives; and may even fail; but it must be made on the grounds of honour, if not on those of policy. We are going to try almost immediately, for there is no time to be lost.

'The sands,' to quote Mr. Chamberlain on another subject, 'are running down in the glass.'

Ladysmith has stood two months' siege and bombardment. Food and ammunition stores are dwindling. Disease is daily increasing. The strain on the garrison has been, in spite of their pluck and stamina, a severe one. How long can they hold out? It is difficult to say precisely, because after the ordinary rations are exhausted determined men will eat horses and rats and beetles, and such like odds and ends, and so continue the defence.

But another month must be the limit of their endurance, and then if no help comes Sir George White will have to fire off all his ammunition, blow up his heavy guns, burn waggons and equipment, and sally out with his whole force in a fierce endeavour to escape southwards.

Perhaps half the garrison might succeed in reaching our lines, but the rest, less the killed and wounded, would be sent to occupy the new camp at Waterfall, which has been already laid out—such is the intelligent anticipation of the enemy—for their accommodation.

So we are going to try to force the Tugela within the week, and I dare say my next letter will give you some account of our fortunes.

Meanwhile all is very quiet in the camps. From Chieveley, where there are two brigades of infantry, a thousand horse of sorts, including the 13th Hussars, and a dozen naval guns, it is quite possible to see the Boer positions, and the outposts live within range of each other's rifles.

Yesterday I rode out to watch the evening bombardment which we make on their entrenchments with the naval 4.7-inch guns. From the low hill on which the battery is established the whole scene is laid bare.

The Boer lines run in a great crescent along the hills. Tier above tier of trenches have been scored along their sides, and the brown streaks run across the grass of the open country south of the river.

After tea in the captain's cabin—I should say tent—Commander Limpus of the 'Terrible' kindly invited me to look through the telescope and mark the fall of the shots. The glass was one of great power, and I could plainly see the figures of the Boers walking about in twos and threes, sitting on the embankments,

Chapter XII: Back to the British Lines

or shovelling away to heighten them. We selected one particular group near a kraal, the range of which had been carefully noted, and the great guns were slowly brought to bear on the unsuspecting target.

I looked through the spy-hole at the tiny picture—three dirty beehives for the kraal, a long breastwork of newly thrown up earth, six or seven miniature men gathered into a little bunch, two others skylarking on the grass behind the trench, apparently engaged in a boxing match.

Then I turned to the guns. A naval officer craned along the seventeen-feet barrel, peering through the telescopic sights. Another was pencilling some calculations as to wind and light and other intricate details. The crew, attentive, stood around.

At last all was done. I looked back to the enemy. The group was still intact. The boxers were still playing—one had pushed the other down. A solitary horseman had also come into the picture and was riding slowly across. The desire of murder rose in my heart. Now for a bag!

Bang! I jumped at least a foot, disarranging the telescope, but there was plenty of time to reset it while the shell was hissing and roaring its way through nearly five miles of air.

I found the kraal again and the group still there, but all motionless and alert, like startled rabbits. Then they began to bob into the earth, one after the other. Suddenly, in the middle of the kraal, there appeared a huge flash, a billowy ball of smoke, and clouds of dust.

Bang! I jumped again; the second gun had fired. But before this shell could reach the trenches a dozen little figures scampered away, scattering in all directions. Evidently the first had not been without effect. Yet when I turned the glass to another part of the defences the Boers were working away stolidly, and only those near the explosion showed any signs of disturbance.

The bombardment continued for half an hour, the shells being flung sometimes into the trenches, sometimes among the houses of Colenso, and always directed with marvellous accuracy.

London to Ladysmith via Pretoria

At last, the guns were covered up again in their tarpaulins, the crowd of military spectators broke up and dispersed amid the tents, and soon it became night.

A Naval 4.7 inch gun in action, Natal.

Troops of the Dublin Fusiliers in action, Natal.

CHAPTER XIII
CHRISTMAS AND NEW YEAR

Frere: January 4, 1900.

December 25.—Christmas Day! 'Glory to God in the Highest, and on earth, peace and goodwill towards men.'

So no great shells were fired into the Boer entrenchments at dawn, and the hostile camps remained tranquil throughout the day. Even the pickets forbore to snipe each other, and both armies attended divine service in the morning and implored Heaven's blessing on their righteous causes.

In the afternoon, the British held athletic sports, an impromptu military tournament, and a gymkhana, all of which caused much merriment and diversion, and the Boers profited by the cessation of the shell fire to shovel away at their trenches.

In the evening, there were Christmas dinners in our camp—roast beef, plum pudding, a quart of beer for everyone, and various smoking concerts afterwards. I cannot describe the enemy's festivities.

But since that peaceful day we have had desultory picket firing, and the great guns in the naval battery have spoken whenever an opportunity presented itself.

The opposing outpost lines are drawn so far apart that with the best intentions they can scarcely harm each other. But the long range of the smallbore rifles encourages fancy shooting, so that there is often a brisk fusillade and no one any the worse.

On our side we have only had one infantry soldier wounded. We do not know what the fortunes of the Boers may have been, but it is probable that they lose a few men every day from the bombardment, and certain that on Monday last there were three burghers killed and several wounded and one horse.

It happened in this wise: beyond the strong Infantry pickets which remain in position always, there is a more or less extended line of cavalry outposts, which are sprinkled all along the kopjes to the east and west of the camp, and are sometimes nearly three miles from it.

On the Monday in question—New Year's Day to wit—200 Boers set forth and attacked our picket on the extreme right. The picket, which was composed of the South African Light Horse, fell back with discretion, and the Boers following without their usual caution did not observe that eight troopers had been dropped behind among the rocks and ledges of a donga;[1] so that when twelve of them attempted to make their way up this natural zigzag approach in order to fire upon the retiring picket they were themselves received at 400 yards by a well-directed sputter of musketry, and were glad to make off with five riderless horses, two men upon one horse, and leaving three lying quite still on the ground. Thereafter the picket continued to retreat unmolested.

Indeed, the New Year opened well, and many little things seem to favour the hope that it is the turning point of the war. Besides our tiny skirmish on the right, Captain Gough, of the 16th Lancers, on the left, made his way along a convenient depression, almost to the river bank, and discovered Boers having tea in their camp at scarcely 1,800 yards.

Forthwith he opened fire, causing great commotion; hurried upsetting of the tea, scrambling into tents for rifle, 'confounded impudence of these cursed *rooineks*![2] Come quickly Hans, Pieter, O'Brien, and John Smith, and let us mend their manners. What do they mean by harassing us?'

And in a very few minutes there was a wrathful rattle of firing all along the trenches on the hillside, which spread far away to the right and left as other Boers heard it.

What the deuce is this? Another attack! Till at last the Maxim shell gun caught the infection, and began pom, pom, pom!

---

1 From the Zulu word "udonga." Literally slits in the earth, caused by water erosion.
2 "Rednecks"—a derisory term for Englishmen, who suffered quickly from sunburn in South Africa, hence recognisable through their having red necks.

Chapter XIII: Christmas and New Year

pom, pom, pom! and so on at intervals. Evidently much angry passion was aroused in the Boer camp, and all because Captain Gough had been trying his luck at long range volleys. The situation might have become serious; the event was, however, fortunate. No smoke betrayed the position of the scouting party; no bullets found them. A heavy shower of metal sang and whistled at random in the air.

The donga afforded an excellent line of retreat, and when the adventurous patrol had retired safely into the camp, they were amused to hear the Boers still busy with the supposed chastisement of their audacious assailants.

But these are small incidents which, though they break the monotony of the camp, do not alter nor, each by itself, greatly accelerate the course of the war.

Good news came in on New Year's Day from other quarters. Near Belmont, the Canadians and Queenslanders fell on a raiding or reckless commando, took them on at their own game, hunted them and shot them among the rocks until the white flag was upon the right side for once and hoisted in honest surrender.

Forty prisoners and twenty dead and wounded; excellent news to all of us; but causing amazing joy in Natal, where every colonist goes into an ecstasy over every crumb of British success.

Moreover, we have good news from East London. General Gatacre is stolidly and patiently repairing the opening misfortune of his campaign: has learned by experience much of the new conditions of the war.

Strange that the Boers did not advance after their victory; stranger still that they retired from Dordrecht. Never mind whether their stillness be due to national cautiousness or good defensive arrangements. Since they don't want Dordrecht, let us go there; and there we go accordingly.

Out of this there arises on New Year's Day a successful skirmish, in the account of which the name of De Montmorency[3]

---

3 Raymond de Montmorency (1867–1900), a Canadian-born British Army officer who won a Victoria Cross during the Sudan Campaign in 1898, and

is mentioned. In Egypt the name was associated with madcap courage. Here they talk of prudent skill. The double reputation should be valuable.

And, perhaps, the best news of all comes from Arundel, near Colesberg, where Generals French and Brabazon with the cavalry column—for it is nearly all mounted—are gradually sidling and coaxing the Boers back out of the Colony.

They are a powerful combination: French's distinguished military talents, and Brabazon's long and deep experience of war.

So, with this column there are no frontal attacks—perhaps they are luckier than we in respect of ground—no glorious victories (which the enemy call victories, too); very few people hurt and a steady advance, as we hear on the first day of the year, right up to Colesberg.

Perhaps the tide of war has really begun to turn. Perhaps 1900 is to mark the beginning of a century of good luck and good sense in British policy in Africa.

When I was a prisoner at Pretoria the Boers showed me a large green pamphlet Mr. Reitz[4] had written. It was intended to be an account of the Dutch grounds of quarrel with the English, and was called 'A Century of Wrong.'

Much was distortion and exaggeration, but a considerable part dealt with acknowledged facts.

Wrong in plenty there has been on both sides, but latterly more on theirs than on ours; and the result is war—bitter, bloody war tearing the land in twain; dividing brother from brother, friend from friend, and opening a terrible chasm between the two white races who must live side by side as long as South Africa stands above the ocean, and by whose friendly co-operation alone it can enjoy the fullest measure of prosperity.

---

who in South Africa commanded a scouting unit involved in fighting in the Cape Colony. He was killed in action at the Battle of Stormberg.
4 Francis William Reitz (1844–1934), Fifth President of the Orange Free State and State Secretary of the South African Republic at the time of the Second Anglo-Boer War.

Chapter XIII: Christmas and New Year

'A century of wrong!' British ignorance of South Africa, Boer ignorance of civilisation, British intolerance, Boer brutality, British interference, Boer independence, clash, clash, clash, all along the line! and then fanatical, truth-scorning missionaries, experimental philanthropists, high-handed jingo administrators, colonial ministers who disliked all colonies on the glorious principles of theoretic liberalism, bad generals thinking of their own reputations, not of their country's success, and a series of miserable events recalled sufficiently well by their names—Slagter's Nek, Kimberley, Moshesh, Majuba, Jameson, all these arousing first resentment, then loathing, then contempt, and, finally, a Great Desire, crystallising into a Great Conspiracy for a United Dutch South Africa, free from the flag that has elsewhere been regarded as the flag of freedom.

And so inevitably to war—war with peculiar sadness and horror, in which the line of cleavage springs between all sorts of well-meaning people that used to know one another in friendship; but war which, whatever its fortunes, certainly sweeps the past into obscurity.

We have done with 'a century of wrong.'

God send us now 'a century of right.'

Pom Pom Bridge at Thukela Heights near Ladysmith.

British artillery in action.

CHAPTER XIV
A MILITARY DEMONSTRATION AND SOME GOOD NEWS

Chieveley: January 8, 1900.

BOOM. Thud, thud. Boom. Boom. Thud—thud thud—thud thud thud thud—boom. A long succession of queer moaning vibrations broke the stillness of the sleeping camp.

I became suddenly awake. It was two o'clock on the morning of January 6. The full significance of the sounds came with consciousness.

We had all heard them before—heavy cannonading at Ladysmith. They were at it again. How much longer would the heroic garrison be persecuted? I turned to rest once more. But the distant guns forbade sleep.

The reports grew momentarily more frequent, until at last they merged into one general roar.

This was new. Never before had we heard such bombarding. Louder and louder swelled the cannonade, and presently the deep note of the heavy artillery could scarcely be distinguished above the incessant discharges of field pieces.

So I lay and listened. What was happening eighteen miles away over the hills? Another bayonet attack by the garrison? Or perhaps a general sortie: or perhaps, but this seemed scarcely conceivable, the Boers had hardened their hearts and were delivering the long expected, long threatened assault.

An officer came to my tent with the daylight. Something big happening at Ladysmith—hell of a cannonade—never heard anything like it—worse than Colenso—what do you think of it? But I was without opinion; nor did I find anyone anxious to pronounce. Meanwhile the firing was maintained, and we breakfasted to its accompaniment. Until half-past ten there was not the slightest diminution or intermission.

As the day advanced, however, it gradually died away, showing either that the fight was over, or, as it afterwards turned out, that it had passed into the hands of riflemen.

We all spent an anxious morning speculating on the reason and result of the engagement.

About noon there arrived an unofficial message by heliograph, which the young officer at the signal station confided to his friends. It was brief.

'General attack all sides by Boers—everywhere repulsed—but fight still going on.'

At one o'clock, just as were sitting down to luncheon, came an orderly at full gallop with the order for the whole force in Chieveley to turn out at once. Whereat the camp, till then dormant under the midday sun, sprang to life like a disturbed ant-hill.

Some said we were about to make a regular attack on Colenso, while many of the covering army of Boers were busy at Ladysmith. Others suggested a night assault—with the bayonet. The idea was very pleasant to the hearts of the infantry.

But I soon learned that no serious operation was in contemplation, and that the force was merely to make a demonstration before Colenso with the object of bringing some of the Boers back from Ladysmith, and of so relieving the pressure on Sir George White.

The demonstration was, however, a very imposing affair. First of all the mounted forces threw out a long fringe of patrols all along the front. Behind this the squadrons made a line of black bars. The mounted infantry, Bethune's Horse, and the Natal Carabineers formed the left: the South African Light Horse the centre, and the 13th Hussars and Thorneycroft's Mounted Infantry twisted back to watch the right.

Behind this curtain marched the infantry, Hildyard's brigade on the right, Barton's on the left, line after line of brown men ten yards apart, two hundred yards between the lines, spreading in this open formation over a wide expanse of country, and looking

Chapter XIV: A Military Demonstration

a mighty swarm. Behind these again dark blocks of artillery and waggons moved slowly forward. Behind, and above all, the naval battery began to throw its shells into the village.

The cavalry soon cleared the front, the squadrons wheeled about, the patrols retreated. The South African Light Horse, with whom I now have the honour to serve, were stationed in rear of Gun Hill, a rocky eminence so called because a heavy battery was placed there in the last engagement.

From this feature an excellent view of the operation was afforded, and thence we watched the whole development. Sir Francis Clery, General Hildyard, and their respective Staffs had also taken their position on Gun Hill, so that its crest was thickly crowded with figures peering exhaustively through field glasses and telescopes.

The infantry, who were now moving steadily forward, were literally sprinkled all over the country. In the text-books compiled from the results of past experience the military student reads that armies divide to march and concentrate to fight.

'Nous avons changé tout cela.'[1] Here we concentrate to march and disperse to fight. I asked General Hildyard what formation his brigade was in. He replied, 'Formation for taking advantage of ant-heaps.' This is a valuable addition to the infantry drill.

Meanwhile the demonstration was in progress, and not without effect. Only the well-informed realised that it was a demonstration, and the privates, as they walked phlegmatically on, did not know that they were not about to be plunged into another deluge of fire.

'You watch it, Bill,' I heard one man remark, 'we'll have that —— laughing hyena' (the Vickers-Maxim gun) 'let off at us in a minute.' The Boers, too, seemed to be deceived, or, at any rate, doubtful, for we could see them in twos and threes, and presently in fives and sixes, galloping into their trenches, which were evidently deep enough to shelter horse and man.

---

1 "We have changed all that."

It was most probable that larger bodies had already begun their countermarch from Ladysmith. We were not wasting our time or our trouble. The infantry halted about three thousand yards from the enemy's position, and the artillery, which numbered fourteen guns, trotted forward and came into action.

All these movements, which had been very deliberately made, had taken a long time, and it was now nearly five o'clock. Dark thunder-clouds and a drizzle of rain descended on the silent Boer position, and the range of hills along which it stretched lay in deep shadow as if under the frown of Heaven.

Our batteries also were ranged in this gloomy zone, but with the reserves and on the hill whence we were watching there was bright sunlight. The bombardment and the storm broke over the Boer entrenchments simultaneously.

A swift succession of fierce red flashes stabbed out from the patches of gunners, teams, and waggons, and with yellow gleams soft white balls of smoke appeared among the houses of Colenso and above the belts of scrub which extend on either side.

The noise of explosions of gun and projectile came back to us on the hill in regular order, and above them rang the startling discharges of the 4.7-inch naval guns, whose shells in bursting raised huge brown dust clouds from houses, trench, or hillside.

At the same time the thunder began to rumble, and vivid streaks of blue light scarred the sombre hills. We watched the impressive spectacle in safety and the sunlight.

Besides creating a diversion in favour of Ladysmith the object of our demonstration was to make the enemy reveal his position and especially the positions of his guns.

In this latter respect, however, we were defeated. Though they must have suffered some loss and more annoyance from the bombardment, and though much of the infantry was well within the range of their guns, the Boers declined to be drawn, and during two hours' shelling they did not condescend to give a single shot in reply.

Chapter XIV: A Military Demonstration

It needs a patient man to beat a Dutchman at waiting. So about seven o'clock we gave up trying.

It had been intended to leave the troops on the enemy's front until night and withdraw them after dark, the idea being to make him anxious lest a night attack should be designed.

But as some of the battalions had turned out without having their dinners, Sir Francis Clery decided not to keep them under arms longer, and the whole force withdrew gracefully and solemnly to camp.

Here we found news from Ladysmith. 'Enemy everywhere repulsed for the present.'

For the present! Hold on only a little longer, gallant garrison, and if it be in the power of 25,000 British soldiers to help you, your troubles and privations shall soon be ended—and what a dinner we will have together then!

That night we tried to congratulate or encourage Ladysmith, and the searchlight perseveringly flashed the Morse code on the clouds. But before it had been working half an hour the Boer searchlight saw it and hurried to interfere, flickering, blinking, and crossing to try to confuse the dots and dashes, and appeared to us who watched this curious aerial battle—Briton and Boer fighting each other in the sky with vibrations of ether—to confuse them very effectually.

Next morning, however, the sun came out for uncertain periods, and Ladysmith was able to tell her own story briefly and jerkily, but still a very satisfactory account.

At two o'clock, according to Sir George White, the Boers in great numbers, evidently reinforced from Colenso, surprised the pickets and began a general attack on the outpost line round the town, particularly directing their efforts on Cæsar's Camp and Waggon Hill.

The fighting became very close, and the enemy, who had after all hardened their hearts, pushed the attack with extraordinary daring and vigour.

Some of the trenches on Waggon Hill were actually taken three times by the assailants. But every time General Hamilton—the skilful Hamilton as he has been called—flung them out again by counterattacks.

At one place, indeed, they succeeded in holding on all day, nor was it until the dusk of the evening, when the rain and thunderstorm which we saw hanging over Colenso broke on Ladysmith, that Colonel Park led forth the Devon Regiment—who, having had half their officers killed or wounded by a shell some days before, were probably spiteful—and drove the Dutchmen helter skelter at the point of the bayonet.

So that by night the Boers were repulsed at every point, with necessarily great slaughter, greater at any rate than on our side. Their first experience of assaulting! Encore!

Battles now-a-days are fought mainly with firearms, but no troops, however brave, however well directed, can enjoy the full advantage of their successes if they exclude the possibilities of cold steel and are not prepared to maintain what they have won, if necessary with their fists.

The moral strength of an army which welcomes the closest personal encounter must exceed that of an army which depends for its victories only on being able to kill its foes at a distance.

The bayonet is the most powerful weapon we possess out here. Firearms kill many of the enemy, but it is the white weapon that makes them run away. Rifles can inflict the loss, but victory depends, for us at least, on the bayonets.

Of the losses we as yet know nothing, except that Lord Ava is seriously wounded, a sad item for which the only consolation is that the Empire is worth the blood of its noblest citizens.

But for the general result we rejoice.

Ladysmith, too, is proud and happy. Only ten thousand of us, and look what we do! A little reproachfully, perhaps; for it is dull work fighting week after week without alcohol or green vegetables.

Chapter XIV: A Military Demonstration

Well, it looks as if their trials were very nearly over. Sir Charles Warren's Division marches to Frere to-day. All the hospitals have been cleared ready for those who may need them. If all's well we shall have removed the grounds of reproach by this day week.

The long interval between the acts has come to an end. The warning bell has rung. Take your seats, ladies and gentlemen. The curtain is about to rise.

'High time, too,' say the impatient audience, and with this I must agree; for, looking from my tent as I write, I can see the smoke-puff bulging on Bulwana Hill as 'Long Tom' toils through his seventy-second day of bombardment, and the white wisp seems to beckon the relieving army onward.

Much to the Boers' astonishment, the British Army routinely deployed observation balloons to help determine battlefield strategy.

CHAPTER XV
THE DASH FOR POTGIETER'S FERRY

Spearman's Hill: January 13, 1900.

Secrets usually leak out in a camp, no matter how many people are employed to keep them. For two days before January 10, rumours of an impending move circulated freely. There are, moreover, certain signs by which anyone who is acquainted with the under machinery of an army can tell when operations are imminent.

On the 6th, we heard that orders had been given to clear the Pietermaritzburg hospitals of all patients, evidently because new inmates were expected.

On the 7th, it was reported that the hospitals were all clear.

On the 8th, an ambulance train emptied the field hospitals at Frere, and that same evening there arrived seven hundred civilian stretcher-bearers—brave men who had volunteered to carry wounded under fire, and whom the army somewhat ungratefully nicknames the 'Body-snatchers.'

Nor were these grim preparations the only indications of approaching activity. The commissariat told tales of accumulations of supplies—twenty-one days' packed in waggons—of the collection of transport oxen and other details, meaningless by themselves, but full of significance when viewed side by side with other circumstances.

Accordingly, I was scarcely surprised when, chancing to ride from Chieveley to Frere on the afternoon of the 10th, I discovered the whole of Sir Charles Warren's division added to the already extensive camp.

This was the first move of the complicated operations by which Sir Redvers Buller designed to seize the passage of the Tugela at Potgieter's Ferry: Warren (seven battalions, comprising Coke's and Woodgate's Brigades and five batteries) from Estcourt

Chapter XV: The Dash for Potgieter's Ferry

to Frere. When I got back to Chieveley all was bustle in the camp. Orders to march at dawn had arrived. At last the long pause was finished; waiting was over; action had begun.

So far as Chieveley was concerned, the following was the programme: Barton's Brigade to entrench itself strongly and to remain before Colenso, covering the head of the line of communications, and demonstrating against the position; Hildyard's Brigade to move westward at daylight on the 11th to Pretorius's Farm; cavalry, guns, and baggage (miles of it) to take a more circuitous route to the same place.

Thither also Hart was to move from Frere, joining Hildyard and forming Clery's division.

Warren was to rest until the next day.

The force for the relief of Ladysmith, exclusive of Barton's Brigade and communication troops, was organised as follows:

Commander-in-Chief: SIR REDVERS BULLER

CLERY'S DIVISION	Warren's Division
consisting of	consisting of
Hildyard's Brigade,	Lyttelton's Brigade,
Hart's Brigade,	Woodgate's Brigade,
1 squad. 13th Hussars,	1 squad. 15th Hussars,
3 batteries,	3 batteries,
R.E.	R.E.

CORPS TROOPS
Coke's Brigade (3 battalions),
1 field battery R.A.,
1 howitzer battery R.A.,
2 4.7-inch naval guns and Naval Brigade,
8 long-range naval 12-pounder guns,
1 squadron 13th Hussars,
R.E., &c.

CAVALRY (DUNDONALD)
1st Royal Dragoons.
14th Hussars.
4 squadrons South African Light Horse.

1 squadron Imperial Light Horse.
Bethune's Mounted Infantry.
Thorneycroft's Mounted Infantry.
1 squadron Natal Carabineers.
1 squadron Natal Police.
1 company K.R.R.
  Mounted Infantry.
6 machine guns.

Or, to sum the whole up briefly, 19,000 infantry, 3,000 cavalry, and 60 guns.

All were busy with their various tasks—Barton's Brigade entrenching, making redoubts and shelter pits, or block-houses of railway iron; the other brigades packing up ready for the march as night closed in.

In the morning we started. The cavalry were responsible for the safety of the baggage convoy, and with Colonel Byng, who commanded the column, I waited and watched the almost interminable procession defile.

Ox waggons piled high with all kinds of packages, and drawn sometimes by ten or twelve pairs of oxen, mule waggons, Scotch carts, ambulance waggons, with huge Red Cross flags, ammunition carts, artillery, slaughter cattle, and, last of all, the naval battery, with its two enormous 4.7-inch pieces, dragged by long strings of animals, and guarded by straw-hatted khaki-clad bluejackets, passed in imposing array, with here and there a troop of cavalry to protect them or to prevent straggling.

And here let me make an unpleasant digression. The vast amount of baggage this army takes with it on the march hampers its movements and utterly precludes all possibility of surprising the enemy.

I have never before seen even officers accommodated with tents on service, though both the Indian frontier and the Soudan lie under a hotter sun than South Africa. But here to day, within striking distance of a mobile enemy whom we wish to circumvent, every private soldier has canvas shelter, and the other ar-

Chapter XV: The Dash for Potgieter's Ferry

rangements are on an equally elaborate scale. The consequence is that roads are crowded, drifts are blocked, marching troops are delayed, and all rapidity of movement is out of the question.

Meanwhile, the enemy completes the fortification of his positions, and the cost of capturing them rises. It is a poor economy to let a soldier live well for three days at the price of killing him on the fourth.[1]

We marched off with the rearguard at last, and the column twisted away among the hills towards the west. After marching about three miles we reached the point where the track from Frere joined the track from Chieveley, and here two streams of waggons flowed into one another like the confluence of rivers.

Shortly after this, all the mounted forces with the baggage were directed to concentrate at the head of the column, and, leaving the tardy waggons to toil along at their own pace, we trotted swiftly forward.

Pretorius's Farm was reached at noon—a tin-roofed house, a few sheds, a dozen trees, and an artificial pond filled to the brim by the recent rains. Here drawn up in the spacious plain were the Royal Dragoons—distinguished from the Colonial Corps by the bristle of lances bare of pennons above their ranks and by their great horses—one squadron of the already famous Imperial Light Horse, and Bethune's Mounted Infantry.

The Dragoons remained at the farm, which was that night to be the camping place of Clery's division. But all the rest of the mounted forces, about a thousand men, and a battery of artillery were hurried forward to seize the bridge across the Little Tugela at Springfield.

So on we ride, 'trot and walk,' lightly and easily over the good turf, and winding in scattered practical formations among the beautiful verdant hills of Natal. Presently, we topped a ridge and entered a very extensive basin of country—a huge circular val-

---

1 This complaint was not in one respect justified by what followed, for after we left Spearman's we only saw our tents for a day or two, and at rare intervals, until Ladysmith was relieved. [Original footnote by author]

ley of green grass with sloping hills apparently on all sides and towards the west, bluffs, rising range above range, to the bright purple wall of the Drakensberg.

Other valleys opened out from this, some half veiled in thin mist, others into which the sun was shining, filled with a curious blue light, so that one seemed to be looking down into depths of clear water, and everyone rejoiced in the splendours of the delightful landscape.

But now we approached Springfield, and perhaps at Springfield we should find the enemy. Surely if they did not oppose the passage they would blow up the bridge.

Tiny patrols—beetles on a green baize carpet—scoured the plain, and before we reached the crease—scarcely perceptible at a mile's distance, in which the Little Tugela flows—word was brought that no Dutchmen were anywhere to be seen.

Captain Gough, it appeared, with one man had ridden over the bridge in safety; more than that, had actually explored three miles on the further side: did not believe there was a Boer this side of the Tugela: would like to push on to Potgieter's and make certain: 'Perhaps we can seize Potgieter's to-night. They don't like having a flooded river behind them.'

So we come safely to Springfield—three houses, a long wooden bridge 'erected by public subscription, at a cost of 4,300*l.*'—half a dozen farms with their tin roofs and tree clumps seen in the neighbourhood—and no Boers.

Orders were to seize the bridge: seized accordingly; and after all had crossed and watered in the Little Tugela—swollen by the rains to quite a considerable Tugela, eighty yards wide—we looked about for something else to do.

Meanwhile more patrols came in; all told the same tale: no Boers anywhere. Well, then, let us push on. Why not seize the heights above Potgieter's? If held, they would cost a thousand men to storm; now, perhaps, they might be had for nothing. Again, why not? Orders said, 'Go to Springfield;' nothing about Potgieter's at all.

Chapter XV: The Dash for Potgieter's Ferry

Never mind—if cavalry had never done more than obey their orders how different English history would have been! Captain Birdwood, 11th Bengal Lancers, glorious regiment of the Indian frontier, now on Lord Dundonald's[2] staff, was for pushing on.

All and sundry were eager to get on. 'Have a dash for it.'

It is very easy to see what to do in the field of war until you put on the thick blue goggles of responsibility. Dundonald reflected, reflected again, and finally resolved. *Vorwärts!* So on we went accordingly.

Three hundred men and two guns were left to hold the Springfield bridge, seven hundred men and four guns hurried on through the afternoon to Potgieter's Ferry, or, more properly speaking, the heights commanding it, and reached them safely at six o'clock, finding a strong position strengthened by loopholed stone walls, unguarded and unoccupied.

The whole force climbed to the top of the hills, and with great labour succeeded in dragging the guns with them before night. Then we sent back to announce what we had done and to ask for reinforcements.

The necessity for reinforcements seemed very real to me, for I have a wholesome respect for Boer military enterprise; and after the security of a great camp the dangers of our lonely unsupported perch on the hills came home with extra force.

'No Boers this side of the Tugela.' How did we know? We had not seen any, but the deep valleys along the river might easily conceal two thousand horsemen.

I said to myself, the Boer has always a reason for everything he does. He left the Springfield bridge standing. It would have cost him nothing to blow it up. Why, then, had he neglected this obvious precaution?

Again, the position we had seized had actually been fortified by the enemy.

---

2 Lieutenant General Douglas Cochrane, 12th Earl of Dundonald (1852–1935), served in Egypt and the Sudan before being deployed to South Africa.

Why, then, had they abandoned it to a parcel of horsemen without a shot fired? I could quite understand that the flooded Tugela was not a satisfactory feature to fight in front of, but it seemed certain that they had some devilry prepared for us somewhere. The uninjured bridge appeared to me a trap: the unguarded position a bait.

Suppose they were, we should be attacked at daylight. Nothing more than a soldier should always expect; but what of the position? The line we had to hold to cover the approaches to our hill-top was far greater than seven hundred men could occupy.

Had we been only cavalry and mounted men we could have fallen back after the position became untenable, but we were encumbered with four field-guns—a source of anxiety, not of strength.

So I began to long for infantry. Two thousand good infantry would make everything absolutely secure. And ten miles away were infantry by thousands, all delighted to march every mile nearer the front.

We passed a wet and watchful night without food or sleep, and were glad to find the break of day unbroken by the musketry of a heavy attack.

From our lofty position on the heights the whole country beyond the Tugela was spread like a map. I sat on a great rock which overhung the valley, and searched the landscape inch by inch with field glasses. After an hour's study my feeling of insecurity departed.

I learned the answer to the questions which had perplexed the mind. Before us lay the 'devilry' the Boers had prepared, and it was no longer difficult to understand why the Springfield bridge had been spared and the heights abandoned.

The ground fell almost sheer six hundred feet to the flat bottom of the valley. Beneath, the Tugela curled along like a brown and very sinuous serpent. Never have I seen such violent twists and bends in a river. At times the waters seemed to loop back on themselves.

Chapter XV: The Dash for Potgieter's Ferry

One great loop bent towards us, and at the arch of this the little ferry of Potgieter's floated, moored to ropes which looked through the field glasses like a spider's web. The ford, approached by roads cut down through the steep bank, was beside it, but closed for the time being by the flood.

The loop of river enclosed a great tongue of land which jutted from the hills on the enemy's side almost to our feet. A thousand yards from the tip of this tongue rose a line of low kopjes crowned with reddish stones. The whole tongue was virtually ours. Our guns on the heights or on the bank could sweep it from flank to flank, enfilade and cross fire.

Therefore the passage of the river was assured. We had obtained what amounted to a practical bridgehead, and could cross whenever we thought fit. But the explanation of many things lay beyond.

At the base of the tongue, where it sprang from the Boer side of the valley, the ground rose in a series of gentle grassy slopes to a long horseshoe of hills, and along this, both flanks resting securely on unfordable reaches of the river, out of range from our heights of any but the heaviest guns, approachable by a smooth grass glacis, which was exposed to two or three tiers of cross-fire and converging fire, ran the enemy's position.

Please look at the sketch below, which shows nothing but what it is meant to.

Plan of Potgieter's Ferry

It will be seen that there is no difficulty in shelling the Boers out of the little kopjes, of fortifying them, and of passing the army on to the tip of the tongue; but to get off the tongue on to the smooth plateau that runs to Ladysmith it was necessary to force the tremendous Boer position enclosing the tongue.

In technical language the possession of the heights virtually gave us a bridgehead on the Tugela, but the debouches from that bridgehead were barred by an exterior line of hills fortified and occupied by the enemy.

What will Sir Redvers Buller do? In a few hours we shall know.

To cross and deliver a frontal attack will cost at least three thousand men. Is a flank attack possible? Can the position be turned? Fords few and far between, steep banks, mighty positions on the further banks: such are some of the difficulties. But everyone has confidence in the general. An officer who had been serving on the Kimberley side came here.

'I don't understand,' he said, 'how it is you are all so cheerful here after Colenso. You should hear the troops at Modder River.'

But it is a poor army that cannot take a repulse and come up smiling, and when the private soldiers put their faith in any man they are very constant. Besides, Buller's personality impresses everyone with the idea of some great reserve of force. Certainly he has something up his sleeve.

The move to Potgieter's has been talked of for a month and executed with the greatest ostentation and deliberation. Surely something lies behind it all. So at least we all believe, and in the meanwhile trust wholeheartedly.

But some part of the army will certainly cross at Potgieter's; and as I looked down on the smooth smiling landscape it seemed very strange to think that in a few days it would blaze into a veritable hell. Yet the dark lines of shelter trenches, the redoubts crowning the hills, the bristle of tiny black figures busily entrenching against the sky line, hundreds of horses grazing in the plain, all promised a fierce and stubborn defence.

Chapter XV: The Dash for Potgieter's Ferry

I turned about. The country to the southward was also visible. What looked to the naked eye like an endless thin rope lay streaked across the spacious veldt, and when I looked through the glass I saw that it was ten or twelve miles of marching men and baggage. The armies were approaching. The collision impended.

Nothing happened during the day except the capture of the ferry, which daring enterprise was carried out by volunteers from the South African Light Horse.

Six swimmers, protected by a covering party of twenty men, swam the flooded Tugela and began to haul the punt back, whereat the Boers concealed in the kopjes opened a brisk fire at long range on the naked figures, but did not hit anyone nor prevent them all from bringing the punt safely to our side: a dashing exploit, of which their regiment—the 'Cockyolibirds,' as the army, with its customary irreverence, calls us on account of the cock's feather cockades we wear in our hats (miserable jealousy!)—are immensely proud.

The falling of the Tugela increased the danger of our position, and I was delighted when I woke up the next morning, the second of our adventurous occupation, to find Colonel Sandbach, to whom I had confided my doubts, outside my tent, saying 'I suppose you'll be happy now. Two battalions have arrived.'

And, sure enough, when I looked southwards, I saw a steady rivulet of infantry trickling through the gorge, and forming a comfortable brown inundation in the hollow where our camp lay.

A few minutes later Sir Redvers Buller and his staff rode up to see things for themselves, and then we knew that all was well. The General made his way to the great stone we call the observatory, and lying down on his back peered through a telescope in silence for the best part of an hour. Then he went off to breakfast with the Cavalry Brigade staff.

A few officers remained behind to take a still more exhaustive view. 'There'll be some wigs on that green before long.'

'What a wonderful sight it will be from here!' 'What a place to see a battle from!' Two artillerymen were loitering near.

London to Ladysmith via Pretoria

Said one: 'We ought to have the Queen up here, in her little donkey carriage.'

'Ah, we'd do it all right then,' replied his comrade.

But when I looked at the peaceful plain and reflected on the storm and tumult presently to burst upon it, I could not help being glad that no gentle eye would view that bloody panorama.

Winston Churchill at the front.

General White and staff, Ladysmith.

CHAPTER XVI
TRICHARDT'S DRIFT AND THE AFFAIR OF ACTON HOMES

Venter's Spruit: January 22, 1900.

On Thursday, January 11, Sir Redvers Buller began his operations for forcing the Tugela and relieving Ladysmith.

Barton's Brigade entrenched itself at Chieveley, guarding the line of railway communication.

Hildyard's Brigade marched westward six miles to Pretorius's Farm, where they were joined by the cavalry, the naval guns, three batteries Field Artillery, and Hart's Brigade from Frere.

The infantry and two batteries remained and encamped, making Clery's division, while the mounted forces under Dundonald moved forward to take the bridge across the Little Tugela at Springfield, and, finding this unoccupied, pushed on and seized the heights overlooking Potgieter's Drift on the Tugela.

On the 12th, Warren's division, comprising the brigades of Lyttelton and Woodgate, with three batteries, marched to Springfield, where they camped. On the 13th, the mounted troops, holding the heights above Potgieter's Drift, were strengthened by the arrival of two battalions of Lyttelton's Brigade from Springfield. Sir Redvers Buller established his headquarters in this camp.

On the 14th, the rest of the brigade followed, and the same day the corps troops, consisting of Coke's Brigade, one howitzer, and one field battery, reached Springfield.

On the 15th, Coke moved to the position before Potgieter's, and the naval guns were established on the heights commanding the ford. All this while the Boers contented themselves with fortifying their horseshoe position which enclosed the debouches from Potgieter's Drift, and only picket firing disturbed the general peace. Such was the situation when I wrote my last letter.

It was soon to develop, though in a most leisurely and deliberate manner. The mounted forces, which had arrived at Spearman's Hill, as the position before Potgieter's was called, on the 11th, passed nearly a week of expectation.

Daily we watched the enemy fortifying his position, and observed the long lines of trenches which grew and spread along the face of the opposite hills. Daily, we made reconnoitring expeditions both east and west along the Tugela, expeditions always attended with incident, sometimes with adventure.

One day, Colonel Byng crawled with two squadrons to the summit of a high hill which overlooked the road from Colenso to Potgieter's, and a long and patient vigil was rewarded by the arrival of five Boer ox waggons toiling sluggishly along with supplies, on which we directed a rapid and effective fire till they found some refuge in a cutting.

Another day, we strengthened ourselves with two guns, and, marching nearly to the junction of the Tugelas, gave the Boers camped there an honest hour's shelling, and extricated a patrol of Bethune's Mounted Infantry from a rather disagreeable position, so that they were able to bring off a wounded trooper.

Nightly the cavalry camp went to sleep in the belief that a general attack would open on the enemy's position at dawn. Day after day the expected did not happen.

Buller had other resources than to butt his head against the tremendous entrenchments which were springing up before him.

Everyone discussed every conceivable alternative, and in the meanwhile it was always 'battle to-morrow,' but never 'battle to-day.' And so it has continued until this moment, and the great event—the main trial of strength—still impends. But though there has been but little powder burned the situation has materially altered, and its alteration has been entirely to our advantage.

We have crossed the Tugela. The river which for two months has barred the advance of the relieving army lies behind us now. The enemy entrenched and entrenching in a strong position still confronts us, but the British forces are across the Tugela, and

Chapter XVI: Trichardt's Drift

have deployed on the northern bank. With hardly any loss Sir Redvers Buller has gained a splendid advantage.

The old inequality of ground has been swept away, and the strongest army yet moved under one hand in South Africa stands face to face with the Boers on the ordinary terms of attack and defence.

Let me describe the steps by which this result has been obtained. On the afternoon of the 16th, as we were sitting down to luncheon, we noticed a change in the appearance of the infantry camps on the reverse slopes of Spearman's Hill.

There was a busy bustling of men; the tents began to look baggy, then they all subsided together; the white disappeared, and the camping grounds became simply brown patches of moving soldiery.

Lyttelton's Brigade had received orders to march at once. Whither? It was another hour before this part of the secret transpired. They were to cross the river and seize the near kopjes beyond Potgieter's Drift.

Orders for cavalry and guns to move arrived in quick succession; the entire cavalry force, excepting only Bethune's Mounted Infantry, to march at 5.30 P.M., with five days' rations, 150 rounds per man, and what they stood up in—tents blankets, waterproof sheets, picketing gear, all to be left behind.

Our camp was to remain standing. The infantry had struck theirs. I puzzled over this for some time, in fact until an officer pointed out that our camp was in full view of the Boer outposts on Spion Kop, while the infantry camps were hidden by a turn of the hill. Evidently a complex and deeply laid scheme was in progress.

In the interval, while the South African Light Horse were preparing for the march, I rode up to Gun Hill to watch the operation of seizing the near kopjes, which stood on the tongue of land across the river, and as nearly as possible in the centre of the horseshoe position of the enemy.

The sailors were hauling their two great guns to the crest of the hill ready to come into action to support the infantry attack. Far below, the four battalions crept through the scrub at the foot of the hills towards the ferry.

As they arrived at the edge of the open ground the long winding columns dissolved into sprays of skirmishers, line behind line of tiny dashes, visible only as shadows on the smooth face of the veldt, strange formations, the result of bitter practical experience.

Presently the first line—a very thin line—men twenty paces apart—reached the ferry punt and the approaches to the Waggon Drift, and scrambled down to the brim of the river.

A single man began to wade and swim across, carrying a line. Two or three others followed. Then a long chain of men, with arms locked—a sort of human caterpillar—entered the water, struggled slowly across, and formed up under the shelter of the further bank.

All the time the Boers, manning their trenches and guns, remained silent. The infantry of the two leading battalions were thus filtering uneventfully across when the time for the cavalry column to start arrived. There was a subdued flutter of excitement as we paraded, for though both our destination and object were unknown, it was clearly understood that the hour of action had arrived.

Everything was moving. A long cloud of dust rose up in the direction of Springfield. A column of infantry—Coke's Brigade—curled out of its camp near Spearman's Hill, and wound down towards the ferry at Potgieter's.

Eight curiously proportioned guns (naval 12-pounders), with tiny wheels and thin elongated barrels, were passed in a string, each tied to the tail of a waggon drawn by twenty oxen. The howitzer battery hurried to follow; its short and squat pieces, suggesting a row of venomous toads, made a striking contrast.

As the darkness fell the cavalry column started. On all sides men were marching through the night: much important business was toward, which the reader may easily understand by studying

Chapter XVI: Trichardt's Drift

the map, but cannot without such attention. Having placed his army within striking distance of the various passages across the Tugela, Sir Redvers Buller's next object was to cross and debouch. To this end his plan appears to have been—for information is scarcely yet properly codified—something as follows:

Lyttelton's Brigade, the corps troops forming Coke's Brigade, the ten naval guns, the battery of howitzers, one field battery, and Bethune's Mounted Infantry to demonstrate in front of the Potgieter position, keeping the Boers holding the horseshoe in expectation of a frontal attack, and masking their main position; Sir Charles Warren to march by night from Springfield with the brigades of Hart, Woodgate, and Hildyard, the Royal Dragoons, six batteries of artillery, and the pontoon train to a point about five miles west of Spearman's Hill, and opposite Trichardt's Drift on the Tugela.

Here he was to meet the mounted forces from Spearman's Hill, and with these troops he was next day, the 17th, to throw bridges, force the passage of the river, and operate at leisure and discretion against the right flank of the enemy's horseshoe before Potgieter's, resting on Spion Kop, a commanding mountain, ultimately joining hands with the frontal force from Spearman's Hill at a point on the Acton Homes-Ladysmith road.

To sum up briefly, seven battalions, twenty-two guns, and three hundred horse under Lyttelton to mask the Potgieter position; twelve battalions, thirty-six guns, and sixteen hundred horse to cross five miles to the westward, and make a turning movement against the enemy's right.

The Boer covering army was to be swept back on Ladysmith by a powerful left arm, the pivoting shoulder of which was at Potgieter's, the elbow at Trichardt's Drift, and the enveloping hand—the cavalry under Lord Dundonald—stretching out towards Acton Homes.

So much for the plan; now for its execution or modifications.

One main feature has characterised the whole undertaking—its amazing deliberation. There was to be absolutely no hurry of any kind whatever. Let the enemy entrench and fortify. If necessary, we were prepared to sap up to his positions. Let him discover where the attack impended. Even then all his resistance should be overborne. And it seems now that this same deliberation which was so punctiliously observed, when speed appeared an essential to success, baffled the enemy almost as much as it mystified the troops.

However, the event is not yet decided. After about two, hours' easy marching the cavalry reached the point of rendezvous among the hills opposite Trichardt's Drift, and here we halted and awaited developments in the blackness.

An hour passed. Then there arrived Sir Charles Warren and staff.

'Move the cavalry out of the way—fifteen thousand men marching along this road to-night.'

So we moved accordingly and waited again.

Presently the army began to come. I remember that it poured with rain, and there was very little to look at in the gloom, but, nevertheless, it was not possible to stand unmoved and watch the ceaseless living stream—miles of stern-looking men marching in fours so quickly that they often had to run to keep up, of artillery, ammunition columns, supply columns, baggage, slaughter cattle, thirty great pontoons, white-hooded, red-crossed ambulance waggons, all the accessories of an army hurrying forward under the cover of night—and before them a guiding star, the red gleam of war.

We all made quite sure that the bridges would be built during the night, so that with the dawn the infantry could begin to cross and make an immediate onfall. But when morning broke the whole force was revealed spread about the hills overlooking the drift and no sound of artillery proclaimed the beginning of an action.

Of course, since a lightning blow had been expected, we all wondered what was the cause of the delay. Some said folly, others incapacity, others even actual laziness. But so far as the opera-

Chapter XVI: Trichardt's Drift

tions have proceeded I am not inclined to think that we have lost anything by not hurrying on this occasion.

As I write all is going well, and it would have been a terrible demand to make of infantry that they should attack, after a long night march, such a position as lay and still lies in part before us.

In fact it was utterly impossible to do anything worth doing that day beyond the transportation; so that, though the Boers were preparing redoubts and entrenchments with frantic energy, we might just as well take our time.

At about eight o'clock, a patrol of the Imperial Light Horse, under Captain Bridges, having ascertained that only a few Dutch scouts were moving within range on the further bank, the passage of the river began.

Two battalions of Hildyard's Brigade, the West Yorkshires and the Devons, moved towards the drift in the usual open formation, occupied the houses, and began to entrench themselves in the fields.

Six batteries came into action from the wooded heights commanding the passage. The pontoons advanced. Two were launched, and in them the West Yorkshire Regiment began to cross, accumulating gradually in the shelter of the further bank.

Then the sappers began to build the bridges. Half a dozen Boers fired a few shots at long range, and one unfortunate soldier in the Devons was killed.

The batteries opened on the farms, woods, and kopjes beyond the river, shelling them assiduously, though there was not an enemy to be seen, and searching out the ground with great thoroughness.

I watched this proceeding of making 'sicker' from the heights. The drift was approached from the ground where we had bivouacked by a long, steep, descending valley.

At nine o'clock the whole of Hart's Brigade poured down this great gutter and extended near the water. The bridge was growing fast—span after span of pontoons sprang out at the ends as it lay along the bank. Very soon it would be long enough to tow into position across the flood.

Moreover, the infantry of the West Yorks and Devons had mostly been ferried across, and were already occupying the lately well-shelled farms and woods.

At eleven o'clock, the bridge was finished, the transported infantry were spreading up the hills, and Woodgate's Brigade moved forward down the valley. It soon became time for the cavalry to cross, but they were not accommodated, as were the infantry, with a convenient bridge. About a quarter of a mile down stream from Trichardt's Drift there is a deep and rather dangerous ford, called the Waggon Drift.

Across this at noon the mounted men began to make their way, and what with the uneven bottom and the strong current there were a good many duckings.

The Royal Dragoons mounted on their great horses, indeed, passed without much difficulty, but the ponies of the Light Horse and Mounted Infantry were often swept off their feet, and the ridiculous spectacle of officers and men floundering in the torrent or rising indignantly from the shallows provided a large crowd of spectators—who had crossed by the bridge—with a comedy.

Tragedy was not, however, altogether excluded, for a trooper of the 13th Hussars was drowned, and Captain Tremayne, of the same regiment, who made a gallant attempt to rescue him, was taken from the water insensible.

During the afternoon, the busy Engineers built a second bridge across the river, and by this and the first the artillery, the ammunition columns, and the rest of the mass of wheeled transport defiled.

All that day and through the night this monotonous business of passing the waggons across continued. The cavalry had bivouacked—all tents and even waterproofs were now left behind—within the infantry picket lines, and we awoke at the break of day expecting to hear the boom of the first gun.

Chapter XVI: Trichardt's Drift

'Quite right to wait until there was a whole day to make the attack in. Suppose that was the reason we did not hurry yesterday.'

But no guns fired near Trichardt's Drift, and only the frontal force at Potgieter's began its usual bombardment.

Sir Charles Warren, moreover, said that his artillery had not finished crossing—one battery still to cross—and that there was no hurry. Deliberation was the order of the day. So again, everyone was puzzled, and not a few were critical, for in modern times everyone thinks, and even a native camp follower has his views on tactics and strategy.

A very complete consolation awaited the cavalry. All that Warren did with his infantry on this day, the 18th, was to creep cautiously forward about two miles towards the Boer position, which with its left resting on Spion Kop stretched along the edge and crest of a lofty plateau, from which long gently sloping spurs and *arêtes* ran down to the river.

For us, however, there was more diverting employment.

'The mounted brigade will guard the left flank of the infantry.'

Such was the order; and is not offence the surest defence? Accordingly, all the irregular cavalry moved in a considerable column westward across the front of the Boer position, endeavouring to find where its flank rested, and prying with inquisitive patrols at every object of interest.

The order of march was as follows: First, the composite regiment (one squadron of Imperial Light Horse, the 60th Rifles, Mounted Infantry, and one squadron of Natal Carabineers), 350 of the very best; next, four squadrons of the South African Light Horse, good shooting high-class colonial Volunteers with officers of experience; then Thorneycroft's Mounted Infantry.

'Lived in Natal all our lives! Know every inch of it, sir!' And behind these alert mounted riflemen moved the ponderous and terrible regulars, 13th Hussars and Royals, with the dreaded *arme blanche*, 'Wait till we get among them.'

Altogether a formidable brigade.

There were many halts, and no one hurried, so that at two o'clock the whole cavalry formed a line of observation along the lower kopjes by the river about five miles long.

The composite regiment was not, however, to be seen. Major Graham, who commanded it, had been observed trotting swiftly off to the westward. Two hundred Boers had also been reported moving in that direction. Presently came the sound of distant musketry—not so very distant either. Everyone pricked up his ears.

Two miles away to the left was a green hill broken by rocky kopjes. Looking through my glasses I could see ten or twelve riderless horses grazing. A mile further on a group of Boers sheltering behind a kopje from the continual fire was visible. Suddenly one galloped away madly, and even at the distance it was possible to see the cloud of dust from pursuing bullets.

A straggling column of Boers was trekking away across the plain back to their main position. Then came reports and rumours. 'Ambuscaded the Dutchmen—shot 'em to bits—some of them cut off—come and bag the lot.'

Behind the rumours Barnes, adjutant of the Imperial Light Horse, joyful, with a breathless horse; he explained how they had seen two hundred Boers moving towards distant hills, to make sure of their line of retreat by the Acton Homes road into the Free State; galloped to cut them off; reached the hills first, with just five minutes to spare; dismounted, commanding the road, and waited.

The Boers admitted afterwards that they thought that the squadrons visible on the other hills two miles back were the head of our column, and they also blamed their scouts, particularly one, an Austrian.

'It all comes of trusting these cursed foreigners! If we had only had a *veldt* Boer out we should never have been caught.' Caught, however, they undoubtedly were.

The Carabineers and the Imperial Light Horse held their fire until the scouts walked into their midst, and then let drive at the

Chapter XVI: Trichardt's Drift

main body, 300 yards range, mounted men, smooth open grass plain. There was a sudden furious, snapping fusillade. The Boer column stopped paralysed; then they broke and rushed for cover. The greater number galloped fast from the field; some remained on the ground dead or wounded.

Others took refuge among the rocks of the kopjes and apparently proposed to hold out until dark, and hence the arrival of Lieutenant Barnes demanding reinforcements, 60th Rifles, Mounted Infantry, and anything else, so as to attack these fellows in flank and 'bag the lot.'

Meanwhile Lord Dundonald had arrived on our hill. 'Certainly, every man we can spare.' Off gallops the Mounted Infantry and one squadron of the South African Light Horse, and later on some of Thorneycroft's, and later still the Brigadier himself.

I arrived in time to see the end. The Boers—how many we could not tell—were tenaciously holding the black rocks of a kopje and were quite invisible. The British riflemen curved round them in a half-moon, firing continually at the rocks.

The squadron of South African Light Horse had worked almost behind the enemy, and every Dutchman who dared make a dash for liberty ran a terrible gauntlet.

Still the surrender did not come. The white flag flickered for a moment above the rocks, but neither side stopped firing. Evidently a difference of opinion among the enemy. What do we care for that? Night is coming on. Let us rush them with the bayonet and settle the matter.

This from the Rifles—nobody else had bayonets. So a section pushes forward against the rocks, crawling along the ground.

Anxious to see the surrender, I followed on my pony, but on the instant, there broke out a savage fire from the kopje, and with difficulty I found shelter in a donga. Here were two of the Natal Carabineers—one a bearded man of the well-to-do farmer class, the other a young fair-haired gentleman—both privates, both as cool as ice.

'Vewy astonishing outburst of fire,' said the younger man in a delicate voice. 'I would recommend your remaining here with your horse for the present.'

Accordingly, we lay still on the grass slope and awaited developments. The young gentleman put his helmet over the crest on the end of his rifle, and was much diverted to hear the bullets whistle round it. At intervals he substituted his head for the helmet and reported the state of the game. 'Bai Jove, the Rifles are in a hot place.'

I peered cautiously. A hundred yards away the Mounted Infantry section were extended. The dust spurts rose around the men, who remained pinned to the earth, scarcely able to raise their heads to fire. Whatever passed over them came whizzing in our direction.

The Natal Volunteer, however, was too much interested in the proceedings to forego his view. 'Deah, deah, they've fixed bayonets! Why, they're coming back. They've had someone hurt.'

I looked again for a moment. The line of riflemen was certainly retiring, wriggling backwards slowly on their bellies. Two brown forms lay still and hunched in the abandoned position.

Then suddenly the retiring Riflemen sprang up and ran for shelter in our donga. One lad jumped right in among us laughing and panting, and the whole party turned at once and lined the bank. First-class infantry can afford to retire at the double, sure that they will stop at a word.

'We got to within fifty yards of the Dutchmen,' they said; 'but it was too hot to go further. They've shot two fellows through the head.' Eventually we all retired to the main position on the ridge above us. Lord Dundonald and his staff had just arrived.

'There! there's the white flag again. Shoot the devils!' cried a soldier, and the musketry crashed out fiercely.

'What's to be done, sir?' said the Captain, turning to the Brigadier; 'the white flag has been up off and on for the last half-hour, but they don't stop firing, and they've just killed two of my men.'

Chapter XVI: Trichardt's Drift

'Give them one more chance.'

'Cease fire—cease fire there, will you?' for the men were very angry, and so at last the musketry died away, and there was silence.

Then from among the rocks three dark figures stood up holding up their hands, and at this tangible evidence of surrender we got on our horses and galloped towards them waving pocket handkerchiefs and signalling flags to show them that their surrender was accepted.

Altogether there were twenty-four prisoners—all Boers of the most formidable type—a splendid haul, and I thought with delight of my poor friends the prisoners at Pretoria. This might redeem a few.

Then we searched the ground, finding ten dead or dying and twenty loose horses, ten dead and eight badly wounded men. The soldiers crowded round these last, covering them up with blankets or mackintoshes, propping their heads with saddles for pillows, and giving them water and biscuits from their bottles and haversacks. Anger had turned to pity in an instant. The desire to kill was gone. The desire to comfort replaced it.

A little alert officer—Hubert Gough, now a captain, soon to command a regiment—came up to me. Two minutes before his eyes were bright and joyous with the excitement of the man hunt. He had galloped a mile—mostly under fire—to bring the reinforcements to surround the Boers. 'Bag the lot, you know.'

Now he was very sad. 'There's a poor boy dying up there—only a boy, and so cold—who's got a blanket?'

So the soldiers succoured the Boer wounded, and we told the prisoners that they would be shown courtesy and kindness worthy of brave men and a famous quarrel.

The Boer dead were collected and a flag of truce was sent to the enemy's lines to invite a burying and identification party at dawn. I have often seen dead men, killed in war—thousands at Omdurman—scores elsewhere, black and white, but the Boer dead aroused the most painful emotions. Here by the rock under which he had fought lay the Field Cornet of Heilbronn, Mr. de Mentz—a grey-haired man of over sixty years, with firm aquiline features and a short beard. The stony face was grimly calm, but it bore the stamp of unalterable resolve; the look of a man who had thought it all out, and was quite certain that his cause was just, and such as a sober citizen might give his life for.

Nor was I surprised when the Boer prisoners told me that Mentz had refused all suggestions of surrender, and that when his left leg was smashed by a bullet he had continued to load and fire until he bled to death; and they found him, pale and bloodless, holding his wife's letter in his hand. Beside him was a boy of about seventeen shot through the heart.

Further on, lay our own two poor riflemen with their heads smashed like eggshells; and I suppose they had mothers or wives far away at the end of the deep-sea cables.

Ah, horrible war, amazing medley of the glorious and the squalid, the pitiful and the sublime, if modern men of light and leading saw your face closer, simple folk would see it hardly ever.

It could not be denied that the cavalry had scored a brilliant success. We had captured twenty-four, killed ten, and wounded eight—total, forty-two.

Moreover, we had seen the retreating Boers dragging and supporting their injured friends from the field, and might fairly claim fifteen knocked out of time, besides those in our hands, total fifty-seven; a fine bag, for which we had had to pay scarcely anything.

Two soldiers of the Mounted Infantry killed; one trooper of the Imperial Light Horse slightly, and one officer, Captain Shore—the twenty-third officer of this regiment hit during the last three months—severely wounded.

CHAPTER XVII
THE BATTLE OF SPION KOP

Venter's Spruit: January 25, 1900.

It is the remarkable characteristic of strong races, as of honourable men, to keep their tempers in the face of disappointment, and never to lose a just sense of proportion; and it is, moreover, the duty of every citizen in times of trouble to do or say or even to think nothing that can weaken or discourage the energies of the State.

Sir Redvers Buller's army has met with another serious check in the attempt to relieve Ladysmith. We have approached, tested, and assailed the Boer positions beyond the Tugela, fighting more or less continuously for five days, and the result is that we find they cannot be pierced from the direction of Trichardt's Drift any more than at Colenso.

With the loss of more than two thousand men out of a small army, we find it necessary to recross the river and seek for some other line of attack; and meanwhile the long and brave resistance of Ladysmith must be drawing to a close.

Indeed, it is the opinion of many good judges that further efforts to relieve the town will only be attended with further loss. As to this I do not pronounce, but I am certain of one thing—that further efforts must be made, without regard to the loss of life which will attend them.

I have seen and heard a good deal of what has passed here. I have often been blamed for the freedom with which I have written of other operations and criticised their commanders.

I respectfully submit that I am as venomous an amateur strategist as exists at this time. It is very easy—and much more easy than profitable—when freed from all responsibility to make daring suggestions and express decided opinions. I assert that I would not hesitate to criticise mercilessly if I was not myself sobered by the full appreciation of the extraordinary difficulties which the relief of Ladysmith presents; and if there be anyone who has any confidence in my desire to write the truth I appeal to him to be patient and calm, to recognise that perhaps the task before Sir Redvers Buller and his subordinates is an actual impossibility, that if these generals are not capable men—among the best that our times produce—it is difficult to know where and how others may be obtained, and finally to brutally face the fact that Sir George White and his heroic garrison may be forced to become the prisoners of the Boers, remembering always that nothing that happens, either victory or defeat, in northern Natal can affect the ultimate result of the war.

In a word, let no one despair of the Empire because a few thousand soldiers are killed, wounded, or captured Now for the story, as plainly and briefly as possible.

When Buller had arrived at Potgieter's he found himself confronted by a horseshoe position of great strength, enclosing and closing the debouches from the ford where he had secured a practical bridgehead.

He therefore masked Potgieter's with seven battalions and twenty-four guns, and sent Warren with twelve battalions and thirty-six guns to turn the right, which rested on the lofty hill—almost mountain—of Spion Kop.

The Boers, to meet this turning movement, extended their line westwards along the heights of the Tugela valley almost as far as Acton Homes. Their whole position was, therefore, shaped like a note of interrogation laid on its side, —/\, the curve in front of General Lyttelton, the straight line before Sir Charles Warren. At the angle formed by the junction of the curve and the line stands Spion Kop— 'look-out hill.'

The curved position in front of General Lyttelton has been already described in a previous letter. The straight position in front of Sir Charles Warren ran in two lines along the edge and crest of a plateau which rises steeply two miles from the river, but is approachable by numerous long *arêtes* and dongas.

Chapter XVII: The Battle of Spion Kop

These letters have completed the chronicle down to the evening of the 18th, when the successful cavalry action was fought on the extreme left.

I do not know why nothing was done on the 19th, but it does not appear that anything was lost by the delay. The enemy's entrenchments were already complete, and neither his numbers nor the strength of his positions could increase.

On the 20th Warren, having crept up the *arêtes* and dongas, began his attack. The brigades of Generals Woodgate and Hart pushed forward on the right, and the Lancashire and Irish regiments, fighting with the usual gallantry of her Majesty's troops, succeeded, in spite of a heavy fire of rifles and artillery, in effecting lodgments at various points along the edge of the plateau, capturing some portions of the enemy's first line of entrenchments.

On the extreme left, the cavalry under Lord Dundonald demonstrated effectively, and the South African Light Horse under Colonel Byng actually took and held without artillery support of any kind a high hill, called henceforward 'Bastion Hill,' between the Dutch right and centre.

Major Childe, the officer whose squadron performed this daring exploit, was killed on the summit by the shell fire to which the successful assailants were subjected by the Boers.

In the evening infantry reinforcements of Hildyard's Brigade arrived, and at dawn the cavalry handed over the hill to their charge.

The losses during the day did not exceed three hundred and fifty officers and men wounded—with fortunately, a small proportion of killed—and fell mainly on the Lancashire Fusiliers, the Dublin Fusiliers (always in the front), and the Royal Lancaster Regiment. They were not disproportioned to the apparent advantage gained.

On the 21st the action was renewed. Hart's and Woodgate's brigades on the right made good and extended their lodgments, capturing all the Boer trenches of their first defensive line along the edge of the plateau. To the east of 'Bastion Hill' there runs a deep *re-entrant*, which appeared to open a cleft between the right and centre of the Boer position.

The tendency of General Hildyard's action, with five battalions and two batteries, on the British left this day was to drive a wedge of infantry into this cleft and so split the Boer position in two. But as the action developed, the great strength of the second line of defence gradually revealed itself.

It ran along the crest of the plateau, which rises about a thousand yards from the edge in a series of beautiful smooth grassy slopes of concave surface, forming veritable glacis for the musketry of the defence to sweep; and it consisted of a line of low rock and earth redoubts and shelter trenches, apparently provided with overhead cover, and cleverly arranged to command all approaches with fire—often with cross-fire, sometimes with converging fire.

Throughout the 21st, as during the 20th, the British artillery, consisting of six field batteries and four howitzers, the latter apparently of tremendous power, bombarded the whole Boer position ceaselessly, firing on each occasion nearly three thousand shells.

They claim to have inflicted considerable loss on the enemy, and must have inflicted some, but failed utterly and painfully to silence the musketry, to clear the trenches, or reach and overpower the Dutch artillery, which did not number more than seven or eight guns and two Maxim shell-guns, but which were better served and manoeuvred and of superior quality.

The losses in the action of the 20th were about one hundred and thirty officers and men killed and wounded, but this must be regarded as severe in the face of the fact that no serious collision or even contact took place.

During the 22nd and 23rd, the troops held the positions they had won, and the infantry were subjected to a harassing shell fire from the Boer guns, which, playing from either flank, searched the *re-entrants* in which the battalions sheltered, and which,

Chapter XVII: The Battle of Spion Kop

though they did not cause a greater loss than forty men on the 22nd and twenty-five on the 23rd, nevertheless made their position extremely uncomfortable.

It was quite evident that the troops could not be fairly required to endure this bombardment, against which there was no protection, indefinitely. Nor was any good object, but rather the contrary, to be gained by waiting.

Three alternatives presented themselves to the council of war held on the 22nd.

First, to attack the second Boer position frontally along the crest by moonlight. This would involve a great slaughter and a terrible risk. Secondly, to withdraw again, beyond the Tugela, and look elsewhere for a passage: a moral defeat and a further delay in the relief of Ladysmith; and thirdly, to attack by night the mountain of Spion Kop, and thence to enfilade and command the Boer entrenchments.

Sir Redvers Buller, who has always disdained effect, was for the second course—unpalatable as it must have been to a fearless man; miserable as it is to call off infantry after they have made sacrifices and won positions, and to call them off a second time.

The discussion was an informal one, and no votes were taken, but the General yielded to the advice of his subordinate, rightly, I hold, because now at least we know the strength of the enemy's position, whereas before we only dreaded it; and knowledge is a better reason for action than apprehension.

It was therefore decided to attack Spion Kop by night, rush the Boer trenches with the bayonet, entrench as far as possible before dawn, hold on during the day, drag guns up at night, and thus dominate the Boer lines.

There is, of course, no possible doubt that Spion Kop is the key of the whole position, and the reader has only to think of the horizontal note of interrogation, and remember that the mountain at the angle divides, commands, and enfilades the enemy's lines, to appreciate this fact.

The questions to be proved were whether the troops could hold out during the day, and whether the place could be converted into a fort proof against shell fire and armed with guns during the following night. Fate has now decided both.

General Woodgate was entrusted with the command, and Colonel Thorneycroft with much of the arrangement and direction of the night attack. It does not seem that anything but good resulted from this too soon broken co-operation.

Thorneycroft declined to attack on the night of the 22nd because the ground had not been reconnoitered, and he wanted to be sure of his way. The infantry therefore had another day's shelling on the 23rd.

Good reconnaissances were, however, made, Lyttelton was strengthened by two Fusilier battalions from Chieveley, Warren was reinforced by Talbot Coke's Brigade and the Imperial Light Infantry, and at one o'clock on the morning of January 24 General Woodgate started from his camp with the Lancashire Fusiliers, the Royal Lancaster Regiment, two companies of the South Lancashires, and Thorneycroft's Mounted Infantry.

Guided by Colonel Thorneycroft the force made its way successfully up the southern spur of the mountain, over most difficult and dangerous ground, and surprised the Boers guarding the entrenchments on the summit.

At three o'clock those listening in the plain heard the sudden outburst of musketry, followed by the loud cheers of the troops, and knew that the position had been carried. Ten soldiers were killed and wounded in the firing. Six Boers perished by the bayonet.

The force then proceeded to fortify itself, but the surface of the hill was extremely unsuited to defence. The rocks which covered the summit made digging an impossibility, and were themselves mostly too large to be built into sangars. Such cover, however, as had been made by the Boers was utilised and improved.

Morning broke, and with it the attack. The enemy, realising the vital importance of the position, concentrated every man and gun at his disposal for its recapture. A fierce and furious shell fire was opened forthwith on the summit, causing immediate and continual loss.

General Woodgate was wounded, and the command devolved on a regimental officer, who, at half-past six, applied for reinforcements in a letter which scarcely displayed that composure and determination necessary in such a bloody debate.

Sir Redvers Buller then took the extreme step of appointing Major Thorneycroft—already only a local lieutenant-colonel—local Brigadier-General commanding on the summit of Spion Kop.

The Imperial Light Infantry, the Middlesex Regiment, and a little later the Somersets, from General Talbot Coke's Brigade, were ordered to reinforce the defence, but General Coke was directed to remain below the summit of the hill, so that the fight might still be conducted by the best fighting man.

The Boers followed, and accompanied their shells by a vigorous rifle attack on the hill, and about half-past eight the position became most critical. The troops were driven almost entirely off the main plateau and the Boers succeeded in reoccupying some of their trenches.

A frightful disaster was narrowly averted. About twenty men in one of the captured trenches abandoned their resistance, threw up their hands, and called out that they would surrender.

Colonel Thorneycroft, whose great stature made him everywhere conspicuous, and who was from dawn till dusk in the first firing line, rushed to the spot.

The Boers advancing to take the prisoners—as at Nicholson's Nek—were scarcely thirty yards away. Thorneycroft shouted to the Boer leader: 'You may go to hell. I command on this hill and allow no surrender. Go on with your firing.'

Which latter they did with terrible effect, killing many. The survivors, with the rest of the firing line, fled two hundred yards, were rallied by their indomitable commander, and, being reinforced by two brave companies of the Middlesex Regiment, charged back, recovering all lost ground, and the position was maintained until nightfall.

No words in these days of extravagant expression can do justice to the glorious endurance which the English regiments—for they were all English—displayed throughout the long dragging hours of hell fire. Between three and four o'clock the shells were falling on the hill from both sides, as I counted, at the rate of seven a minute, and the strange discharges of the Maxim shell guns—the 'pom-poms' as these terrible engines are called for want of a correct name—lacerated the hillsides with dotted chains of smoke and dust.

A thick and continual stream of wounded flowed rearwards. A village of ambulance waggons grew up at the foot of the mountain. The dead and injured, smashed and broken by the shells, littered the summit till it was a bloody, reeking shambles.

Thirst tormented the soldiers, for though water was at hand the fight was too close and furious to give even a moment's breathing space. But nothing could weaken the stubborn vigour of the defence. The Dorset Regiment—the last of Talbot Coke's Brigade—was ordered to support the struggling troops.

The gallant Lyttelton of his own accord sent the Scottish Rifles and the 3rd King's Royal Rifles from Potgieter's to aid them. But though their splendid attack did not help the main action; though the British artillery, unable to find or reach the enemy's guns, could only tear up the ground in impotent fury; though the shell fire and rifle fire never ceased for an instant—the magnificent infantry maintained the defence, and night closed in with the British still in possession of the hill.

I find it convenient, and perhaps the reader will allow me, to break into a more personal account of what followed.

It drove us all mad to watch idly in camp the horrible shelling that was directed on the captured position, and at about four o'clock I rode with Captain R. Brooke, 7th Hussars, to Spion Kop, to find out what the true situation was. We passed through the

Chapter XVII: The Battle of Spion Kop

ambulance village, and leaving our horses climbed up the spur. Streams of wounded met us and obstructed the path. Men were staggering along alone, or supported by comrades, or crawling on hands and knees, or carried on stretchers.

Corpses lay here and there. Many of the wounds were of a horrible nature. The splinters and fragments of the shell had torn and mutilated in the most ghastly manner.

I passed about two hundred while I was climbing up. There was, moreover, a small but steady leakage of unwounded men of all corps. Some of these cursed and swore. Others were utterly exhausted and fell on the hillside in stupor. Others again seemed drunk, though they had had no liquor. Scores were sleeping heavily.

Fighting was still proceeding, and stray bullets struck all over the ground, while the Maxim shell guns scourged the flanks of the hill and the sheltering infantry at regular intervals of a minute. The 3rd King's Royal Rifles were out of reach. The Dorset Regiment was the only battalion not thrown into the fight, and intact as an effective unit.

I had seen some service and Captain Brooke has been through more fighting than any other officer of late years. We were so profoundly impressed by the spectacle and situation that we resolved to go and tell Sir Charles Warren what we had seen.

The fight had been so close that no proper reports had been sent to the General, so he listened with great patience and attention. One thing was quite clear—unless good and efficient cover could be made during the night, and unless guns could be dragged to the summit of the hill to match the Boer artillery, the infantry could not, perhaps would not, endure another day. The human machine will not stand certain strains for long.

The questions were, could guns be brought up the hill; and, if so, could the troops maintain themselves? The artillery officers had examined the track. They said 'No,' and that even if they could reach the top of the hill they would only be shot out of action.

Two long-range naval 12-pounders, much heavier than the field-guns, had arrived. The naval lieutenant in charge said he could go anywhere, or would have a try any way. He was quite sure that if he could get on the top of the hill he would knock out the Boer guns or be knocked out by them, and that was what he wanted to find out.

I do not believe that the attempt would have succeeded, or that the guns could have been in position by daylight, but the contrast in spirit was very refreshing.

Another informal council of war was called. Sir Charles Warren wanted to know Colonel Thorneycroft's views. I was sent to obtain them. The darkness was intense. The track stony and uneven. It was hopelessly congested with ambulances, stragglers, and wounded men. I soon had to leave my horse, and then toiled upwards, finding everywhere streams of men winding about the almost precipitous sides of the mountain, and an intermittent crackle of musketry at the top.

Only one solid battalion remained—the Dorsets. All the others were intermingled. Officers had collected little parties, companies and half-companies; here and there larger bodies had formed, but there was no possibility, in the darkness, of gripping anybody or anything.

Yet it must not be imagined that the infantry were demoralised. Stragglers and weaklings there were in plenty. But the mass of the soldiers were determined men. One man I found dragging down a box of ammunition quite by himself. 'To do something,' he said.

A sergeant with twenty men formed up was inquiring what troops were to hold the position. Regimental officers everywhere cool and cheery, each with a little group of men around him, all full of fight and energy. But the darkness and the broken ground paralysed everyone.

I found Colonel Thorneycroft at the top of the mountain. Everyone seemed to know, even in the confusion, where he was. He was sitting on the ground surrounded by the remnants of the

Chapter XVII: The Battle of Spion Kop

regiment he had raised, who had fought for him like lions and followed him like dogs. I explained the situation as I had been told and as I thought.

Naval guns were prepared to try, sappers and working parties were already on the road with thousands of sandbags. What did he think? But the decision had already been taken. He had never received any messages from the General, had not had time to write any. Messages had been sent him, he had wanted to send others himself.

The fight had been too hot, too close, too interlaced for him to attend to anything, but to support this company, clear those rocks, or line that trench. So, having heard nothing and expecting no guns, he had decided to retire. As he put it tersely: 'Better six good battalions safely down the hill than a mop up in the morning.'

Then we came home, drawing down our rearguard after us very slowly and carefully, and as the ground grew more level the regiments began to form again into their old solid blocks. Such was the fifth of the series of actions called the Battle of Spion Kop.

It is an event which the British people may regard with feelings of equal pride and sadness.

It redounds to the honour of the soldiers, though not greatly to that of the generals. But when all that will be written about this has been written, and all the bitter words have been said by the people who never do anything themselves, the wise and just citizen will remember that these same generals are, after all, brave, capable, noble English gentlemen, trying their best to carry through a task which may prove to be impossible, and is certainly the hardest ever set to men.

The Lancashire Fusiliers, the Imperial Light Infantry—whose baptism of fire it was—Thorneycroft's, and the Middlesex Regiment sustained the greater part of the losses.

We will have another try, and, if it pleases God, do better next time.

CHAPTER XVIII
THROUGH THE FIVE DAYS' ACTION

Venter's Spruit: January 25, 1900.

The importance of giving a general and comprehensive account of the late actions around and on Spion Kop prevented me from describing its scenes and incidents.

Events, like gentlemen at a levee, in these exciting days tread so closely on each other's heels that many pass unnoticed, and most can only claim the scantiest attention. But I will pick from the hurrying procession a few—distinguished for no other reason than that they have caught my eye—and from their quality the reader may judge of the rest.

The morning of the 20th discovered the cavalry still encamped behind the hills near the Acton Homes road, on which they had surprised the Boers two days before.

The loud and repeated discharge of the artillery advised us that the long-expected general action had begun.

What part were the cavalry to play? No orders had been sent to Lord Dundonald except that he was to cover the left flank of the infantry. But the cavalry commander, no less than his brigade, proposed to interpret these instructions freely.

Accordingly, at about half-past nine, the South African Light Horse, two squadrons of the 13th Hussars, and a battery of four machine guns moved forward towards the line of heights along the edge and crest of which ran the Boer position with the intention of demonstrating against them, and the daring idea—somewhere in the background—of attacking and seizing one prominent feature which jutted out into the plain, and which, from its boldness and shape, we had christened 'Bastion Hill.'

The composite regiment, who watched the extreme left, were directed to support us if all was clear in their front at one o'clock, and Thorneycroft's Mounted Infantry, who kept touch between

Chapter XVIII: Through the Five Day's Action

the main cavalry force and the infantry left flank, had similar orders to co-operate.

At ten o'clock Lord Dundonald ordered the South African Light Horse to advance against Bastion Hill. If the resistance was severe they were not to press the attack, but to content themselves with a musketry demonstration. If, however, they found it convenient to get on they were to do so as far as they liked.

Colonel Byng thereon sent two squadrons under Major Childe to advance, dismounted frontally on the hill, and proposed to cover their movements by the fire of the other two squadrons, who were to gallop to the shelter of a wood and creep thence up the various dongas to within effective range.

Major Childe accepted his orders with alacrity, and started forth on what seemed, as I watched from a grassy ridge, a most desperate enterprise. The dark brown mass of Bastion Hill appeared to dominate the plain. On its crest the figures of the Boers could be seen frequently moving about. Other spurs to either flanks looked as if they afforded facilities for cross fire. And to capture this formidable position we could dismount only about a hundred and fifty men; and had, moreover, no artillery support of any kind.

Yet as one examined the hill it became evident that its strength was apparent rather than real. Its slopes were so steep that they presented no good field of fire. Its crest was a convex curve, over and down which the defenders must advance before they could command the approaches, and when so advanced they would be exposed without shelter of any kind to the fire of the covering troops.

The salient was so prominent and jutted out so far from the general line of hills, and was besides shaped so like a blunted redan, that its front face was secure from flanking fire.

In fact there was plenty of dead ground in its approaches, and, moreover, dongas—which are the same as nullahs in India or gullies in Australia—ran agreeably to our wishes towards the hill in all directions.

When first we had seen the hill three days before we had selected it as a weak point in the Dutch line. It afterwards proved that the Boers had no illusions as to its strength and had made their arrangements accordingly.

So soon as the dismounted squadrons had begun their advance, Colonel Byng led the two who were to cover it forward. The wood we were to reach and find shelter in was about a thousand yards distant, and had been reported unoccupied by the Boers, who indeed confined themselves strictly to the hills after their rough handling on the 18th by the cavalry.

We moved off at a walk, spreading into a wide open order, as wise colonial cavalry always do. And it was fortunate that our formation was a dispersed one, for no sooner had we moved into the open ground than there was the flash of a gun faraway among the hills to the westward.

I had had some experience of artillery fire in the armoured train episode, but there the guns were firing at such close quarters that the report of the discharge and the explosion of the shell were almost simultaneous. Nor had I ever heard the menacing hissing roar which heralds the approach of a long-range projectile.

It came swiftly, passed overhead with a sound like the rending of thin sheets of iron, and burst with a rather dull explosion in the ground a hundred yards behind the squadrons, throwing up smoke and clods of earth. We broke into a gallop, and moved in curving course towards the wood. I suppose we were a target a hundred yards broad by a hundred and fifty deep. The range was not less than seven thousand yards, and we were at the gallop.

Think of this, Inspector-General of Artillery: the Boer gunners fired ten or eleven shells, every one of which fell among or within a hundred yards of our ranks. Between us and the wood ran a deep donga with a river only fordable in places flowing through it.

Some confusion occurred in crossing this, but at last the whole regiment was across, and found shelter from the terrible

Chapter XVIII: Through the Five Day's Action

gun—perhaps there were two—on the further bank. Thanks to our dispersed formation only two horses had been killed, and it was possible to admire without having to deplore the skill of the artillerists who could make such beautiful practice at such a range.

Colonel Byng thought it advisable to leave the horses in the cover of the protecting river bank, and we therefore pushed on, dismounted, and, straggling through the high maize crop without presenting any target to the guns, reached the wood safely.

Through this we hurried as far as its further edge. Here the riflemen on the hill opened with long-range fire. It was only a hundred yards into the donga, and the troopers immediately began running across in twos and threes.

In the irregular corps all appearances are sacrificed to the main object of getting where you want to without being hurt. No one was hurt.

Colonel Byng made his way along the donga to within about twelve or fourteen hundred yards, and from excellent cover opened fire on the Boers holding the summit of the hill.

A long musketry duel ensued without any loss to our side, and with probably no more to the enemy. The colonial troopers, as wary as the Dutch, showed very little to shoot at, so that, though there were plenty of bullets, there was no bloodshed. Regular infantry would probably have lost thirty or forty men.

I went back for machine guns, and about half an hour later they were brought into action at the edge of the wood.

Boers on the sky-line at two thousand yards—tat-tat-tat-tat-tat half a dozen times repeated; Boers galloping to cover; one—yes, by Jupiter!—one on his back on the grass; after that no more targets to shoot at; continuous searching of the sky-line, however, on the chance of killing someone, and, in any case, to support the frontal attack.

We had altogether three guns—the 13th Hussars' Maxim under Lieutenant Clutterbuck, detached from the 4th Hussars; one of Lord Dundonald's battery of Colts under Mr. Hill, who is a member of Parliament, and guides the majestic course of Empire besides managing machine guns; and our own Maxim, all under Major Villiers. These three machines set up a most exhilarating splutter, flaring and crackling all along the edge of the wood, and even attracted the attention of the Boers.

All of a sudden there was a furious rush and roar overhead; two or three little cassarina trees and a shower of branches fell to the ground. What on earth could this be? The main action was crashing away on the right. Evidently a shell had passed a few feet over our heads, but was it from our guns shelling the hills in front, or from the enemy? In another minute the question was answered by another shell.

It was our old friend the gun to the westward, who, irritated by the noisy Maxims, had resolved to put his foot down.

Whizz! Bang! came a third shot, exploding among the branches just behind the Colt gun, to the great delight of Mr. Hill, who secured a large fragment which I have advised him to lay on the table in the smoking-room of the House for the gratification, instruction, and diversion of other honourable members.

The next shell smashed through the roof of a farmhouse which stood at the corner of the wood, and near which two troops of the 13th Hussars, who were escorting the Maxims and watching the flanks, had left their led horses. The next, in quick succession, fell right among them, killing one, but luckily, very luckily, failed to burst.

The officer then decided to move the horses to a safer place. The two troops mounted and galloped off. They were a tiny target, only a moving speck across the plain. But the Boer gunners threw a shell within a yard of the first troop leader. All this at seven thousand yards! English artillery experts, please note and if possible, copy.

While these things were passing the advancing squadrons had begun to climb the hill, and found to their astonishment that they were scarcely fired at. It was of great importance, however, that

Chapter XVIII: Through the Five Day's Action

the Boers should be cleared from the summit by the Maxim fire, and lest this should be diverted on our own men by mistake, I left the wood for the purpose of signalling back how far the advance had proceeded and up to what point the guns could safely fire.

The ground was broken; the distance considerable.

Before I reached the hill the situation had changed. The enemy's artillery had persuaded the Maxims that they would do better to be quiet—at any rate until they could see something to shoot at.

Major Childe had reached the top of the hill, one man of his squadron, ten minutes in front of anyone else, waving his hat on his rifle at the summit to the admiration of thousands of the infantry, all of whom saw this act of conspicuous recklessness and rejoiced.

Lord Dundonald had galloped up to support the attack with Thorneycroft's Mounted Infantry and the rest of the 13th Hussars.

We, the South African Light Horse, had taken Bastion Hill. To advance further forward, however, proved quite impossible. The Boers had withdrawn to a second position a thousand yards in rear of the top of the hill. From this they directed a most accurate and damnable fire on all who showed themselves on the plateau.

Beneath the crest, one sat in safety and listened to the swish of bullets passing overhead. Above, the men were content to lie quite still underneath the rocks and wait for darkness.

I had a message for Major Childe and found him sitting on this dangerous ground, partly sheltered by a large rock—a serene old gentleman, exhausted with his climb, justly proud of its brilliant success.

I found no reason to remain very long on the plateau, and had just returned to the Brigadier when the Boer guns began to shell the tip of the hill. The first two or three projectiles skimmed over the surface, and roared harmlessly away. But the Boers were not long in striking their mark.

Two percussion shells burst on the exposed side of the hill, and then a well-exploded shrapnel searched its summit, searched and found what it sought. Major Childe was instantly killed by a fragment that entered his brain, and half a dozen troopers were more or less seriously wounded. After that, as if satisfied, the enemy's gun turned its attention elsewhere.

I think this death of Major Childe was a very sad event even among the inevitable incidents of war. He had served many-years ago in the Blues, and since then a connection with the Turf had made him not unknown and well liked in sporting circles. Old and grey as he was, the call to arms had drawn him from home, and wife, and comfort, as it is drawing many of all ages and fortunes now.

And so he was killed in his first fight against the Boers after he had performed an exploit—his first and last in war—which would most certainly have brought him honourable distinction.

He had a queer presentiment of impending fate, for he had spoken a good deal to us of the chances of death, and had even selected his own epitaph, so that on the little wooden cross which stands at the foot of Bastion Hill—the hill he himself took and held—there is written: 'Is it well with the child? It is well!'

The coign of vantage which I found on the side of the hill was not only to a great extent sheltered from the bullets, but afforded an extensive view of the general action, and for the rest of the day I remained with Lord Dundonald watching its development.

But a modern action is very disappointing as a spectacle. There is no smoke except that of the bursting shells. The combatants are scattered, spread over a great expanse of ground, concealed wherever possible, clad in neutral tint.

All the pomp and magnificence of Omdurman, the solid lines of infantry, the mighty Dervish array, bright with flashing spears and waving flags, were excluded.

Rows of tiny dots hurried forward a few yards and vanished into the brown of the earth. Bunches and clusters of brown things huddled among the rocks or in sheltered spots. The six batteries of artillery unlimbered, and the horses, hidden in some safe place, were scarcely visible.

Once I saw, in miniature, through glasses, a great wave of infantry surge forward along a spur and disappear beyond a crest line. The patter of the Mauser rifles swelled into a continuous rumbling like a train of waggons passing over a pontoon bridge, and presently the wave recoiled; the minute figures that composed it squeezed themselves into cover among some rocks, a great many groups of men began carrying away black objects.

A trickle of independent dots dispersed itself. Then we groaned. There had been a check. The distant drama continued.

The huddling figures began to move again—lithe, active forms moved about rearranging things—officers, we knew, even at the distance. Then the whole wave started again full of impetus—started—went forward, and never came back. And at this we were all delighted, and praised the valour of our unequalled infantry, and wished we were near enough to give them a cheer.

So we watched until nightfall, when some companies of the Queen's, from General Hildyard's Brigade, arrived, and took over the charge of our hill from us, and we descended to get our horses, and perhaps some food, finding, by good luck, all we wanted, and lay down on the ground to sleep, quite contented with ourselves and the general progress of the army.

The action of the 21st had begun before I awoke, and a brisk fusillade was going on all along the line. This day the right attack stood still, or nearly so, and the activity was confined to the left, where General Hildyard, with five battalions and two batteries, skilfully felt and tested the enemy's positions and found them most unpleasantly strong.

The main difficulty was that our guns could not come into action to smash the enemy in his trenches without coming under his rifle fire, because the edge of the plateau was only a thousand yards from the second and main Boer position, and unless the guns were on the edge of the plateau they could see very little and do less.

The cavalry guarded the left flank passively, and I remember no particular incident except that our own artillery flung the fragments of two premature shells among us and wounded a soldier in the Devonshire Regiment.

The following fact, however, is instructive.

Captain Stewart's squadron of the South African Light Horse dismounted, held an advanced kopje all day long under a heavy fire, and never lost a man.

Two hundred yards further back was another kopje held by two companies of regular infantry under equal fire. The infantry had more than twenty men hit.

On the 22nd, the action languished and the generals consulted. The infantry had made themselves masters of all the edge of the plateau, and the regiments clustered in the steep re-entrants like flies on the side of a wall. The Boers endeavoured to reach them with shells, and a desultory musketry duel also proceeded.

During the afternoon, I went with Captain Brooke to visit some of the battalions of General Hart's Brigade and see what sort of punishment they were receiving. As we rode up the watercourse which marks the bottom of the valley a shrapnel shell cleared the western crest line and exploded among one of the battalions.

At first it seemed to have done no harm, but as we climbed higher and nearer we met a stretcher carried by six soldiers. On it lay a body with a handkerchief thrown across the face. The soldiers bearing the stretcher were all covered with blood.

We proceeded and soon reached the battalions. A company of the Dublin Fusiliers were among those captured in the armoured train, and I have the pleasure of knowing most of the officers of this regiment.

So we visited them first—a dozen gentlemen—begrimed, unwashed, unshaven, sitting on the hillside behind a two-foot wall of rough stones and near a wooden box, which they called the 'Officers' Mess.'

Chapter XVIII: Through the Five Day's Action

They were in capital spirits in spite of every abominable circumstance.

'What did you lose in the action?'

'Oh, about fifty. Poor Hensley was killed, you know; that was the worst of it.'

Captain Hensley was one of the smallest and bravest men in the Army, and the Dublin Fusiliers, who should be good judges, regarded him as their very best officer for all military affairs, whether attack, retreat, or reconnaissance.

Each had lost a friend, but collectively as a regiment they had lost a powerful weapon.

'Very few of us left now,' said the colonel, surveying his regiment with pride.

'How many?'

'About four hundred and fifty.'

'Out of a thousand?'

'Well, out of about nine hundred.'

This war has fallen heavily on some regiments.

Scarcely any has suffered more severely, none has won greater distinction, than the Dublin Fusiliers—everywhere at the front—Dundee, Lombard's Kop, Colenso, Chieveley, Colenso again, and even here at Spion Kop.

Half the regiment, more than half the officers killed or wounded or prisoners. But the survivors were as cheery as ever.

'Do these shells catch anyone?'

'Only two or three an hour. They don't come always: every half-hour we get half a dozen. That last one killed an officer in the next regiment. Rather bad luck, picking an officer out of all these men—only one killed to-day so far, a dozen wounded.'

I inquired how much more time remained before the next consignment of shells was due. They said about ten minutes. I thought that would just suit me, and bade them good morning, for I have a horror of being killed when not on duty; but Captain

Brooke was anxious to climb to the top and examine the Boer position, and since we had come so far it was perhaps worthwhile going on.

So we did, and with great punctuality the shells arrived. We were talking to the officers of another regiment when they began. Two came in quick succession over the eastern wall of the valley and then one over the western. All three burst—two on impact, one in the air.

A fourth ripped along a stone shelter behind which skirmishers were firing. A fifth missed the valley altogether and screeched away into the plain clear of the hills.

The officers and men were quite callous. They scarcely troubled to look up. The soldiers went on smoking or playing cards or sleeping as if nothing had happened.

Personally, I felt no inclination to any of these pursuits, and I thought to sit and wait indefinitely, for the caprice of one of these shrieking iron devils would be most trying to anyone. But apparently you can get accustomed to anything.

The regiment where the officer had been killed a few minutes before was less cheerful and callous. The little group of officers crouching in the scanty shelter had seen one of their number plucked out of their midst and slain—uselessly as it seemed.

They advised us to take cover, which we would gladly have done had there been any worth speaking of; for at this moment the Boers discharged their Vickers-Maxim gun—the 'pom-pom'—and I have never heard such an extraordinary noise.

Seven or eight bangs, a rattle, an amazing cluttering and whistling overhead, then the explosions of the little shells, which scarred the opposite hillside in a long row of puffs of brown dust and blue-white smoke, suggesting a lash from a knotted scourge.

'Look out!' we were told, 'they always follow that with a shell.'

And so they did, but it passed overhead without harming anyone. Again the Vickers-Maxim flung its covey of projectiles. Again we crouched for the following shell; but this time it did

Chapter XVIII: Through the Five Day's Action

not come—immediately. I had seen quite enough, however, so we bade our friends good luck—never good-bye on active service—and hurried, slowly, on account of appearances, from this unhealthy valley.

As we reached our horses I saw another shell burst among the infantry. After that there was another interval.

Further on we met a group of soldiers returning to their regiment One lad of about nineteen was munching a biscuit. His right trouser leg was soaked with blood, I asked whether he was wounded.

'No, sir; it's only blood from an officer's head,' he answered, and went on—eating his biscuit.

Such were the fortunes for four days of the two brigades forming Warren's left attack.

I have already written a general account of the final action of Spion Kop on January 24, and have little to add.

As soon as the news spread through the camps that the British troops were occupying the top of the mountain I hurried to Gun Hill, where the batteries were arrayed, and watched the fight from a flank.

The spectacle was inconsiderable but significant. It was like a shadow peep-show. Along the mighty profile of the hill a fringe of little black crotchets advanced.

Then there were brown and red smudges of dust from shells striking the ground and white puffs from shrapnel bursting in the air—variations from the black and white.

Presently, a stretcher borne by five tiny figures jerks slowly forward, silhouetted on the sky-line; more shells; back goes the stretcher laden, a thicker horizontal line than before.

Then—a rush of crotchets rearwards—one leading two mules, mules terrified, jibbing, hanging back—all in silhouette one moment, the next all smudged with dust cloud; God help the driver; shadows clear again; driver still dragging mules—no, only one mule now; other figures still running rearwards.

Suddenly reinforcements arrive, hundreds of them; the whole sky-line bristles with crotchets moving swiftly along it, bending forward almost double, as if driving through a hailstorm. Thank heaven for that—only just in time too—and then more smudges on the shadow screen.

Sir Charles Warren was standing near me with his staff. One of his officers came up and told me that they had been disturbed at breakfast by a Boer shell, which had crashed through their waggon, killing a servant and a horse.

Presently the General himself saw me. I inquired about the situation, and learned for the first time of General Woodgate's wound—death it was then reported—and that Thorneycroft had been appointed brigadier-general.

'We have put what we think is the best fighting man in command regardless of seniority. We shall support him as he may request. We can do no more.'

I will only relate one other incident—a miserable one.

The day before the attack on Spion Kop, I had chanced to ride across the pontoon bridge. I heard my name called, and saw the cheery face of a boy I had known at Harrow—a smart, clean-looking young gentleman—quite the rough material for Irregular Horse.

He had just arrived and pushed his way to the front; hoped, so he said, 'to get a job.' This morning they told me that an unauthorised Press correspondent had been found among the killed on the summit. At least they thought at first it was a Press correspondent, for no one seemed to know him. A man had been found leaning forward on his rifle, dead. A broken pair of field glasses, shattered by the same shell that had killed their owner, bore the name 'M'Corquodale.'

The name and the face flew together in my mind. It was the last joined subaltern of Thorneycroft's Mounted Infantry—joined in the evening, shot at dawn. Poor gallant young Englishman! he had soon 'got his job.' The great sacrifice had been required of the Queen's latest recruit.

CHAPTER XIX
A FRESH EFFORT AND AN ARMY CHAPLAIN

Spearman's Hill: February 4, 1900

The first gleams of daylight crept underneath the waggon, and the sleepers, closely packed for shelter from the rain showers, awoke. Those who live under the conditions of a civilised city, who lie abed till nine and ten of the clock in artificially darkened rooms, gain luxury at the expense of joy.

But the soldier, who fares simply, sleeps soundly, and rises with the morning star, wakes in an elation of body and spirit without an effort and with scarcely a yawn. There is no more delicious moment in the day than this, when we light the fire and, while the kettle boils, watch the dark shadows of the hills take form, perspective, and finally colour, knowing that there is another whole day begun, bright with chance and interest, and free from all cares.

All cares—for who can be worried about the little matters of humdrum life when he may be dead before the night? Such a one was with us yesterday—see, there is a spare mug for coffee in the mess—but now gone for ever. And so it may be with us to-morrow.

What does it matter that this or that is misunderstood or perverted; that so-and-so is envious and spiteful; that heavy difficulties obstruct the larger schemes of life, clogging nimble aspiration with the mud of matters of fact? Here, life itself, life at its best and healthiest, awaits the caprice of the bullet.

Let us see the development of the day. All else may stand over, perhaps for ever. Existence is never so sweet as when it is at hazard. The bright butterfly flutters in the sunshine, the expression of the philosophy of Omar Khayyám, without the potations. But we awoke on the morning of the 25th in most gloomy spirits. I had seen the evacuation of Spion Kop during the night, and I did not doubt that it would be followed by the abandonment of all efforts to turn the Boer left from the passages of the Tugela at and near Trichardt's Drift. Nor were these forebodings wrong.

Before the sun was fairly risen orders arrived, 'All baggage to move east of Venter's Spruit immediately. Troops to be ready to turn out at thirty minutes' notice.'

General retreat, that was their meaning. Buller was withdrawing his train as a preliminary to disengaging, if he could, the fighting brigades, and retiring across the river.

Buller! So it was no longer Warren! The Commander-in-Chief had arrived, in the hour of misfortune, to take all responsibility for what had befallen the army, to extricate it, if possible, from its position of peril, to encourage the soldiers, now a second time defeated without being beaten, to bear the disappointment.

Everyone knows how all this, that looked so difficult, was successfully accomplished. The army was irritated by the feeling that it had made sacrifices for nothing. It was puzzled and disappointed by failure which it did not admit nor understand.

The enemy were flushed with success. The opposing lines in many places were scarcely a thousand yards apart. As the infantry retired the enemy would have commanding ground from which to assail them at every point.

Behind flowed the Tugela, a deep, rapid, only occasionally fordable river, eighty-five yards broad, with precipitous banks.

We all prepared ourselves for a bloody and even disastrous rearguard action. But now, I repeat, when things had come to this pass, Buller took personal command. He arrived on the field calm, cheerful, inscrutable as ever, rode hither and thither with a weary staff and a huge notebook, gripped the whole business in his strong hands, and so shook it into shape that we crossed the river in safety, comfort, and good order, with most remarkable mechanical precision, and without the loss of a single man or a pound of stores.

Chapter XIX: A Fresh Effort

The fighting troops stood fast for two days, while the train of waggons streamed back over the bridges and parked in huge black squares on the southern bank.

Then, on the night of the 26th, the retreat began. It was pitch dark, and a driving rain veiled all lights. The ground was broken. The enemy near. It is scarcely possible to imagine a more difficult operation. But it was performed with amazing ease.

Buller himself—not Buller by proxy or Buller at the end of a heliograph—Buller himself managed it. He was the man who gave orders, the man whom the soldiers looked to. He had already transported his train. At dusk he passed the Royals over the ford.

By ten o'clock all his cavalry and guns were across the pontoon bridges. At ten he began disengaging his infantry, and by daylight the army stood in order on the southern bank.

While the sappers began to take the pontoon bridges to pieces the Boers, who must have been astonished by the unusual rapidity of the movement, fired their first shell at the crossing. We were over the river none too soon.

A successful retreat is a poor thing for a relieving army to boast of when their gallant friends are hard pressed and worn out. But this withdrawal showed that this force possesses both a leader and machinery of organisation, and it is this, and this alone, that has preserved our confidence.

We believe that Buller gauged the capacity of one subordinate at Colenso, of another at Spion Kop, and that now he will do things himself, as he was meant to do. I know not why he has waited so long. Probably some pedantic principle of military etiquette: 'Commander-in-Chief should occupy a central position; turning movements should be directed by subordinates.'

But the army believes that this is all over now, and that for the future Buller will trust no one but himself in great matters; and it is because they believe this that the soldiers are looking forward with confidence and eagerness to the third and last attempt—for the sands at Ladysmith have run down very low—to shatter the

Boer lines. We have waited a week in the camp behind Spearman's Hill. The General has addressed the troops himself. He has promised that we shall be in Ladysmith soon. To replace the sixteen hundred killed and wounded in the late actions, drafts of twenty-four hundred men have arrived.

A mountain battery, A Battery R.H.A., and two great fortress guns have strengthened the artillery. Two squadrons of the 14th Hussars have been added to the cavalry, so that we are actually to-day numerically stronger by more than a thousand men than when we fought at Spion Kop, while the Boers are at least five hundred weaker—attrition *versus* recuperation.

Everyone has been well fed, reinforced and inspirited, and all are prepared for a supreme effort, in which we shall either reach Ladysmith or be flung back truly beaten with a loss of six or seven thousand men.

I will not try to foreshadow the line of attack, though certain movements appear to indicate where it will be directed. But it is generally believed that we fight to-morrow at dawn, and as I write this letter seventy guns are drawing up in line on the hills to open the preparatory bombardment.

It is a solemn Sunday, and the camp, with its white tents looking snug and peaceful in the sunlight, holds its breath that the beating of its heart may not be heard.

On such a day as this the services of religion would appeal with passionate force to thousands. I attended a church parade this morning. What a chance this was for a man of great soul who feared God! On every side were drawn up deep masses of soldiery, rank behind rank—perhaps, in all, five thousand.

In the hollow square stood the General, the man on whom everything depended. All around were men who within the week had been face to face with Death, and were going to face him again in a few hours.

Life seemed very precarious, in spite of the sunlit landscape. What was it all for? What was the good of human effort? How should it befall a man who died in a quarrel he did not understand? All the anxious questionings of weak spirits. It was one of those occasions when a fine preacher might have given comfort and strength where both were sorely needed, and have printed on many minds a permanent impression.

The bridegroom Opportunity had come. But the Church had her lamp untrimmed.

A chaplain with a raucous voice discoursed on the details of 'The siege and surrender of Jericho.' The soldiers froze into apathy, and after a while the formal perfunctory service reached its welcome conclusion.

As I marched home, an officer said to me: 'Why is it, when the Church spends so much on missionary work among heathens, she does not take the trouble to send good men to preach in time of war? The medical profession is represented by some of its greatest exponents. Why are men's wounded souls left to the care of a village practitioner?'

Nor could I answer; but I remembered the venerable figure and noble character of Father Brindle[1] in the River War, and wondered whether Rome was again seizing the opportunity which Canterbury disdained—the opportunity of telling the glad tidings to soldiers about to die.

---

1 Bishop Robert Brindle, a Roman Catholic priest who famously marched with his regiment, the Royal Irish, during the Sudan campaign of 1884.

CHAPTER XX
THE COMBAT OF VAAL KRANTZ

General Buller's Headquarters: February 9, 1900.

During the ten days that passed peacefully after the British retreat from the positions beyond Trichardt's Drift, Sir Redvers Buller's force was strengthened by the arrival of a battery of Horse Artillery, two powerful siege guns, two squadrons of the 14th Hussars, and drafts for the Infantry battalions, amounting to 2,400 men.

Thus not only was the loss of 1,600 men in the five days' fighting round Spion Kop made good, but the army was actually a thousand stronger than before its repulse.

Good and plentiful rations of meat and vegetables were given to the troops, and their spirits were restored by the General's public declaration that he had discovered the key to the enemy's position, and the promise that within a week from the beginning of the impending operation Ladysmith should be relieved.

The account of the straits to which the gallant garrison was now reduced by famine, disease, and war increased the earnest desire of officers and men to engage the enemy and, even at the greatest price, to break his lines.

In spite of the various inexplicable features which the actions of Colenso and Spion Kop presented, the confidence of the army in Sir Redvers Buller was still firm, and the knowledge that he himself would personally direct the operations, instead of leaving their conduct to a divisional commander, gave general satisfaction and relief.

On the afternoon of February 4, the superior officers were made acquainted with the outlines of the plan of action to be followed.

The reader will, perhaps, remember the description in a former letter of the Boer position before Potgieter's and Trichardt's

Chapter XX: The Combat of Vaal Krantz

Drift as a horizontal note of interrogation, of which Spion Kop formed the centre angle—/\.

The fighting of the previous week had been directed towards the straight line, and on the angle.

The new operation was aimed at the curve. The general scheme was to seize the hills which formed the left of the enemy's position and roll him up from left to right.

It was known that the Boers were massed mainly in their central camp behind Spion Kop, and that, as no demonstration was intended against the position in front of Trichardt's Drift, their whole force would be occupying the curve and guarding its right flank.

The details of the plan were well conceived. The battle would begin by a demonstration against the Brakfontein position, which the Boers had fortified by four tiers of trenches, with bombproof casemates, barbed wire entanglements, and a line of redoubts, so that it was obviously too strong to be carried frontally.

This demonstration would be made by Wynne's Brigade (formerly Woodgate's), supported by six batteries of Artillery, the Howitzer Battery, and the two 4.7-inch naval guns.

These troops crossed the river by the pontoon bridge at Potgieter's on the 3rd and 4th, relieving Lyttelton's Brigade which had been in occupation of the advanced position on the low kopjes.

A new pontoon bridge was thrown at the angle of the river a mile below Potgieter's, the purpose of which seemed to be to enable the frontal attack to be fully supported.

While the Artillery preparation of the advance against Brakfontein and Wynne's advance were going on, Clery's Division (consisting of Hart's Brigade and Hildyard's) and Lyttelton's Brigade were to mass near the new pontoon bridge (No. 2), as if about to support the frontal movement.

When the bombardment had been in progress for two hours, these three brigades were to move, not towards the Brakfontein position, but eastwards to Munger's Drift, throw a pontoon bridge covered first by one battery of Field Artillery withdrawn from the demonstration, secondly by the fire of guns which had been dragged to the summit of Swartkop, and which formed a powerful battery of fourteen pieces, viz., six 12-pounder long range naval guns, two 15-pounder guns of the 64th Field Battery, six 9-pounder mountain guns, and lastly by the two 50-pounder siege guns.

As soon as the bridge was complete, Lyttelton's Brigade would cross, and, ignoring the fire from the Boer left, extended along the Doornkloof heights, attack the Vaal Krantz ridge, which formed the left of the horseshoe curve around the debouches of Potgieter's.

This attack was to be covered on its right by the guns already specified on Swartkop and the 64th Field Battery, and prepared by the six artillery batteries employed in the demonstration, which were to withdraw one by one at intervals of ten minutes, cross No. 2 pontoon bridge, and take up new positions opposite to the Vaal Krantz ridge.

If and when Vaal Krantz was captured, all six batteries were to move across No. 3 bridge and take up positions on the hill, whence they could prepare and support the further advance of Clery's Division, which, having crossed, was to move past Vaal Krantz, pivot to the left on it, and attack the Brakfontein position from its left flank.

The 1st Cavalry Brigade under Burn-Murdoch (Royals, 13th and 14th Hussars, and A Battery R.H.A.) would also cross and run the gauntlet of Doornkloof and break out on to the plateau beyond Clery's Division.

The 2nd Cavalry Brigade (South African Light Horse, Composite Regiment, Thorneycroft's, and Bethune's Mounted Infantry, and the Colt Battery) were to guard the right and rear of the attacking troops from any attack coming from Doornkloof.

Wynne was to co-operate as opportunity offered. Talbot Coke was to remain in reserve. Such was the plan, and it seemed to all who heard it good and clear.

Chapter XX: The Combat of Vaal Krantz

It gave scope to the whole force, and seemed to offer all the conditions for a decisive trial of strength between the two armies.

On Sunday afternoon, the Infantry Brigades began to move to their respective positions, and at daylight on the 5th the Cavalry Division broke its camp behind spearman's.

At nine minutes past seven he bombardment of the Brakfontein position began, and by half-past seven all the Artillery except the Swartkop guns were firing in a leisurely fashion at the Boer redoubts and entrenchments.

At the same time Wynne's Brigade moved forward in dispersed formation towards the enemy, and the Cavalry began to defile across the front and to mass near the three Infantry Brigades collected near No. 2 pontoon bridge.

For some time, the Boers made no reply, but at about ten o'clock their Vickers-Maxim opened on the batteries firing from the Potgieter's plain, and the fire gradually increased as other guns, some of great range, joined in, until the Artillery was sharply engaged in an unsatisfactory duel—fifty guns exposed in the open against six or seven guns concealed and impossible to find.

The Boer shells struck all along the advanced batteries, bursting between the guns, throwing up huge fountains of dust and smoke, and covering the gunners at times completely from view.

Shrapnel shells were also flung from both flanks and ripped the dusty plain with their scattering bullets. But the Artillery stood to their work like men, and though they apparently produced no impression on the Boer guns, did not suffer as severely as might have been expected, losing no more than fifteen officers and men altogether.

At intervals of ten minutes the batteries withdrew in beautiful order and ceremony and defiled across the second pontoon bridge.

Meanwhile Wynne's Brigade had advanced to within twelve hundred yards of the Brakfontein position and retired, drawing the enemy's heavy fire; the three brigades under Clery had moved to the right near Munger's Drift; the Cavalry were massed in the hollows at the foot of Swartkop; and the Engineers had constructed the third pontoon bridge, performing their business with excellent method and despatch under a sharp fire from Boer skirmishers and a Maxim.

The six batteries and the howitzers now took up positions opposite Vaal Krantz, and seventy guns began to shell this ridge in regular preparation and to reply to three Boer guns which had now opened from Doornkloof and our extreme right. A loud and crashing cannonade developed.

At midday the Durham Light Infantry of Lyttelton's Brigade crossed the third pontoon bridge and advanced briskly along the opposite bank on the Vaal Krantz ridge. They were supported by the 3rd King's Royal Rifles, and behind these the other two battalions of the Brigade strengthened the attack.

The troops moved across the open in fine style, paying no attention to the enemy's guns on Doornkloof, which burst their shrapnel at seven thousand yards (shrapnel at seven thousand yards!) with remarkable accuracy. In an hour the leading companies had reached the foot of the ridge, and the active riflemen could be seen clambering swiftly up.

As the advance continued one of the Boer Vickers-Maxim guns which was posted in rear of Vaal Krantz found it wise to retire and galloped off unscathed through a tremendous fire from our artillery: a most wonderful escape.

The Durham Light Infantry carried the hill at the point of the bayonet, losing seven officers and sixty or seventy men, and capturing five Boer prisoners, besides ten horses and some wounded.

Most of the enemy, however, had retired before the attack, unable to endure the appalling concentration of artillery which had prepared it.

Among those who remained to fight to the last were five or six armed Kaffirs, one of whom shot an officer of the Durhams. To these no quarter was given. Their employment by the Dutch in this war shows that while they furiously complain of Khama's de-

Chapter XX: The Combat of Vaal Krantz

fence of his territory against their raiding parties on the ground that white men must be killed by white men, they have themselves no such scruples.[1]

There is no possible doubt about the facts set forth above, and the incident should be carefully noted by the public.

By nightfall, the whole of General Lyttelton's Brigade had occupied Vaal Krantz, and were entrenching themselves.

The losses in the day's fighting were not severe, and though no detailed statement has yet been compiled, I do not think they exceeded one hundred and fifty.

Part of Sir Redvers Buller's plan had been successfully executed. The fact that the action had not been opened until 7 A.M. and had been conducted in a most leisurely manner left the programme only half completed.

It remained to pass Clery's Division across the third bridge, to plant the batteries in their new position on Vaal Krantz, to set free the 1st Cavalry Brigade in the plain beyond, and to begin the main attack on Brakfontein. It remained and it still remains.

During the night of the 5th Lyttelton's Brigade made shelters and traverses of stones, and secured the possession of the hill; but it was now reported that field guns could not occupy the ridge because, first, it was too steep and rocky—though this condition does not apparently prevent the Boers dragging their heaviest guns to the tops of the highest hills—and, secondly, because the enemy's long-range rifle fire was too heavy. The hill, therefore, which had been successfully captured, proved of no value whatever.

Beyond it was a second position which was of great strength, and which if it was ever to be taken must be taken by the Infantry without Artillery support.

---

1 If the author's version is correct, then this is the first indication of Africans being armed to fight in the war, by either side. It is however more likely that these were so-called "agterryers", or servants, traditionally brought along by Boers even into battle, and who got caught up in the conflict. As the author pointed out, the attitude of the Boers towards the Africans was hardly charitable, and the likelihood that they would arm them for conflict is unlikely.

This was considered impossible or at any rate too costly and too dangerous to attempt.

During the next day the Boers continued to bombard the captured ridge, and also maintained a harassing long-range musketry fire. A great gun firing a hundred-pound 6-in. shell came into action from the top of Doornkloof, throwing its huge projectiles on Vaal Krantz and about the bivouacs generally; one of them exploded within a few yards of Sir Redvers Buller.

Two Vickers-Maxims from either side of the Boer position fired at brief intervals, and other guns burst shrapnel effectively from very long range on the solitary brigade which held Vaal Krantz.

To this bombardment the Field Artillery and the naval guns—seventy-two pieces in all, both big and little—made a noisy but futile response. The infantry of Lyttelton's Brigade, however, endured patiently throughout the day, in spite of the galling crossfire and severe losses.

At about four in the afternoon the Boers made a sudden attack on the hill, creeping to within short range, and then opened a quick fire. The Vickers-Maxim guns supported this vigorously.

The pickets at the western end of the hill were driven back with loss, and for a few minutes it appeared that the hill would be retaken. But General Lyttelton ordered half a battalion of the Durham Light Infantry, supported by the King's Royal Rifles, to clear the hill, and these fine troops, led by Colonel Fitzgerald, rose up from their shelters and, giving three rousing cheers—the thin, distant sound of which came back to the anxious, watching army—swept the Boers back at the point of the bayonet. Colonel Fitzgerald was, however, severely wounded.

While these things were passing a new pontoon bridge was being constructed at a bend of the Tugela immediately under the Vaal Krantz ridge, and by five o'clock this was finished. Nothing else was done during the day, but at nightfall Lyttelton's Brigade was relieved by Hildyard's, which marched across the new pontoon (No. 4) under a desultory shell fire from an extreme range.

Chapter XX: The Combat of Vaal Krantz

Lyttelton's Brigade returned under cover of darkness to a bivouac underneath the Zwartkop guns. Their losses in the two days' operations had been 225 officers and men.

General Hildyard, with whom was Prince Christian Victor, spent the night in improving the defences of the hill and in building new traverses and head cover.

At midnight the Boers made a fresh effort to regain the position, and the sudden roar of musketry awakened the sleeping army. The attack, however, was easily repulsed.

At daybreak the shelling began again, only now the Boers had brought up several new guns, and the bombardment was much heavier. Owing, however, to the excellent cover which had been arranged the casualties during the day did not exceed forty.

The Cavalry and Transport, who were sheltering in the hollows underneath Zwartkop, were also shelled, and it was thought desirable to move them back to a safer position.

In the evening, Sir Redvers Buller, who throughout these two days had been sitting under a tree in a somewhat exposed position, and who had bivouacked with the troops, consulted with his generals.

Many plans were suggested, but there was a general consensus of opinion that it was impossible to advance further along this line.

At eleven at night, Hildyard's Brigade was withdrawn from Vaal Krantz, evacuating the position in good order, and carrying with them their wounded, whom till dark it had been impossible to collect.

Orders were issued for the general retirement of the army to Springfield and Spearman's, and by ten o'clock on the 8th this operation was in full progress. With feelings of bitter disappointment at not having been permitted to fight the matter out, the Infantry, only two brigades of which had been sharply engaged, marched by various routes to their former camping grounds, and only their perfect discipline enabled them to control their grief and anger.

The Cavalry and Artillery followed in due course, and thus the fourth attempt to relieve Ladysmith, which had been begun with such hopes and enthusiasm, fizzled out into failure.

It must not, however, be imagined that the enemy conducted his defence without proportionate loss.

What I have written is a plain record of facts, and I am so deeply conscious of their significance that I shall attempt some explanation.

The Boer covering army numbers at least 12,000 men, with perhaps a dozen excellent guns. They hold along the line of the Tugela what is practically a continuous position of vast strength.

Their superior mobility, and the fact that they occupy the chord, while we must move along the arc of the circle, enables them to forefront us with nearly their whole force wherever an attack is aimed, however it may be disguised. Therefore there is no way of avoiding a direct assault.

Now, according to Continental experience the attacking force should outnumber the defence by three to one. Therefore Sir Redvers Buller should have 36,000 men. Instead of this he has only 22,000.

Moreover, behind the first row of positions, which practically runs along the edge of an unbroken line of steep flat-topped hills, there is a second row standing back from the edge at no great distance.

Any attack on this second row the Artillery cannot support, because from the plain below they are too far off to find the Boer guns, and from the edge they are too close to the enemy's riflemen.

The ground is too broken, in the opinion of many generals, for night operations. Therefore the attacking Infantry of insufficient strength must face unaided the fire of cool, entrenched riflemen, armed with magazine weapons and using smokeless powder.

Nevertheless, so excellent is the quality of the Infantry that if the whole force were launched in attack, it is not impossible that

Chapter XX: The Combat of Vaal Krantz

they would carry everything before them. But after this first victory it will be necessary to push on and attack the Boers investing Ladysmith.

The line of communications must be kept open behind the relieving army or it will be itself in the most terrible danger.

Already the Boers' position beyond Potgieter's laps around us on three sides. What if we should break through, only to have the door shut behind us? At least two brigades would have to be left to hold the line of communications. The rest, weakened by several fierce and bloody engagements, would not be strong enough to effect the relief.

The idea of setting all on the turn of the battle is very grateful and pleasant to the mind of the army, which only asks for a decisive trial of strength, but Sir Redvers Buller has to remember that his army, besides being the Ladysmith Relief Column, is also the only force which can be spared to protect South Natal.

Is he, therefore, justified in running the greatest risks? On the other hand, how can we let Ladysmith and all its gallant defenders fall into the hands of the enemy? It is agonising to contemplate such a conclusion to all the efforts and sacrifices that have been made.

I believe and trust we shall try again. As long as there is fighting one does not reflect on this horrible situation.

I have tried to explain some of the difficulties which confront the General. I am not now concerned with the attempts that have been made to overcome them.

A great deal is incomprehensible, but it may be safely said that if Sir Redvers Buller cannot relieve Ladysmith with his present force, we do not know of any other officer in the British Service who would be likely to succeed.

CHAPTER XXI
HUSSAR HILL

General Buller's Headquarters: February 15, 1900.

When Sir Redvers Buller broke off the combat of Vaal Krantz, and for the third time ordered his unbeaten troops to retreat, it was clearly understood that another attempt to penetrate the Boer lines was to be made without delay.

The army has moved from Spearman's and Springfield to Chieveley, General Lyttelton, who had succeeded Sir Francis Clery, in command of the 2nd Division and 4th Brigade, marching via Pretorius's Farm on the 9th and 10th, Sir Charles Warren covering the withdrawal of the supplies and transport and following on the 10th and 11th.

The regular Cavalry Brigade, under Burn-Murdoch, was left with two battalions to hold the bridge at Springfield, beyond which place the Boers, who had crossed the Tugela in some strength at Potgieter's, were reported to be showing considerable activity.

The left flank of the marching Infantry columns was covered by Dundonald's Brigade of Light Horse, and the operations were performed without interruption from the enemy.

On the 12th, orders were issued to reconnoitre Hussar Hill, a grassy and wooded eminence four miles to the east of Chieveley, and the direction of the next attack was revealed.

The reader of the accounts of this war is probably familiar with the Colenso position and understands its great strength. The proper left of this position rests on the rocky, scrub-covered hill of Hlangwani, which rises on the British side of the Tugela.

If this hill can be captured and artillery placed on it, and if it can be secured from cross fire, then all the trenches of Fort Wylie and along the river bank will be completely enfiladed, and the Colenso position will become untenable, so that Hlangwani is

Chapter XXI: Hussar Hill

the key of the Colenso position. In order, however, to guard this key carefully the Boers have extended their left—as at Trichardt's Drift they extended their right—until it occupies a very lofty range of mountains four or five miles to the east of Hlangwani, and along all this front works have been constructed on a judicious system of defence.

The long delays have given ample time to the enemy to complete his fortifications, and the trenches here are more like forts than field works, being provided with overhead cover against shells and carefully made loopholes.

In front of them stretches a bare slope, on either side rise formidable hills from which long-range guns can make a continual cross-fire. Behind this position, again, are others of great strength. But there are also encouraging considerations.

We are to make—at least in spite of disappointments we hope and believe we are to make—a supreme effort to relieve Ladysmith. At the same time we are the army for the defence of South Natal.

If we had put the matter to the test at Potgieter's and failed, our line of communications might have been cut behind us, and the whole army, weakened by the inevitable heavy losses of attacking these great positions, might have been captured or dispersed.

Here we have the railway behind us. We are not as we were at Potgieter's 'formed to a flank.'

We derive an accession of strength from the fact that the troops holding Railhead are now available for the general action. Besides these inducements this road is the shortest way.

Buller, therefore, has elected to lose his men and risk defeat—without which risk no victory can be won—-on this line.

Whether he will succeed or not were foolish to prophesy, but it is the common belief that this line offers as good a chance as any other and that at last the army will be given a fair run, and permitted to begin a general engagement and fight it out to the end.

If Buller goes in and wins, he will have accomplished a wonderful feat of arms, and will gain the lasting honour and gratitude of his country. If he is beaten, he will deserve the respect and sympathy of all true soldiers as a man who has tried to the best of his ability to perform a task for which his resources were inadequate.

I hasten to return to the chronicle.

Hussar Hill—so-called because a small post of the 13th Hussars was surprised on it six weeks ago and lost two men killed—is the high ground opposite Hlangwani and the mountainous ridges called Monte Cristo and Cingolo, on which the Artillery must be posted to prepare the attack.

Hence the reconnaissance of the 12th.

At eight o'clock—we never get up early in this war—Lord Dundonald started from the cavalry camp near Stuart's Farm with the South African Light Horse, the Composite Regiment, Thorneycroft's Mounted Infantry, the Colt Battery, one battalion of Infantry, the Royal Welsh Fusiliers, and a battery of Field Artillery.

The Irregular Horse were familiar with the ground, and we soon occupied Hussar Hill, driving back a small Boer patrol which was watching it, and wounding two of the enemy.

A strong picket line was thrown out all round the captured ground and a dropping musketry fire began at long range with the Boers, who lay hidden in the surrounding dongas.

At noon Sir Redvers Buller arrived, and made a prolonged reconnaissance of the ground with his telescope.

At one o'clock we were ordered to withdraw, and the difficult task of extricating the advanced pickets from close contact with the enemy was performed under a sharp fire, fortunately without the loss of a man.

After you leave Hussar Hill on the way back to Chieveley camp it is necessary to cross a wide dip of ground. We had withdrawn several miles in careful rearguard fashion, the guns and the bat-

Chapter XXI: Hussar Hill

talion had gone back, and the last two squadrons were walking across this dip towards the ridge on the homeward side.

Perhaps we had not curled in our tail quite quick enough, or perhaps the enemy has grown more enterprising of late, in any case just as we were reaching the ridge a single shot was fired from Hussar Hill, and then without more ado a loud crackle of musketry burst forth.

The distance was nearly two thousand yards, but the squadrons in close formation were a good target.

Everybody walked for about twenty yards, and then without the necessity of an order broke into a brisk canter, opening the ranks to a dispersed formation at the same time.

It was very dry weather, and the bullets striking between the horsemen raised large spurts of dust, so that it seemed that many men must surely be hit. Moreover, the fire had swelled to a menacing roar.

I chanced to be riding with Colonel Byng in rear, and looking round saw that we had good luck. For though bullets fell among the troopers quite thickly enough, the ground two hundred yards further back was all alive with jumping dust. The Boers were shooting short.

We reached the ridge and cover in a minute, and it was very pretty to see these irregular soldiers stop their horses and dismount with their carbines at once without any hesitation.

Along the ridge Captain Hill's Colt Battery was drawn up in line, and as soon as the front was clear the four little pink guns began spluttering furiously.

The whole of the South African Light Horse dismounted and, lining the ridge, opened fire with their rifles.

Thorneycroft's Mounted Infantry came into line on our left flank, and brought two tripod Maxims into action with them.

Lord Dundonald sent back word to the battery to halt and fire over our heads, and Major Gough's Regiment and the Royal Welsh Fusiliers, who had almost reached cover, turned round of their own accord and hurried eagerly in the direction of the firing, which had become very loud on both sides.

There now ensued a strange little skirmish, which would have been a bloody rifle duel but for the great distance which separated the combatants and for the cleverness with which friends and foes concealed and sheltered themselves.

Not less than four hundred men on either side were firing as fast as modern rifles will allow. Between us stretched the smooth green dip of ground. Beyond there rose the sharper outlines of Hussar Hill, two or three sheds, and a few trees. That was where the Boers were.

But they were quite invisible to the naked eye, and no smoke betrayed their positions. With a telescope they could be seen—a long row of heads above the grass.

We were equally hidden. Still their bullets—a proportion of their bullets—found us, and I earnestly trust that some of ours found them. Indeed there was a very hot fire, in spite of the range. Yet no one was hit.

Ah, yes, there was one, a tall trooper turned sharply on his side, and two of his comrades carried him quickly back behind a little house, shot through the thigh.

A little further along the firing line another was being helped to the rear. The Colt Battery drew the cream of the fire, and Mr. Garrett, one of the experts sent out by the firm, was shot through the ankle, but he continued to work his gun.

Captain Hill walked up and down his battery exposing himself with great delight, and showing that he was a very worthy representative of an Irish constituency.

I happened to pass along the line on some duty or other when I noticed my younger brother, whose keen desire to take some part in the public quarrel had led me, in spite of misgivings, to procure him a lieutenancy, lying on the ground, with his troop. As I approached I saw him start in the quick, peculiar manner of a stricken man.

Chapter XXI: Hussar Hill

I asked him at once whether he was hurt, and he said something—he thought it must be a bullet—had hit him on the gaiter and numbed his leg. He was quite sure it had not gone in, but when we had carried him away we found—as I expected—that he was shot through the leg. The wound was not serious, but the doctors declared he would be a month in hospital.

It was his baptism of fire, and I have since wondered at the strange caprice which strikes down one man in his first skirmish and protects another time after time. But I suppose all pitchers will get broken in the end.

Outwardly I sympathised with my brother in his misfortune, which he mourned bitterly, since it prevented him taking part in the impending battle, but secretly I confess myself well content that this young gentleman should be honourably out of harm's way for a month.

It was neither our business nor our pleasure to remain and continue this long-range duel with the Boers.

Our work for the day was over, and all were anxious to get home to luncheon. Accordingly, as soon as the battery had come into action to cover our withdrawal we commenced withdrawing squadron by squadron and finally broke off the engagement, for the Boers were not inclined to follow further.

At about three o'clock, our loss in this interesting affair was one officer, Lieutenant John Churchill, and seven men of the South African Light Horse wounded and a few horses.

Thorneycroft's Mounted Infantry also had two casualties, and there were two more in the Colt detachments.

The Boers were throughout invisible, but two days later when the ground was revisited, we found one dead burgher—so that at any rate they lost more heavily than we.

The Colt guns worked very well, and the effect of the fire of a whole battery of these weapons was a marked diminution in the enemy's musketry. They were mounted on the light carriages patented by Lord Dundonald, and the advantage of these in enabling the guns to be run back by hand, so as to avoid exposing the horses, was very obvious.

I shall leave the great operation which, as I write, has already begun, to another letter, but since gaiety has its value in these troublous times, let the reader pay attention to the story of General Hart and the third-class shot.

Major-General Hart, who commands the Irish Brigade, is a man of intrepid personal courage—indeed, to his complete contempt for danger the heavy losses among his battalions, and particularly in the Dublin Fusiliers, must be to some extent attributed.

After Colenso there were bitter things said on this account. But the reckless courage of the General was so remarkable in subsequent actions that, being brave men themselves, they forgave him everything for the sake of his daring.

During the first day at Spion Kop, General Hart discovered a soldier sitting safely behind a rock and a long way behind the firing line.

'Good afternoon, my man,' he said in his most nervous, apologetic voice; 'what are you doing here?'

'Sir,' replied the soldier, 'an officer told me to stop here, sir.'

'Oh! Why?'

'I'm a third-class shot, sir.'

'Dear me,' said the General after some reflection, 'that's an awful pity, because you see you'll have to get quite close to the Boers to do any good. Come along with me and I'll find you a nice place,' and a mournful procession trailed off towards the most advanced skirmishers.

CHAPTER XXII
THE ENGAGEMENT OF MONTE CRISTO

Cingolo Neck: February 19, 1900.

Not since I wrote the tale of my escape from Pretoria, have I taken up my pen with such feelings of satisfaction and contentment as I do to-night. The period of doubt and hesitation is over. We have grasped the nettle firmly, and as shrewdly as firmly, and have taken no hurt. It remains only to pluck it.

For heaven's sake, no over-confidence or premature elation; but there is really good hope that Sir Redvers Buller has solved the Riddle of the Tugela—at last.

At last! I expect there will be some who will inquire—'Why not "at first"?' All I can answer is this: There is certainly no more capable soldier of high rank in all the army in Natal than Sir Redvers Buller.

For three months, he has been trying his best to pierce the Boer lines and the barrier of mountain and river which separates Ladysmith from food and friends; trying with an army—magnificent in everything but numbers, and not inconsiderable even in that respect—trying at a heavy price of blood in Africa, of anxiety at home.

Now, for the first time, it seems that he may succeed. Knowing the General and the difficulties, I am inclined to ask, not whether he might have succeeded sooner, but rather whether anyone else would have succeeded at all. But to the chronicle!

Anyone who stands on Gun Hill near Chieveley can see the whole of the Boer position about Colenso sweeping before him in a wide curve. The mountain wall looks perfectly unbroken. The river lies everywhere buried in its gorge, and is quite invisible.

To the observer, there is only a smooth green bay of land sloping gently downward, and embraced by the rocky, scrub-covered hills. Along this crescent of high ground runs—or rather, by God's grace, ran the Boer line, strong in its natural features, and entrenched from end to end.

When the map is consulted, however, it is seen that the Tugela does not flow uniformly along the foot of the hills as might be expected, but that after passing Colenso village, which is about the centre of the position, it plunges into the mountainous country, and bends sharply northward; so that, though the left of the Boer line might appear as strong as the right, there was this difference, that the Boer right had the river on its front, the Boer left had it in its rear.

The attack of the 15th of December had been directed against the Boer right, because after reconnaissance Sir Redvers Buller deemed that, in spite of the river advantage, the right was actually the weaker of the two flanks.

The attack of the 15th was repulsed with heavy loss. It might, therefore, seem that little promise of success attended an attack on the Boer left. The situation, however, was entirely altered by the great reinforcements in heavy artillery which had reached the army, and a position which formerly appeared unassailable now looked less formidable.

Let us now consider the Boer left by itself. It ran in a chain of sangars, trenches, and rifle pits, from Colenso village, through the scrub by the river, over the rugged hill of Hlangwani, along a smooth grass ridge we called 'The Green Hill,' and was extended to guard against a turning movement on to the lofty wooded ridges of Monte Cristo and Cingolo and the neck joining these two features.

Sir Redvers Buller's determination was to turn this widely extended position on its extreme left, and to endeavour to crumple it from left to right. As it were, a gigantic right arm was to reach out to the eastward, its shoulder at Gun Hill, its elbow on Hussar Hill, its hand on Cingolo, its fingers, the Irregular Cavalry Bri-

Chapter XXII: The Engagement of Monte Cristo

gade, actually behind Cingolo. On February 12th, a reconnaissance in force of Hussar Hill was made by Lord Dundonald.

On the 14th the army moved east from Chieveley to occupy this ground. General Hart with one brigade held Gun Hill and Railhead. The First Cavalry Brigade watched the left flank at Springfield, but with these exceptions the whole force marched for Hussar Hill.

The Irregular Cavalry covered the front, and the South African Light Horse, thrown out far in advance, secured the position by half-past eight, just in time to forestall a force of Boers which had been despatched, so soon as the general movement of the British was evident, to resist the capture of the hill.

A short sharp skirmish followed, in which we lost a few horses and men, and claim to have killed six Boers, and which was terminated after half an hour by the arrival of the leading Infantry battalion—the Royal Welsh Fusiliers.

During the day, the occupation was completed, and the brigades of Generals Wynne, Coke, and Barton, then joining Warren's Division with the Artillery, entrenched themselves strongly and bivouacked on the hill.

Meanwhile Lyttelton's Division marched from its camp in the Blue Krantz Valley, east of Chieveley, along the valley to a position short of the eastern spurs of Hussar Hill. These spurs are more thickly wooded and broken than the rest of the hill, and about four o'clock in the afternoon some hundred Boers established themselves among the rocks and opened a sharp fire.

They were, however, expelled from their position by the Artillery and by the fire of the advanced battalions of Lyttelton's Division operating from the Blue Krantz Valley.

During the 15th and 16th, a desultory artillery duel proceeded on both sides with slight loss to us.

The water question presented some difficulty, as the Blue Krantz River was several miles from Hussar Hill and the hill itself was waterless. A system of iron tanks mounted on ox waggons was arranged, and a sufficient though small supply maintained. The heavy artillery was also brought into action and strongly entrenched.

The formidable nature of the enemy's position and the evident care with which he had fortified it may well have added to the delay by giving cause for the gravest reflection.

On the afternoon of the 16th, Sir Redvers Buller resolved to plunge, and orders were issued for a general advance at dawn.

Colonel Sandbach, under whose supervision the Intelligence Department has attained a new and a refreshing standard of efficiency, made comprehensive and, as was afterwards proved, accurate reports of the enemy's strength and spirit, and strongly recommended the attack on the left flank.

Two hours before dawn the army was on the move. Hart's Brigade, the 6-inch and other great guns at Chieveley, guarded Railhead.

Hlangwani Hill, and the long line of entrenchments rimming the Green Hill, were masked and fronted by the display of the field and siege batteries, whose strength in guns was as follows:

	Guns
Four 5-inch siege guns............................	4
Six naval twelve-pounder long-range guns........	6
Two 4.7-inch naval guns...............................	2
One battery howitzers............................	6
One battery corps artillery (R.F.A.).............	6
Two brigade divisions R.F.A	36
One mountain battery............................	<u>6</u>
	66

and which were also able to prepare and support the attack on Cingolo Neck and Monte Cristo Ridge. Cingolo Ridge itself, however, was almost beyond their reach.

Lyttelton's Division with Wynne's Fusilier Brigade was to stretch out to the eastward and, by a wide turning movement pivoting on the guns and Barton's Brigade, attack the Cingolo Ridge.

Chapter XXII: The Engagement of Monte Cristo

Dundonald's Cavalry Brigade was to make a far wider detour and climb up the end of the ridge, thus making absolutely certain of finding the enemy's left flank at last.

By daybreak all were moving, and as the Irregular Cavalry forded the Blue Krantz stream on their enveloping march we heard the boom of the first gun. The usual leisurely bombardment had begun, and I counted only thirty shells in the first ten minutes, which was not very hard work for the gunners considering that nearly seventy guns were in action.

But the Artillery never hurry themselves, and indeed I do not remember to have heard in this war a really good cannonade, such as we had at Omdurman, except for a few minutes at Vaal Krantz.

The Cavalry Brigade marched ten miles eastward through most broken and difficult country, all rock, high grass, and dense thickets, which made it imperative to move in single file, and the sound of the general action grew fainter and fainter.

Gradually, however, we began to turn again towards it. The slope of the ground rose against us. The scrub became more dense. To ride further was impossible. We dismounted and led our horses, who scrambled and blundered painfully among the trees and boulders.

So scattered was our formation that I did not care to imagine what would have happened had the enemy put in an appearance. But our safety lay in these same natural difficulties.

The Boers doubtless reflected, 'No one will ever try to go through such ground as that'—besides which war cannot be made without running risks. The soldier must chance his life. The general must not be afraid to brave disaster.

But how tolerant the arm-chair critics should be of men who try daring *coups* and fail! You must put your head into the lion's mouth if the performance is to be a success.

And then I remembered the attacks on the brave and capable General Gatacre after Stormberg, and wondered what would be said of us if we were caught 'dismounted and scattered in a wood.' At length we reached the foot of the hill and halted to reconnoitre the slopes as far as was possible.

After half an hour, since nothing could be seen, the advance was resumed up the side of a precipice and through a jungle so thick that we had to cut our road.

It was eleven o'clock before we reached the summit of the ridge and emerged on to a more or less open plateau, diversified with patches of wood and heaps of great boulders. Two squadrons had re-formed on the top and had deployed to cover the others.

The troopers of the remaining seven squadrons were working their way up about four to the minute. It would take at least two hours before the command was complete: and meanwhile! Suddenly there was a rifle shot. Then another, then a regular splutter of musketry. Bullets began to whizz overhead. The Boers had discovered us.

Now came the crisis. There might be a hundred Boers on the hill, in which case all was well. On the other hand, there might be a thousand, in which case——! and retreat down the precipice was, of course, quite out of the question.

Luckily there were only about a hundred, and after a skirmish, in which one of the Natal Carabineers was unhappily killed, they fell back, and we completed our deployment on the top of the hill.

The squadron of Imperial Light Horse and the Natal Carabineers now advanced slowly along the ridge, clearing it of the enemy, slaying and retrieving one field cornet and two burghers, and capturing ten horses.

Half-way along the Queen's, the right battalion of Hildyard's attack, which, having made a smaller detour, had now rushed the top, came into line and supported the dismounted men.

The rest of the Cavalry descended into the plain on the other side of the ridge, outflanking and even threatening the retreat of its defenders, so that in the end the Boers, who were very weak

Chapter XXII: The Engagement of Monte Cristo

in numbers, were hunted off the ridge altogether, and Cingolo was ours.

Cingolo and Monte Cristo are joined together by a neck of ground from which both heights rise steeply. On either side of Monte Cristo and Cingolo long spurs run at right angles to the main hill.

By the operations of the 17th the Boer line had been twisted off Cingolo, and turned back along the subsidiary spurs of Monte Cristo, and the British forces had placed themselves diagonally across the left of the Boer position thus:

Plan of position at Monte Cristo

The advantages of this situation were to be enjoyed on the morrow.

Finding our further advance barred by the turned-back position the enemy had adopted, and which we could only attack frontally, the Cavalry threw out a line of outposts which were soon engaged in a long-range rifle duel, and prepared to bivouac for the night.

Cingolo Ridge was meanwhile strongly occupied by the Infantry, whose line ran from its highest peak slantwise across the valley of the Gomba Stream to Hussar Hill, where it found its pivot in Barton's Brigade and the Artillery.

The Boers, who were much disconcerted by the change in the situation, showed themselves ostentatiously on the turned-back ridge of their position as if to make themselves appear in great strength, and derisively hoisted white flags on their guns.

The Colonial and American troopers (for in the South African Light Horse we have a great many Americans, and one even who served under Sheridan) made some exceedingly good practice at the extreme ranges. So the afternoon passed, and the night came in comparative quiet.

At dawn the artillery began on both sides, and we were ourselves awakened by Creusot shells bursting in our bivouac. The enemy's fire was chiefly directed on the company of the Queen's which was holding the top of Cingolo, and only the good cover which the great rocks afforded prevented serious losses. As it was several men were injured.

But we knew that we held the best cards; and so did the Boers.

At eight o'clock Hildyard's Brigade advanced against the peak of the Monte Cristo ridge which lay beyond the neck. The West Yorks led, the Queen's and East Surrey supported.

The musketry swelled into a constant crackle like the noise of a good fire roaring up the chimney, but, in spite of more than a hundred casualties, the advance never checked for an instant, and by half-past ten o'clock the bayonets of the attacking infantry began to glitter among the trees of the summit.

The Boers, who were lining a hastily-dug trench half way along the ridge, threatened in front with an overwhelming force and assailed in flank by the long-range fire of the Cavalry, began to fall back.

By eleven o'clock, the fight on the part of the enemy resolved itself into a rearguard action.

Under the pressure of the advancing and enveloping army this degenerated very rapidly.

When the Dutchman makes up his mind to go, he throws all dignity to the winds, and I have never seen an enemy leave the

Chapter XXII: The Engagement of Monte Cristo

field in such a hurry as did these valiant Boers who found their flank turned, and remembered for the first time that there was a deep river behind them.

Shortly after twelve o'clock, the summit of the ridge of Monte Cristo was in our hands.

The spurs which started at right angles from it were, of course, now enfiladed and commanded. The Boers evacuated both in great haste.

The eastern spur was what I have called the 'turned-back' position. The Cavalry under Dundonald galloped forward and seized it as soon as the enemy were seen in motion, and from this advantageous standpoint we fired heavily into their line of retreat. They scarcely waited to fire back, and we had only two men and a few horses wounded.

The spur on the Colenso or western side was none other than the Green Hill itself, and judging rightly that its frowning entrenchments were now empty of defenders Sir Redvers Buller ordered a general advance frontally against it. Two miles of trenches were taken with scarcely any loss. The enemy fled in disorder across the river.

A few prisoners, some wounded, several cartloads of ammunition and stores, five camps with all kinds of Boer material, and last of all, and compared to which all else was insignificant, the dominating Monte Cristo ridge stretching northward to within an easy spring of Bulwana Hill, were the prize of victory.

The soldiers, delighted at the change of fortune, slept in the Boer tents—or would have done had these not been disgustingly foul and stinking.

From the captured ridge we could look right down into Ladysmith, and at the first opportunity I climbed up to see it for myself. Only eight miles away stood the poor little persecuted town, with whose fate there is wrapped up the honour of the Empire, and for whose sake so many hundred good soldiers have given life or limb—a twenty-acre patch of tin houses and blue gum trees, but famous to the uttermost ends of the earth.

The victory of Monte Cristo has revolutionised the situation in Natal. It has laid open a practicable road to Ladysmith.

Great difficulties and heavy opposition have yet to be encountered and overcome, but the word 'impossible' must no longer be—should, perhaps, never have been used.

The success was won at the cost of less than two hundred men killed and wounded, and surely no army more than the Army of Natal deserves a cheaply bought triumph.

Area of operations Colenso - Ladysmith.

CHAPTER XXIII
THE PASSAGE OF THE TUGELA

Hospital Ship 'Maine': March 4, 1900.

Since I finished my last letter, on February the 21st, I have found no time to sit down to write until now, because we have passed through a period of ceaseless struggle and emotion, and I have been seeing so many things that I could not pause to record anything.

It has been as if a painter prepared himself to paint some portrait, but was so fascinated by the beauty of his model that he could not turn his eyes from her face to the canvas; only that the spectacles which have held me have not always been beautiful.

Now the great event is over, the long and bloody conflict around Ladysmith has been gloriously decided, and I take a few days' leisure on the good ship *Maine*, where everyone is busy getting well, to think about it all and set down some things on paper.

First and foremost, there was the Monte Cristo ridge, that we had captured on the 18th, which gave us the Green Hill, Hlangwani Hill, and, when we chose to take it, the whole of the Hlangwani plateau.

The Monte Cristo ridge is the centrepiece to the whole of this battle. As soon as we had won it I telegraphed to the *Morning Post* that now at last success was a distinct possibility.

With this important feature in our possession it was certain that we held the key to Ladysmith, and though we might fumble a little with the lock, sooner or later, barring the accidents of war, we should open the door.

As Monte Cristo had given Sir Redvers Buller Hlangwani, so Hlangwani rendered the whole of the western section (the eastern section was already in our hands) of the Colenso position untenable by the enemy, and they, finding themselves commanded and enfiladed, forthwith evacuated it.

On the 19th, General Buller made good his position on Green Hill, occupied Hlangwani with Barton's Brigade, built or improved his roads and communications from Hussar Hill across the Gomba Valley, and brought up his heavy guns.

The Boers, who were mostly on the other side of the river, resisted stubbornly with artillery, with their Vickers-Maxim guns and the fire of skirmishers, so that we suffered some slight loss, but could not be said to have wasted the day.

On the 20th, the south side of the Tugela was entirely cleared of the enemy, who retired across the bridge they had built, and, moreover, a heavy battery was established on the spurs of Hlangwani to drive them out of Colenso.

In the afternoon Hart's Brigade advanced from Chieveley, and his leading-battalion, under Major Stuart-Wortley, occupied Colenso village without any resistance.

The question now arose—Where should the river be crossed? Sir Redvers Buller possessed the whole of the Hlangwani plateau, which, as the reader may perceive by looking at the map on page 230, fills up the re-entrant angle made opposite Pieters by the Tugela after it leaves Colenso. From this Hlangwani plateau he could either cross the river where it ran north and south or where it ran east and west.

Sir Redvers Buller determined to cross the former reach beyond Colenso village. To do this he had to let go his hold on the Monte Cristo ridge and resign all the advantages which its possession had given him, and had besides to descend into the low ground, where his army must be cramped between the high hills on its left and the river on its right.

There was, of course, something to be said for the other plan, which was advocated strongly by Sir Charles Warren. The crossing, it was urged, was absolutely safe, being commanded on all sides by our guns, and the enemy could make no opposition except with artillery.

Moreover, the army would get on its line of railway and could 'advance along the railroad.'

Chapter XXIII: The Passage of the Tugela

This last was a purely imaginary advantage, to be sure, because the railway had no rolling-stock, and was disconnected from the rest of the line by the destruction of the Tugela bridge.

But what weighed with the Commander-in-Chief much more than the representations of his lieutenant was the accumulating evidence that the enemy were in full retreat.

The Intelligence reports all pointed to this situation. Boers had ridden off in all directions. Waggons were seen trekking along every road to the north and west. The camps between us and Ladysmith began to break up.

Everyone said, 'This is the result of Lord Roberts's advance: the Boers find themselves now too weak to hold us off. They have raised the siege.' But this conclusion proved false in the sense that it was premature. Undoubtedly the Boers had been reduced in strength by about 5,000 men, who had been sent into the Free State for its defence.

Until the Monte Cristo ridge was lost to them, they deemed themselves quite strong enough to maintain the siege. When, however, this position was captured, the situation was revolutionised. They saw that we had found their flank, and thoroughly appreciated the significance and value of the long high wedge of ground, which cut right across the left of their positions, and seemed to stretch away almost to Bulwana Mountain.

They knew perfectly well that if we advanced by our right along the line of this ridge, which they called 'the Bush Kop,' supporting ourselves by it as a man might rest his hand on a balustrade, we could turn their Pieters position just as we had already turned their entrenchments at Colenso.

Therein lay the true reason of their retirement, and in attributing it either to Lord Roberts's operations or to the beating we had given them on the 18th, we made a mistake, which was not repaired until much blood had been shed.

I draw a rough diagram to assist the reader who will take the trouble to study the map.

It is only drawn from memory, and its object is to show how completely the Monte Cristo ridge turned both the line of entrenchments through Colenso and that before Pieters. But no diagrams, however exaggerated, would convince so well as would the actual ground.

Plan of the Colenso Position

In the belief, however, that the enemy were in retreat the General resolved to cross the river at A by a pontoon bridge and follow the railway line.

On the 21st, therefore, he moved his army westward across the Hlangwani plateau, threw his bridge, and during the afternoon passed his two leading infantry brigades over it.

As soon as the Boers perceived that he had chosen this line of advance their hopes revived. 'Oh,' we may imagine them saying, 'if you propose to go that way, things are not so bad after all.'

So they returned to the number of about nine thousand burghers, and manned the trenches of the Pieters position, with

Chapter XXIII: The Passage of the Tugela

the result that Wynne's Lancashire Brigade, which was the first to cross, soon found itself engaged in a sharp action among the low-kopjes, and suffered a hundred and fifty casualties, including its General, before dark. Musketry fire was continuous throughout the night.

The 1st Cavalry Brigade had been brought in from Springfield on the 20th, and on the morning of the 22nd both the Regular and Irregular Cavalry were to have crossed the river.

We accordingly marched from our camp at the neck between Cingolo and Monte Cristo and met the 1st Cavalry Brigade, which had come from Chieveley, at the pontoon bridge.

A brisk action was crackling away beyond the river, and it looked as if the ground scarcely admitted of our intervention.

Indeed, we had hardly arrived when a Staff Officer came up, and brought us orders to camp near Hlangwani Hill, as we should not cross that day. Presently I talked to the Staff Officer, who chanced to be a friend of mine, and chanced, besides, to be a man with a capacity for sustained thought, an eye for country, and some imagination.

He said: 'I don't like the situation; there are more of them than we expected. We have come down off our high ground. We have taken all the big guns off the big hills. We are getting ourselves cramped up among these kopjes in the valley of the Tugela. It will be like being in the Coliseum and shot at by every row of seats.'

Sir Redvers Buller, however, still believing he had only a rearguard in front of him, was determined to persevere. It is, perhaps, his strongest characteristic obstinately to pursue his plan in spite of all advice, in spite, too, of his horror of bloodshed, until himself convinced that it is impracticable.

The moment he is satisfied that this is the case no considerations of sentiment or effect prevent him from coming back and starting afresh. No modern General ever cared less for what the world might say. However unpalatable and humiliating a retreat might be, he would make one so soon as he was persuaded that adverse chances lay before him.

'To get there in the end,' was his guiding principle. Nor would the General consent to imperil the ultimate success by asking his soldiers to make a supreme effort to redress a false tactical move. It was a principle which led us to much blood and bitter disappointment, but in the end to victory.

Not yet convinced, General Buller, pressing forward, moved the whole of his infantry, with the exception of Barton's Brigade, and nearly all the artillery, heavy and field, across the river, and in the afternoon sent two battalions from Norcott's Brigade and the Lancashire Brigade—to the vacant command of which Colonel Kitchener had been appointed—forward against the low kopjes.

By nightfall a good deal of this low, rolling ground was in our possession, though at some cost in men and officers.

At dusk the Boers made a fierce and furious counter-attack. I was watching the operations from Hlangwani Hill through a powerful telescope. As the light died my companions climbed down the rocks to the Cavalry camp and left me alone staring at the bright flashes of the guns which stabbed the obscurity on all sides.

Suddenly, above the booming of the cannon, there arose the harsh rattling roar of a tremendous fusillade. Without a single intermission this continued for several hours. The Howitzer Battery, in spite of the darkness, evidently considered the situation demanded its efforts, and fired salvoes of lyddite shells, which, bursting in the direction of the Boer positions, lit up the whole scene with flaring explosions.

I went anxiously to bed that night, wondering what was passing beyond the river, and the last thing I can remember was the musketry drumming away with unabated vigour.

There was still a steady splutter at dawn on the 23rd, and before the light was full grown the guns joined in the din.

We eagerly sought for news of what had passed. Apparently, the result was not unfavourable to the army. 'Push for Ladysmith to-day, horse, foot, and artillery' was the order, 'Both cavalry brigades to cross the river at once.'

Chapter XXIII: The Passage of the Tugela

Details were scarce and doubtful. Indeed, I cannot yet give any accurate description of the fighting on the night of the 22nd, for it was of a confused and desperate nature, and many men must tell their tale before any general account can be written.

What happened, briefly described, was that the Boers attacked heavily at nightfall with rifle fire all along the line, and, in their eagerness to dislodge the troops, came to close quarters on several occasions at various points.

At least two bayonet charges are recorded. Sixteen men of Stuart Wortley's Composite Battalion of Reservists of the Rifle Brigade and King's Royal Rifles showed blood on their bayonets in the morning. About three hundred officers and men were killed or wounded. The Boers also suffered heavily, leaving dead on the ground, among others, a grandson of President Kruger.

Prisoners were made and lost, taken and rescued by both sides; but the daylight showed that victory rested with the British, for the infantry were revealed still tenaciously holding all their positions.

At eight o'clock the cavalry crossed the river under shell fire directed on the bridge, and were massed at Fort Wylie, near Colenso.

I rode along the railway line to watch the action from one of the low kopjes. A capricious shell fire annoyed the whole army as it sheltered behind the rocky hills, and an unceasing stream of stretchers from the front bore true witness to the serious nature of the conflict, for this was the third and bloodiest day of the seven days' fighting called the battle of Pieters.

I found Sir Redvers Buller and his Staff in a somewhat exposed position, whence an excellent view could be obtained.

The General displayed his customary composure, asked me how my brother's wound was getting on, and told me that he had just ordered Hart's Brigade, supported by two battalions from Lyttelton's Division, to assault the hill marked '3' on my diagram, and hereinafter called Inniskilling Hill.

'I have told Hart to follow the railway. I think he can get round to their left flank under cover of the river bank,' he said, 'but we must be prepared for a counter-attack on our left as soon as they see what I'm up to;' and he then made certain dispositions of his cavalry, which brought the South African Light Horse close up to the wooded kopje on which we stood.

I must now describe the main Pieters position, one hill of which was about to be attacked.

It ran, as the diagram shows, from the high and, so far as we were concerned, inaccessible hills on the west to the angle of the river, and then along the three hills marked 3, 2, and 1.

I use this inverted sequence of numbers because we were now attacking them in the wrong order.

Sir Redvers Buller's plan was as follows: On the 22nd he had taken the low kopjes, and his powerful artillery gave him complete command of the river gorge. Behind the kopjes, which acted as a kind of shield, and along the river gorge he proposed to advance his infantry until the angle of the river was passed and there was room to stretch out his, till then, cramped right arm and reach round the enemy's left on Inniskilling Hill, and so crumple it.

This perilous and difficult task was entrusted to the Irish Brigade, which comprised the Dublin Fusiliers, the Inniskilling Fusiliers, the Connaught Rangers, and the Imperial Light Infantry, who had temporarily replaced the Border Regiment—in all about three thousand men, supported by two thousand more.

Their commander, General Hart, was one of the bravest officers in the army, and it was generally felt that such a leader and such troops could carry the business through if success lay within the scope of human efforts.

The account of the ensuing operation is so tragic and full of mournful interest that I must leave it to another letter.

CHAPTER XXIV
THE BATTLE OF PIETERS: THE THIRD DAY

Hospital ship 'Maine': March 5, 1900.

At half-past twelve on the 23rd, General Hart ordered his brigade to advance. The battalions, which were sheltering among stone walls and other hastily constructed cover on the reverse slope of the kopje immediately in front of that on which we stood, rose up one by one and formed in rank.

They then moved off in single file along the railroad, the Inniskilling Fusiliers leading, the Connaught Rangers, Dublin Fusiliers, and the Imperial Light Infantry following in succession. At the same time the Durham Light Infantry and the 2nd Rifle Brigade began to march to take the place of the assaulting brigade on the advanced kopje.

Wishing to have a nearer view of the attack, I descended the wooded hill, cantered along the railway—down which the procession of laden stretchers, now hardly interrupted for three days, was still moving—and, dismounting, climbed the rocky sides of the advanced kopje.

On the top, in a little half-circle of stones, I found General Lyttelton, who received me kindly, and together we watched the development of the operation.

Nearly a mile of the railway line was visible, and along it the stream of Infantry flowed steadily. The telescope showed the soldiers walking quite slowly, with their rifles at the slope. Thus far, at least, they were not under fire.

The low kopjes which were held by the other brigades shielded the movement. A mile away, the river and railway turned sharply to the right; the river plunged into a steep gorge, and the railway was lost in a cutting.

There was certainly plenty of cover; but just before the cutting was reached the iron bridge across the Onderbrook Spruit had to be crossed, and this was evidently commanded by the enemy's riflemen.

Beyond the railway and the moving trickle of men the brown dark face of Inniskilling Hill, crowned with sangars and entrenchments, rose up gloomy and, as yet, silent.

The patter of musketry along the left of the army, which reached back from the advanced kopjes to Colenso village, the boom of the heavy guns across the river, and the ceaseless thudding of the Field Artillery making a leisurely preparation, were an almost unnoticed accompaniment to the scene.

Before us, the Infantry were moving steadily nearer to the hill and the open ground by the railway bridge, and we listened amid the comparatively peaceful din for the impending fire storm.

The head of the column reached the exposed ground, and the soldiers began to walk across it.

Then at once above the average fusillade and cannonade rose the extraordinary rattling roll of Mauser musketry in great volume.

If the reader wishes to know exactly what this is like he must drum the fingers of both his hands on a wooden table, one after the other as quickly and as hard as he can.

I turned my telescope on the Dutch defences. They were no longer deserted. All along the rim of the trenches, clear cut and jet black, against the sky stood a crowded line of slouch-hatted men, visible as far as their shoulders, and wielding what looked like thin sticks.

Far below by the red ironwork of the railway bridge—2,000 yards, at least, from the trenches—the surface of the ground was blurred and dusty.

Across the bridge the Infantry were still moving, but no longer slowly—they were running for their lives. Man after man emerged from the sheltered railroad, which ran like a covered

Chapter XXIV: The Battle of Pieters

way across the enemy's front, into the open and the driving hail of bullets, ran the gauntlet and dropped down the embankment on the further side of the bridge into safety again.

The range was great, but a good many soldiers were hit and lay scattered about the ironwork of the bridge.

'Pom-pom-pom,' 'pom-pom-pom,' and so on, twenty times went the Boer automatic gun, and the flights of little shells spotted the bridge with puffs of white smoke. But the advancing Infantry never hesitated for a moment, and continued to scamper across the dangerous ground, paying their toll accordingly. More than sixty men were shot in this short space.

Yet this was not the attack. This was only the preliminary movement across the enemy's front.

The enemy's shells, which occasionally burst on the advanced kopje, and a whistle of stray bullets from the left, advised us to change our position, and we moved a little further down the slope towards the river.

Here the bridge was no longer visible. I looked towards the hill-top, whence the roar of musketry was ceaselessly proceeding.

The Artillery had seen the slouch hats, too, and forgetting their usual apathy in the joy of a live target, concentrated a most hellish and terrible fire on the trenches.

Meanwhile the afternoon had been passing. The Infantry had filed steadily across the front, and the two leading battalions had already accumulated on the eastern spurs of Inniskilling Hill.

At four o'clock General Hart ordered the attack, and the troops forthwith began to climb the slopes. The broken ground delayed their progress, and it was nearly sunset by the time they had reached the furthest position which could be gained under cover.

The Boer entrenchments were about four hundred yards away.

The *arête* by which the Inniskillings had advanced was bare, and swept by a dreadful frontal fire from the works on the summit and a still more terrible flanking fire from the other hills. It was so narrow that, though only four companies were arranged in the firing line, there was scarcely room for two to deploy. There was not, however, the slightest hesitation, and as we watched with straining eyes we could see the leading companies rise up together and run swiftly forward on the enemy's works with inspiring dash and enthusiasm.

But if the attack was superb, the defence was magnificent; nor could the devoted heroism of the Irish soldiers surpass the stout endurance of the Dutch.

The Artillery redoubled their efforts. The whole summit of the hill was alive with shell. Shrapnel flashed into being above the crests, and the ground sprang up into dust whipped by the showers of bullets and splinters.

Again and again, whole sections of the entrenchments vanished in an awful uprush of black earth and smoke, smothering the fierce blaze of the lyddite shells from the howitzers and heavy artillery.

The cannonade grew to tremendous thundering hum. Not less than sixty guns were firing continuously on the Boer trenches. But the musketry was never subdued for an instant. Amid the smoke and the dust the slouch hats could still be seen.

The Dutch, firm and undaunted, stood to their parapets and plied their rifles with deadly effect. The terrible power of the Mauser rifle was displayed. As the charging companies met the storm of bullets they were swept away. Officers and men fell by scores on the narrow ridge.

Though assailed in front and flank by the hideous whispering Death, the survivors hurried obstinately onward, until their own artillery were forced to cease firing, and it seemed that, in spite of bullets, flesh and blood would prevail.

But at the last supreme moment the weakness of the attack was shown. The Inniskillings had almost reached their goal. They were too few to effect their purpose; and when the Boers saw that the attack had withered, they shot all the straighter, and several of the boldest leapt out from their trenches and, running forward to meet the soldiers, discharged their magazines at the closest

Chapter XXIV: The Battle of Pieters

range. It was a frantic scene of blood and fury. Thus confronted, the Irish perished rather than retire. A few men indeed ran back down the slope to the nearest cover, and there savagely turned to bay, but the greater part of the front line was shot down.

Other companies, some from the Connaught Rangers, some headed by the brave Colonel Sitwell, from the Dublin Fusiliers, advanced to renew—it was already too late to support—the attack, and as the light faded another fierce and bloody assault was delivered and was repulsed.

Yet the Irish soldiers would not leave the hill, and, persuaded at length that they could not advance further, they lay down on the ground they had won, and began to build walls and shelters, from behind which they opened a revengeful fire on the exulting Boers.

In the two attacks, both colonels, three majors, twenty officers, and six hundred men had fallen out of an engaged force of scarcely one thousand two hundred. Then darkness pulled down the curtain, and the tragedy came to an end for the day.

All through the night of the 23rd, a heavy rifle fire was maintained by both sides. Stray bullets whistled about the bivouacs, and the South African Light Horse, who had selected a most sheltered spot to sleep in, had a trooper hit. There were a certain number of casualties along the whole front.

As soon as it was daylight I rode out with Captain Brooke to learn what had happened in the night. We knew that the hill had not been carried before dusk, but hoped, since the combatants were so close together, that in the darkness the bayonet would have settled the matter.

We had just reached the hollow behind the advanced kopje from which I had watched the attack on the previous evening, when suddenly a shrapnel shell burst in the air above our heads with a sharp, startling bang.

The hollow and slope of the hill were crowded with Infantry battalions lying down in quarter column. The bullets and splinters of the shell smote the ground on all sides. We were both mounted and in the centre of the cone of dispersion. I was immediately conscious that nothing had happened to me, though the dust around my horse was flicked up, and I concluded that everyone had enjoyed equally good fortune.

Indeed, I turned to Brooke, and was about to elaborate my theory that shrapnel is comparatively harmless, when I saw some stir and turmoil and no less than eight men were picked up killed or wounded by this explosion.

I have only once before seen in war such a successful shell, and on that occasion, I was studying the effect from the other side.

My respect for modern artillery was mightily increased by this example of its power. Two more shells followed in quick succession. The first struck down four men, and broke in two the leg of an Infantry officer's charger, so that the poor beast galloped about in a circle, preventing his rider from dismounting for some time; the second shore along the Howitzer Battery, killing one soldier and wounding an officer, five soldiers, and three horses.

All this occurred in a space of about two minutes, and the three shells between them accounted for nineteen men and four horses. Then the gun, which was firing 'on spec', and could not see the effect of its fire, turned its attention elsewhere; but the thought forced itself on me, 'Fancy if there had been a battery.'

The crowded Infantry waiting in support would certainly have been driven out of the re-entrant with frightful slaughter.

Yet in a European war there would have been not one, but three or four batteries. I do not see how troops can be handled in masses under such conditions, even when in support and on reverse slopes. Future warfare must depend on the individual.

We climbed on to the top of the kopje, which was sprinkled with staff officers and others—all much interested in the exhibition of shell fire, which they discussed as a purely scientific question.

Inniskilling Hill was still crowned with the enemy, though they no longer showed above their trenches. Its slopes were scored

Chapter XXIV: The Battle of Pieters

with numerous brown lines, the stone walls built by the attacking brigade during the night, and behind these the telescope showed the Infantry clustering thickly.

The Boers on their part had made some new trenches in advance of those on the crest of the hill, so that the opposing firing lines were scarcely three hundred yards apart, which meant that everyone in them must lie still or run grave risks.

Thus they remained all day, firing at each other continually, while on the bare ground between them the dead and wounded lay thickly scattered, the dead mixed with the living, the wounded untended, without dressings, food, or water, and harassed by the fire from both sides and from our artillery.

It was a very painful thing to watch these poor fellows moving about feebly and trying to wriggle themselves into some position of safety, and it reminded me of the wounded Dervishes after Omdurman—only these were our own countrymen.

It seems that a misunderstanding, of the rights and wrongs of which the reader shall be himself a judge, arose with the enemy.

When day broke, the Boers, who were much nearer to the wounded than were our troops, came out of their trenches with a Red Cross flag, and the firing thereupon ceased locally.

Our people ought then to have been ready to come forward with another Red Cross flag, and an informal truce might easily have been arranged for an hour or two. Unfortunately, however, there was some delay on our part.

The Boers therefore picked up their own wounded, of whom there were a few, gave some of our men a little water, and took away their rifles. All this was quite correct; but the Boers then proceeded to strip and despoil the dead and wounded, taking off their boots and turning out their pockets, and this so infuriated the watching soldiers behind the wall that they forthwith fired on the Boers, Red Cross flag notwithstanding.

This, of course, was the signal for fighting to recommence fiercely, and during the day neither side would hear of parley.

The Boers behaved cruelly in various instances, and several wounded men who tried to crawl away were deliberately destroyed by being shot at close quarters with many bullets.

During the 24th, there was heavy firing on both sides, but no movement of infantry on either. The army suffered some loss from the Boer artillery, particularly the automatic guns, which were well served, and which enfiladed many of our positions on the slopes of the low kopjes. In this way Colonel Thorold, of the Royal Welsh Fusiliers, and other officers, met their deaths.

The casualties were principally in Hildyard's English and Kitchener's Lancashire Brigades. Hart's six battalions found good cover in the gorge of the Tugela.

Sir Redvers Buller now saw that his plan of filing his army round the angle of the river and across the enemy's front would, in any case, be very costly, and was perhaps impossible. He, therefore, determined to get back to the Hlangwani plateau, and try the extreme left of the enemy's position.

He had the strategic advantage of being on interior lines, and was consequently able to move his troops with great ease from one flank to the other.

His new plan was to pass the brigades of his left and centre across the pontoon bridge from the left to the right, so that Hart, who was formerly the extreme right, would now become almost the extreme left, and, having thus extended his right arm, to cross the river where it flowed east and west, and make a still wider swoop on the enemy's flank.

The first thing to do was to move the heavy guns, and this, with certain redistributions of the cavalry, occupied the whole day. A long-range four-gun naval battery was established on the western slopes of the Monte Cristo ridge. Another similar battery was placed on the spurs of Hlangwani. The 4.7-inch naval guns and the 5 in. fortress battery were brought into line in the centre of the Hlangwani plateau.

All this was good. The big guns were getting back on to the big hills. The firing, which continued all day, swelled into a roar to-

Chapter XXIV: The Battle of Pieters

wards night as the Boers made vigorous attempts to drive Hart's Brigade from its lodgments.

They were, however, foiled in their endeavour to squeeze in between the troops and the river. The battalions, who were attacked frontally, lay down with fixed bayonets and prayed that the Boers might be encouraged by their silence to make an assault.

The latter, however, were fully aware of the eagerness of the soldiers for personal collision, and kept their distance. The firing on both sides was unaimed, and very little harm was done. No one, however, had much sleep.

The condition of the wounded, still lying sore and thirsty on the bare hillside, was now so shocking that Sir Redvers Buller was forced, much against his inclination, at dawn on the 25th, to send in a flag of truce to the Boer commander and ask for an armistice.

This the Boers formally refused, but agreed that if we would not fire on their positions during the day, they would not prevent our bearer companies from removing the wounded and burying the dead.

The arrangement worked well; the enemy were polite to our medical officers, and by noon all the wounded had been brought down and the dead buried. The neglect and exposure for forty-eight hours had much aggravated the case of the former, and the bodies of the dead, swollen, blackened, and torn by the terrible wounds of the expansive bullets,[1] now so generally used by the enemy, were ugly things to see. The fact that no regular armistice was agreed on was an advantage, as we were not thereby debarred from making military movements.

The Boers improved their entrenchments, and Sir Redvers Buller employed the day in withdrawing his train across the river.

---

1 Expansive, or "expanding" bullets, also called "dum-dums," are hollow or soft point bullets which are designed to expand upon impact, causing a larger wound—and helping to prevent deeper penetration (useful in preventing collateral damage). Expansive bullets were outlawed in international warfare by the Hague Convention of 1889, and their continued use by the Boers was a source of much controversy.

This movement, seeming to foreshadow another retreat, sorely disquieted the troops, who were only reassured by the promise of a general onslaught from the other flank at no distant time.

The strange quiet of this Sunday, the first day since the 14th of the month unbroken by musketry and cannonade, was terminated at nine o'clock at night.

The Boers had seen the waggons passing back over the bridge, and were anxious to find out whether or not the infantry were following, and if the low kopjes were evacuated. They therefore opened a tremendous magazine fire at long range on the brigades holding the line from Colenso village to the angle of the river.

The fusillade was returned, and for ten minutes the musketry was louder than at any other time in this campaign. Very few casualties occurred, however, and after a while the Boers, having learned that the positions were still occupied, ceased firing, and the British soon imitated them, so that, except for the ceaseless 'sniping,' silence was restored.

At dawn on the 26th, the artillery re-opened on both sides, and during the day a constant bombardment was maintained, in which we, having more guns, fired the greater number of shells, and the Dutch, having larger targets, hit a greater number of men. The losses were not, however, severe, except in view of the fact that they had to be endured by the infantry idly and passively.

Considerable movements of troops were made. Colenso and the kopjes about Fort Wylie were converted into a bridgehead, garrisoned by Talbot Coke's Brigade. A new line of communications was opened around the foot of Hlangwani. A pontoon bridge (B) was arranged ready to be thrown below the falls of the river, not far from the still intact Boer bridge. Hildyard's English Brigade stood fast on the advanced low kopjes forming the extreme left of the line. Hart's command held its position about the slopes of Inniskilling Hill and in the gorge of the river. Barton's Fusilier Brigade, Kitchener's Lancashire Brigade, and the two remaining battalions of Norcott's (formerly Lyttelton's) Brigade crossed the old bridge to the Hlangwani plateau.

Chapter XXIV: The Battle of Pieters

All was now ready for the final attack on the left of the Pieters position, and in spite of the high quality of the Infantry it was generally recognised throughout the army that the fate of Ladysmith must depend on the success of the next day's operations.

The spirit of the army was still undaunted, but they had suffered much from losses, exposure, and disappointment. Since January 11, a period of more than six weeks, the troops had been continuously fighting and bivouacking.

The peaceful intervals of a few days had merely been in order to replenish stores and ammunition. During this time the only reinforcements to reach the army had been a few drafts, a cavalry regiment, a horse battery, and some heavy guns.

Exclusive of the 1,100 casualties suffered at Colenso in December, the force, rarely more than 20,000 men, had had over 3,500 killed and wounded, had never had a single gleam of success, and had hardly seen the enemy who hit them so hard.

Colenso, Spion Kop, Vaal Krantz, and the third day at Pieters were not inspiring memories, and though everyone was cheered by the good news of the entanglement of Cronje's army[2] on the western side, yet it was felt that the attempt to be made on the morrow would be the last effort the Natal Field Army would be asked or allowed to make.

And oppressed by these reflections we went anxiously to rest on the eve of Majuba Day.

---

2 The prelude to the Boer surrender at Paardeberg, the first great defeat suffered by the Boers in the war.

CHAPTER XXV
UPON MAJUBA DAY

Commandant's Office. Durban: March 6, 1900.

Day broke behind a cloudy sky, and the bang of an early gun reminded us that a great business was on hand. The bivouac of the Irregular Cavalry, which, since they had recrossed the river, had been set at the neck between Monte Cristo and Cingolo, was soon astir.

We arose—all had slept in their boots and had no need to dress—drank some coffee and rejoiced that the day promised to be cool. It would help the infantry, and on the infantry all depended.

At half-past six, Dundonald's Brigade marched towards the northern end of the Hlangwani plateau, where we were to take up positions on the spurs of Monte Cristo and along the bluffs of the south bank of the Tugela, from which we might assist the infantry attack, and particularly the attack of Barton's Brigade, by long-range rifle fire, and by our Colt battery and Maxim guns.

While we marched, the artillery fire grew more rapid, as battery after battery joined in the bombardment; and when we reached the high wooded ridge which we were ordered to line, I could see our shells bursting merrily in the enemy's trenches.

The position which had been assigned to the South African Light Horse afforded a close yet extensive view of the whole scene. Deep in its gorge below our feet flowed the Tugela, with the new pontoon bridge visible to the left, just below a fine waterfall.

Behind us, on a rounded spur of Monte Cristo, one of the long-range batteries was firing away busily. Before us, across the river, there rose from the water's edge first a yellow strip of sandy foreshore, then steep, scrub-covered banks, and then smooth, brown slopes, terminating in the three hills which were to be successively assaulted, and which were surmounted by the dark lines

Chapter XXV: Upon Majuba Day

of the Boer forts and trenches. It was like a stage scene viewed from the dress circle. Moreover, we were very comfortable. There were large convenient rocks to sit behind in case of bullets, or to rest a telescope on, and the small trees which sparsely covered the ridge gave a partial shade from the sun.

Opposite our front, a considerable valley, thickly wooded, ran back from the river, and it was our easy and pleasant task to 'fan' this, as an American officer would say, by scattering a ceaseless shower of rifle and machine-gun bullets throughout its length.

Under these satisfactory circumstances I watched the battle.

It developed very slowly, and with the deliberation which characterises all our manoeuvres. The guns gradually worked themselves into a state of excitement, and what with our musketry, supplemented by that of the Border Regiment and the Composite Battalion, whose duties were the same as ours, and the machine-guns puffing like steam engines, we soon had a capital loud noise, which I think is a most invigorating element in an attack.

Besides this, the enemy's sharpshooters were curiously subdued. They found an unexpected amount of random bullets flying about, and, as they confessed afterwards, it puzzled and disturbed them.

The spectacle of two thousand men firing for half a day at nothing may provoke the comment 'shocking waste of ammunition.'

Very likely there was waste. But all war is waste, and cartridges are the cheapest item in the bill. At any rate, we made it too hot for the 'snipers' to show their heads, which was certainly worth fifty men to the assaulting brigades.

This method of preparing an attack by a great volume of unaimed—not undirected—rifle fire is worthy of the closest attention. I have only once before noticed its employment, and that was when Sir Bindon Blood attacked and took the Tanga Pass.[1]

---

[1] General Sir Bindon Blood (1842–1940) won fame in India when he led the unit which took the Tanga Pass in the north west while on a punitive raid against the Bonerwall tribe.

Then, as now, it was most effective. While we were thus occupied, the Infantry of Barton's Brigade were marching across the pontoon bridge, turning to their right and filing along the sandy foreshore.

The plan of attack to which Sir Redvers Buller had finally committed himself was as follows: Hildyard's Brigade to hold its position on the low kopjes; Barton's Brigade to cross the new pontoon bridge opposite to the left of the enemy's position, and assault the hill marked '3' on my diagram, and hereinafter called Barton's Hill.

Next Kitchener's Brigade was to cross, covered by Barton's fire, to assault the centre hill marked '2,' and called Railway Hill.

Lastly, Norcott's two untouched battalions were to join the rest of their brigade, and, supported by General Hart's Brigade, to attack Inniskilling Hill.

In brief, we were to stretch out our right arm, reach round the enemy's flank, and pivoting on Hildyard's Brigade crumple him from (his) left to right. It was the same plan as before, only that we now had our right hand on the Monte Cristo ridge, from which commanding position our long-range guns could enfilade and even take in reverse some of the enemy's trenches.

The leading brigade was across the river by nine o'clock, and by ten had reached its position ready for attacking at the foot of Barton's Hill. The advance began forthwith and the figures of the Infantry could be seen swarming up the steep slopes of the river gorge.

The Boers did very little to stop the attack. They knew their weakness. One side of Barton's Hill was swept and commanded by the guns on Monte Cristo. The other side, at the back of which was the donga we were 'fanning,' was raked by the heavy artillery on the Hlangwani spur and by the field batteries arranged along the south side of the river.

Observe the influence of the Monte Cristo ridge! It made Barton's Hill untenable by the Boers; and Barton's Hill prepared the way for an attack on Railway Hill, and Railway Hill—but I must

Chapter XXV: Upon Majuba Day

not anticipate. Indeed, next to Monte Cristo, Barton's Hill was the key of the Boer position, and so unfortunate was the enemy's situation that he could not hold this all-important feature once he had lost the Monte Cristo ridge.

What was tactically possible and safe—for the Boer is a cautious warrior—was done. Knowing that his left would be turned he extended a sort of false left in the air beyond the end of the Monte Cristo ridge, and here he brought a gun into action, which worried us among other people but did not, of course, prevent any military movement.

By noon the whole of Barton's Hill was in the possession of his brigade, without, as it seemed to us, any serious opposition. The artillery then turned its attention to the other objectives of the attack.

The Boer detached left was, however, of considerable strength, and as soon as Barton had occupied this hill (which proved, moreover, far more extensive than had been expected), he was heavily attacked by rifle fire from its under features and from a network of dongas to the eastward, and as the Artillery were busy preparing the attack on Railway Hill, the brigade, particularly the Scots and Irish Fusiliers, soon became severely engaged and suffered grievous loss.

The fact that Barton's Hill was in our possession made the Boers on Railway and Inniskilling Hills very insecure. A powerful Infantry force was holding the left of their position, and though it was itself being actively attacked on the eastern face, it could spare at least a battalion to assail their flank and threaten their rear.

Covered by this flanking fire, by the long-range musketry, and by a tremendous bombardment, in which every gun, from the lumbering 5 in. siege guns to the little 9-pounder mountain battery, joined, the main attack was now launched. It proceeded simultaneously against Railway Hill, Inniskilling Hill, and the neck between them, but as the general line was placed obliquely across the Boer front, the attack fell first on Railway Hill and the neck.

The right battalions drew up in many long lines on the sides of the river gorge.

Then men began gradually to work their way upwards, until all the dead patches of ground and every scrap of cover sheltered a fierce little group. Behind the railway embankment, among the rocks, in the scrub, in a cutting, near a ruined house, clusters of men eagerly awaited the decisive moment: and all this time more than seventy guns concentrated their fire on the entrenchments, scattering the stones and earth high in the air.

Then, suddenly, shortly after four o'clock, all further attempts at advancing under cover were abandoned, and the Lancashire Brigade marched proudly into the open ground and on the enemy's works.

The Mauser musketry burst forth at once, and the bullets, humming through the assaulting waves of infantry, reached us on our hillside and wounded a trooper in spite of the distance.

But, bullets or no bullets, we could not take our eyes off the scene.

The Lancashire Brigade advanced on a wide front. Norcott's Riflemen were already prolonging their line to the right. The Boer fire was dispersed along the whole front of attack, instead of converging on one narrow column.

The assault was going to succeed. We stood up on our rocks. Bayonets began to glitter on the distant slope. The moving lines increased their pace. The heads of the Boers bobbing up and down in their trenches grew fewer and fewer. They knew the tide was running too strongly. Death and flight were thinning their ranks.

Then the sky-line of Railway Hill bristled with men, who dropped on their knees forthwith and fired in particular haste at something that was running away down the other side.

There was the sound of cheering. Railway Hill was ours. I looked to the left. The neck between the hills was lined with trenches.

Chapter XXV: Upon Majuba Day

The South Lancashire Regiment had halted, pinned to the ground by the Boer fire. Were they going to lose the day for us when it was already won? The question was soon answered.

In an instant there appeared on the left of the Boer trench a dozen—only a dozen—violent forms rushing forward.

A small party had worked their way to the flank, and were at close quarters with cold steel. And then—by contrast to their former courage—the valiant burghers fled in all directions, and others held out their rifles and bandoliers and begged for mercy, which was sometimes generously given, so that by the time the whole attack had charged forward into the trenches there was a nice string of thirty-two prisoners winding down the hill: at which token of certain victory we shouted loudly.

Inniskilling Hill alone remained, and that was almost in our hands. Its slopes were on three sides alive with the active figures of the Light Brigade, and the bayonets sparkled.

The hill ran into a peak. Many of the trenches were already deserted, but the stone breastwork at the summit still contained defenders. There, painted against the evening sky, were the slouch hats and moving rifles.

Shell after shell exploded among them: overhead, in their faces, in the trench itself, behind them, before them, around them. Sometimes five and six shells were bursting on the very apex at the same instant. Showers of rock and splinters fell on all sides. Yet they held their ground and stayed in greater peril than was ever mortal man before.

But the infantry were drawing very near. At last the Dutchmen fled. One, a huge fellow in a brown jersey, tarried to spring on the parapet and empty his magazine once more into the approaching ranks, and while he did so a 50 lb. lyddite shell burst, as it seemed, in the midst of him, and the last defender of Inniskilling Hill vanished.

Then the artillery put up their sights and began to throw their shells over the crest of hill and ridge, so that they might overtake fugitives. The valleys behind fumed and stewed. Wreaths of dust and smoke curled upward. The infantry crowned the trenches all along the line, some firing their rifles at the flying enemy, others beckoning to nearer folk to surrender, and they all cheered in the triumph of successful attack till the glorious sound came down to us who watched, so that the whole army took up the shout, and all men knew that the battle of Pieters was won.

Forthwith came orders for the cavalry to cross the river, and we mounted in high expectation, knowing that behind the captured hill lay an open plain stretching almost to the foot of Bulwana. We galloped swiftly down to the pontoon bridge, and were about to pass over it, when the General-in-Chief met us. He had ridden to the other bank to see for himself and us.

The Boer artillery were firing heavily to cover the retreat of their riflemen. He would not allow us to go across that night lest we should lose heavily in horses. So the brigade returned disappointed to its former position, watered horses, and selected a bivouac.

I was sent to warn the Naval Battery that a heavy counter-stroke would probably be made on the right of Barton's Brigade during the night, and, climbing the spur of Monte Cristo, on which the guns were placed, had a commanding view of the field.

In the gathering darkness, the Boer artillery, invisible all day, was betrayed by its flashes. Two 'pom-poms' flickered away steadily from the direction of Doorn Kloof, making a regular succession of small bright flame points.

Two more guns were firing from the hills to our left. Another was in action far away on our right. There may have been more, but even so it was not much artillery to oppose our eleven batteries.

But it is almost an open question whether it is better to have many guns to shoot at very little, or few guns to shoot at a great deal; hundreds of shells tearing up the ground or a dozen plunging into masses of men.

Personally, I am convinced that future warfare will be to the few, by which I mean that to escape annihilation soldiers will

Chapter XXV: Upon Majuba Day

have to fight in widely dispersed formations, when they will have to think for themselves, and when each must be to a great extent his own general; and with regard to artillery, it appears that the advantages of defensive action, range, concealment, and individual initiative may easily counterbalance numbers and discipline.

The night fell upon these reflections, and I hastened to rejoin the cavalry. On the way I passed through Sir Charles Warren's camp, and there found a gang of prisoners—forty-eight of them—all in a row almost the same number that the Boers had taken in the armoured train.

Looking at these very ordinary people, who grinned and chattered without dignity, and who might, from their appearance, have been a knot of loafers round a public-house, it was difficult to understand what qualities made them such a terrible foe.

'Only forty-eight, sir,' said a private soldier, who was guarding them, 'and there wouldn't have been so many as that if the orfcers hadn't stopped us from giving them the bayonet. I never saw such cowards in my life; shoot at you till you come up to them, and then beg for mercy. I'd teach 'em.'

With which remark he turned to the prisoners, who had just been issued rations of beef and biscuit, but who were also very thirsty, and began giving them water to drink from his own canteen, and so left me wondering at the opposite and contradictory sides of human nature as shown by Briton as well as Boer.

We got neither food nor blankets that night, and slept in our waterproofs on the ground; but we had at last that which was better than feast or couch, for which we had hungered and longed through many weary weeks, which had been thrice forbidden us, and which was all the more splendid since it had been so long delayed—Victory.

CHAPTER XXVI
THE RELIEF OF LADYSMITH

Commandant's Office, Durban: March 9, 1900.

The successful action of the 27th had given Sir Redvers Buller possession of the whole of the left and centre of the Pieters position, and in consequence of these large sections of their entrenchments having fallen into British hands, the Boers evacuated the remainder and retreated westward on to the high hills and northward towards Bulwana Mountain.

About ninety prisoners were captured in the assault, and more than a hundred bodies were counted in the trenches.

After making allowances for the fact that these men were for the most part killed by shell fire, and that therefore the proportion of killed to wounded would necessarily be higher than if the loss were caused by bullets, it seems probable that no less than three hundred wounded were removed. Forty were collected by British ambulance parties.

Of the Boers who were killed in the retreat no accurate estimate can be formed, but the dongas and kopjes beyond the position were strewn with occasional corpses. Undoubtedly the enemy was hard hit in personnel, and the fact that we had taken two miles of entrenchments as well as considerable stores of ammunition proved that a very definite and substantial success had been won. But we were not prepared for the complete results that followed the operations of the 27th.

Neither the General nor his army expected to enter Ladysmith without another action. Before us a smooth plain, apparently unobstructed, ran to the foot of Bulwana, but from this forbidding eminence a line of ridges and kopjes was drawn to the high hills of Doorn Kloof, and seemed to interpose another serious barrier.

It was true that this last position was within range, or almost within range, of Sir George White's guns, so that its defenders

Chapter XXVI: The Relief of Ladysmith

might be caught between two fires, but we knew, and thought the Boers knew, that the Ladysmith garrison was too feeble from want of food and other privations to count for very much.

So Sir Redvers Buller, facing the least satisfactory assumption, determined to rest his army on the 28th, and attack Bulwana Hill on March 1. He accordingly sent a message by heliograph into Ladysmith to say that he had beaten the enemy thoroughly, and was sending on his cavalry to reconnoitre.

Ladysmith had informed herself, however, of the state of the game. Captain Tilney, from his balloon, observed all that passed in the enemy's lines on the morning of the 28th. At first, when he heard no artillery fire, he was depressed, and feared lest the relieving army had retreated again.

Then, as it became day, he was sure that this was not so, for the infantry in crowds were occupying the Boer position, and the mounted patrols pricked forward into the plain. Presently he saw the Boers rounding up their cattle and driving them off to the north. Next they caught and began to saddle their horses.

The great white tilted waggons of the various laagers filed along the road around the eastern end of Bulwana. Lastly, up went a pair of shears over 'Long Tom,' and at this he descended to the earth with the good news that the enemy were off at last.

The garrison, however, had been mocked by false hopes before, and all steeled themselves to wait 'at least another ten days.'

Meanwhile, since there was no fire from the enemy's side, our cavalry and artillery were rapidly and safely crossing the river. There was a considerable block at the bridge when the South African Light Horse arrived, and we had full leisure to examine the traffic. Guns, men, horses, and mules were hurrying across to the northern bank, and an opposing stream of wounded flowed steadily back to the south. I watched these with interest.

First came a young officer riding a pony and smoking a cigarette, but very pale and with his left arm covered with bloody bandages.

Brooke greeted him and asked, 'Bone?'

'Yes,' replied the subaltern laconically, 'shoulder smashed up.'

We expressed our sympathy.

'Oh, that's all right; good show, wasn't it? The men are awfully pleased;' and he rode slowly on up the hill—the type of an unyielding race—and stoical besides; for wounds, especially shattered bones, grow painful after twelve or fourteen hours.

A string of wounded passed by on stretchers, some lying quite still, others sitting up and looking about them; one, also an officer, a dark, black-moustached captain, whose eyes were covered with a bandage, kept his bearers busy with continual impatient questions.

'Yes, but what I want to know is this, did they get into them with the bayonet?' The volunteer stretcher-bearers could make no satisfactory reply, but said, 'Yes, they give 'em 'ell, sir.'

'Where, on the left of Railway Hill?' 'Oh, everywhere, sir.'

The group passed by, and the last thing I heard was, 'How much of the artillery has crossed? Are they sending the cavalry over? What the...'

Presently came stretchers with wounded Boers. Most of these poor creatures were fearfully shattered. One tall man with a great fierce beard and fine features had a fragment of rock or iron driven through his liver. He was, moreover, stained bright yellow with lyddite, but did not seem in much pain, for he looked very calm and stolid.

The less seriously injured among the soldiers hobbled back alone or assisted by their comrades.

I asked a smart-looking sergeant of the Dublin Fusiliers, who was limping along with a broken foot, whether the regiment had been again heavily engaged. Of course they had.

'Sure, we're always in the thick of it, sorr. Mr. —— was hit; no, not badly; only his wrist, but there's not many of the officers left; only two now who were at Talana.'

Chapter XXVI: The Relief of Ladysmith

At last the time came for the cavalry to cross the bridge, and as we filed on to the floating roadway we were amused to see a large fingerpost at the entrance, on which the engineers had neatly painted, 'To Ladysmith.'

The brigade passed over the neck between Railway and Inniskilling Hills, and we massed in a suitable place on the descending slopes beyond. We looked at the country before us, and saw that it was good. Here at last was ground cavalry could work on at some speed.

Ladysmith was still hidden by the remaining ridges, but we thought that somehow, and with a little luck, we might have a look at it before night.

Under Bulwana the waggons of the Boers and several hundred horsemen could be seen hurrying away. It was clearly our business to try to intercept them unless they had made good covering dispositions.

Patrols were sent out in all directions, and a squadron of Thorneycroft's Mounted Infantry proceeded to Pieters Station, where a complete train of about twenty trucks had been abandoned by the enemy.

While this reconnaissance was going on I climbed up Inniskilling Hill to examine the trenches. It was occupied by the East Surrey Regiment, and the soldiers were very eager to do the honours. They had several things to show: 'Come along here, sir; there's a bloke here without a head; took clean off, sir;' and were mightily disappointed that I would not let them remove the blanket which covered the grisly shape.

The trench was cut deep in the ground, and, unlike our trenches, there was scarcely any parapet. A few great stones had been laid in front, but evidently the Boer believed in getting well into the ground.

The bottom was knee deep in cartridge cases, and every few yards there was an enormous heap of Mauser ammunition, thousands of rounds, all fastened neatly, five at a time, in clips.

A large proportion were covered with bright green slime, which the soldiers declared was poison, but which on analysis may prove to be wax, used to preserve the bullet.

The Boers, however, were not so guiltless of other charges. A field officer of the East Surreys, recognising me, came up and showed me an expansive bullet of a particularly cruel pattern. The tip had been cut off, exposing the soft core, and four slits were scored down the side. Whole boxes of this ammunition had been found.

An officer who had been making calculations told me that the proportion of illegal bullets was nearly one in five. I should not myself have thought it was so large, but certainly the improper bullets were very numerous.

I have a specimen of this particular kind by me as I write, and I am informed by people who shoot big game that it is the most severe bullet of its kind yet invented. Five other sorts have been collected by the medical officers, who have also tried to classify the wounds they respectively produce.

I cannot be accused of having written unfairly about the enemy; indeed, I have only cared to write what I thought was the truth about everybody. I have tried to do justice to the patriotic virtues of the Boers, and it is now necessary to observe that the character of these people reveals, in stress, a dark and spiteful underside. A man—I use the word in its fullest sense—does not wish to lacerate his foe, however earnestly he may desire his life.

The popping of musketry made me hasten to rejoin my regiment. The squadron of mounted infantry had reached Pieters Railway Station, only to be heavily fired on from a low hill to the westward; and they now came scampering back with half a dozen riderless horses.

Happily, the riders mostly arrived on foot after a few minutes. But it was evidently necessary to push forward very carefully. Indeed, it is hard to imagine how pursuits will occur in future war. A hundred bold men with magazine rifles on a ridge can delay a whole army. The cavalry must reconnoitre and retire. Infantry

Chapter XXVI: The Relief of Ladysmith

and guns must push forward. Meanwhile the beaten troops are moving steadily to safety.

In a little while—to revert to the narrative—the horse artillery battery came up, and the offending hill was conscientiously shelled for an hour. Then the patrols crept forward again, but progress was necessarily slow. We were still six miles from Ladysmith at three o'clock.

At this hour, the Boer ambulances had been invited to come for such of their wounded as could be moved, for since the enemy returned our wounded from Spion Kop, we have followed the practice of sending back theirs on all occasions should they prefer it.

Anxious to find out the impression produced on the Boers by the late actions, I hastened to meet the ambulances, which, preceded by three horsemen carrying a large white flag, were now coming from the direction of Bulwana.

They were stopped at our cavalry picket line, and a report of their arrival was sent back to the nearest brigadier. Their leader was a fine old fellow of the genuine veldt Boer type. He spoke English fluently, and we were soon in conversation.

Cronje's surrender[1] had been officially announced to us on the previous day, and I inquired whether he had heard of it. He replied that he knew Cronje was in difficulties, but understood he had managed to escape with his army. As for the surrender, it might be true or it might be false. 'We are told so many lies that we believe nothing.'

But his next remark showed that he realised that the tide had begun to turn. 'I don't know what we poor Afrikanders have done that England won't let us be a nation.' I would have replied that I remembered having heard something about 'driving the English into the sea,' but I have been over this ground before

---

[1] Boer General Piet Cronje had been forced to surrender at Paardeberg Drift on the banks of the Modder River in the Orange Free State near Kimberley on February 27, 1900. The defeat was devastating, as his army contained around ten percent of the entire Boer armed forces.

in every sense, and knew the futility of any discussion. Indeed, when the debate is being conducted with shells, bullets, and bayonets, words are feeble weapons. So I said with an irony which was quite lost on him, 'It must be all those damned capitalists,' and this, of course, won his complete agreement, so that he confided that losing the position we had taken on the 27th was 'a sore and bitter blow.'

It happened that two squadrons of the 13th Hussars had ridden forward beyond us towards Bulwana, and at this moment the Boer artillery began to shell them rather heavily.

We watched the proceedings for a few minutes, and the Boer was much astonished to see soldiers riding leisurely forward in regular though open order without paying the slightest attention to the shrapnel.

Then several more squadrons were ordered to support the reconnaissance. A great company of horsemen jingled past the halted ambulances and cantered off in the direction of the firing.

My companion regarded these steadfastly, then he said: 'Why do they all look so pleased?'

'Because they think they are going to fight; but they will not be allowed to. It is only desired to draw your fire and reconnoitre.'

The whole plain was now occupied by cavalry, both brigades being on the move.

'Little did we think a week ago,' said the Boer, 'that we should see such a sight as this, here in this plain.'

'Didn't you think we should get through?'

'No, we didn't believe it possible.'

'And you find the soldiers brave?'

'They do not care for life.'

'And Ladysmith?'

'Ah,' his eye brightened, 'there's pluck, if you like. Wonderful!'

Then we agreed that it was a sad and terrible war, and whoever won, we would make the gold mines pay, so that 'the damned

Chapter XXVI: The Relief of Ladysmith

capitalists' should not think they had scored, and thus we parted. I afterwards learned that the Boer ambulances removed twenty-seven of their wounded. The condition of the others was too serious to allow of their being moved, and in spite of every attention, they all died while in our hands.

When I rejoined the South African Light Horse the Irregular Brigade had begun to advance again. Major Gough's Composite Regiment had scouted the distant ridge and found it unoccupied.

Now Dundonald moved his whole command thither, and with his staff climbed to the top. But to our disappointment Ladysmith was not to be seen. Two or three other ridges hung like curtains before us.

The afternoon had passed, and it was already after six o'clock. The Boer artillery was still firing, and it seemed rash to attempt to reconnoitre further when the ground was broken and the light fading.

The order was given to retire and the movement had actually begun when a messenger came back from Gough with the news that the last ridge between us and the town was unoccupied by the enemy, that he could see Ladysmith, and that there was, for the moment, a clear run in.

Dundonald immediately determined to go on himself into the town with the two squadrons who were scouting in front, and to send the rest of the brigade back to camp.

He invited me to accompany him, and without delay we started at a gallop. Never shall I forget that ride. The evening was deliciously cool. My horse was strong and fresh, for I had changed him at midday.

The ground was rough with many stones, but we cared little for that. Beyond the next ridge, or the rise beyond that, or around the corner of the hill, was Ladysmith—the goal of all our hopes and ambitions during weeks of almost ceaseless fighting.

Ladysmith—the centre of the world's attention, the scene of famous deeds, the cause of mighty efforts—Ladysmith was within our reach at last. We were going to be inside the town within an hour. The excitement of the moment was increased by the exhilaration of the gallop.

Onward wildly, recklessly, up and down hill, over the boulders, through the scrub, Hubert Gough with his two squadrons, Mackenzie's Natal Carabineers and the Imperial Light Horse, were clear of the ridges already.

We turned the shoulder of a hill, and there before us lay the tin houses and dark trees we had come so far to see and save.

The British guns on Cæsar's Camp were firing steadily in spite of the twilight. What was happening? Never mind, we were nearly through the dangerous ground.

Now we were all on the flat. Brigadier, staff, and troops let their horses go. We raced through the thorn bushes by Intombi Spruit.

Suddenly there was a challenge.

'Halt, who goes there?'

'The Ladysmith Relief Column,' and thereat from out of trenches and rifle pits artfully concealed in the scrub a score of tattered men came running, cheering feebly, and some were crying.

In the half light they looked ghastly pale and thin. A poor, white-faced officer waved his helmet to and fro, and laughed foolishly, and the tall, strong colonial horsemen, standing up in their stirrups, raised a loud resounding cheer, for then we knew we had reached the Ladysmith picket line.

Presently we arranged ourselves in military order, Natal Carabineers and Imperial Light Horse riding two and two abreast so that there might be no question about precedence, and with Gough, the youngest regimental commander in the army, and one of the best, at the head of the column, we forded the Klip River and rode into the town.

That night I dined with Sir George White, who had held the town for four months against all comers, and was placed next to

Chapter XXVI: The Relief of Ladysmith

Hamilton, who won the fight at Elandslaagte and beat the Boers off Waggon Hill, and next but one to Hunter, whom everyone said was the finest man in the world. Never before had I sat in such brave company nor stood so close to a great event.

As the war drives slowly to its close more substantial triumphs, larger battles, wherein the enemy suffers heavier loss, the capture of towns, and the surrender of armies may mark its progress.

But whatever victories the future may have in store, the defence and relief of Ladysmith, because they afford, perhaps, the most remarkable examples of national tenacity and perseverance which our later history contains, will not be soon forgotten by the British people, whether at home or in the Colonies.

Boer artillery outside Ladysmith.

General Buller enters Ladysmith.

CHAPTER XXVII
AFTER THE SIEGE

Durban: March 10, 1900.

Since the road by which Dundonald's squadrons had entered the town was never again closed by the enemy, the siege of Ladysmith may be said to have ended on the last day of February.

During the night the heavy guns fired at intervals, using up the carefully husbanded ammunition in order to prevent the Boers from removing their artillery.

On March 1, the garrison reverted to a full half-ration of biscuits and horseflesh, and an attempt was made to harass the Boers, who were in full retreat towards the Biggarsberg.

Sir George White had made careful inquiries among the regiments for men who would undertake to walk five miles and fight at the end of the march. But so reduced were the soldiers through want of food that, though many volunteered, only two thousand men were considered fit out of the whole garrison.

These were, however, formed into a column, under Colonel Knox, consisting of two batteries of artillery, two squadrons of the 19th Hussars and 5th Lancers, 'all that was left of them,' with horses, and detachments, each about two hundred and fifty strong, from the Manchester, Liverpool, and Devon Regiments, the 60th Rifles, and the Gordon Highlanders, and this force moved out of Ladysmith at dawn on the 1st to attack the Boers on Pepworth's Hill, in the hope of interfering with their entrainment at Modderspruit Station.

The Dutch, however, had left a rear guard sufficient to hold in check so small a force, and it was 2 o'clock before Pepworth's Hill was occupied.

The batteries then shelled Modderspruit Station, and very nearly caught three crowded trains, which just managed to steam out of range in time. The whole force of men and horses was by

Chapter XXVII: After the Siege

this time quite exhausted. The men could scarcely carry their rifles.

In the squadron of 19th Hussars nine horses out of sixty fell down and died, and Colonel Knox therefore ordered the withdrawal into the town.

Only about a dozen men were killed or wounded in this affair, but the fact that the garrison was capable of making any offensive movement after their privations is a manifest proof of their soldierly spirit and excellent discipline.

On the same morning Sir Redvers Buller advanced on Bulwana Hill. Down from the commanding positions which they had won by their courage and endurance marched the incomparable infantry, and by 2 o'clock the plain of Pieters was thickly occupied by successive lines of men in extended order, with long columns of guns and transport trailing behind them.

Shortly before noon it was ascertained that Bulwana Hill was abandoned by the enemy, and the army was thereon ordered to camp in the plain, no further fighting being necessary.

The failure to pursue the retreating Boers when two fine cavalry brigades were standing idle and eager must be noticed.

It is probable that the Boer rearguard would have been sufficiently strong to require both infantry and guns to drive it back. It is certain that sharp fighting must have attended the effort. Nevertheless the opinion generally expressed was that it should have been made.

My personal impression is that Sir Redvers Buller was deeply moved by the heavy losses the troops had suffered, and was reluctant to demand further sacrifices from them at this time.

Indeed, the price of victory had been a high one.

In the fortnight's fighting, from February 14 to February 28, two generals, six colonels commanding regiments, a hundred and five other officers, and one thousand five hundred and eleven soldiers had been killed or wounded out of an engaged force of about eighteen thousand men; a proportion of slightly under

10 per cent. In the whole series of operations for the relief of Ladysmith the losses amounted to three hundred officers and more than five thousand men, out of a total engaged force of about twenty-three thousand, a proportion of rather more than 20 per cent.

Nor had this loss been inflicted in a single day's victorious battle, but was spread over twenty-five days of general action in a period of ten weeks; and until the last week no decided success had cheered the troops.

The stress of the campaign, moreover, had fallen with peculiar force on certain regiments: the Lancashire Fusiliers sustained losses of over 35 per cent., the Inniskillings of 40 per cent., and the Dublin Fusiliers of over 60 per cent.

It was very remarkable that the fighting efficiency of these regiments was in no way impaired by such serious reductions. The casualties among the officers maintained their usual glorious disproportion, six or seven regiments in the army having less than eight officers left alive and unwounded.

Among the cavalry the heaviest losses occurred in Dundonald's Brigade, the South African Light Horse, Thorneycroft's Mounted Infantry, and the squadron of Imperial Light Horse, each losing a little less than a quarter of their strength.

The ceaseless marching and fighting had worn out the clothes and boots of the army, and a certain number of the guns of the field artillery were unserviceable through constant firing.

The troops, besides clothes, needed fresh meat, an exclusive diet of tinned food being unwholesome if unduly prolonged.

Sir Redvers Buller's estimate that a week's rest was needed does not seem excessive by the light of such facts, but still one more effort might have saved much trouble later on.

On March 3 the relieving army made its triumphal entry into Ladysmith, and passing through the town camped on the plain beyond. The scene was solemn and stirring, and only the most phlegmatic were able to conceal their emotions.

Chapter XXVII: After the Siege

The streets were lined with the brave defenders, looking very smart and clean in their best clothes, but pale, thin, and wasp-waisted—their belts several holes tighter than was satisfactory.

Before the little Town Hall, the tower of which, sorely battered, yet unyielding, seemed to symbolise the spirit of the garrison, Sir George White and his staff sat on their skeleton horses. Opposite to them were drawn up the pipers of the Gordon Highlanders.

The townsfolk, hollow-eyed but jubilant, crowded the pavement and the windows of the houses. Everyone who could find a flag had hung it out, but we needed no bright colours to raise our spirits.

At eleven o'clock precisely the relieving army began to march into the town. First of all rode Sir Redvers Buller with his headquarters staff and an escort of the Royal Dragoons.

The infantry and artillery followed by brigades, but in front of all, as a special recognition of their devoted valour, marched the Dublin Fusiliers, few, but proud.

Many of the soldiers, remembering their emerald island, had fastened sprigs of green to their helmets, and all marched with a swing that was wonderful to watch. Their Colonel and their four officers looked as happy as kings are thought to be.

As the regiments passed Sir George White, the men recognised their former general, and, disdaining the rules of the service, waved their helmets and rifles, and cheered him with intense enthusiasm. Some even broke from the ranks.

Seeing this the Gordon Highlanders began to cheer the Dublins, and after that the noise of cheering was continual, every regiment as it passed giving and receiving fresh ovations. All through the morning and on into the afternoon the long stream of men and guns flowed through the streets of Ladysmith, and all marvelled to see what manner of men these were—dirty, war-worn, travel-stained, tanned, their uniforms in tatters, their boots falling to pieces, their helmets dinted and broken, but nevertheless magnificent soldiers, striding along, deep-chested and broad-shouldered, with the light of triumph in their eyes and the blood of fighting ancestors in their veins.

It was a procession of lions. And presently, when the two battalions of Devons met—both full of honours—and old friends breaking from the ranks gripped each other's hands and shouted, everyone was carried away, and I waved my feathered hat, and cheered and cheered until I could cheer no longer for joy that I had lived to see the day.

At length all was over.

The last dust-brown battalion had passed away and the roadway was again clear. Yet the ceremony was incomplete.

Before the staff could ride away, the Mayor of Ladysmith advanced and requested Sir George White to receive an address which the townspeople had prepared and were anxious to present to him.

The General dismounted from his horse, and standing on the steps of the Town Hall, in the midst of the inhabitants whom he had ruled so rigorously during the hard months of the siege, listened while their Town Clerk read their earnest grateful thanks to him for saving their town from the hands of the enemy.

The General replied briefly, complimented them on their behaviour during the siege, thanked them for the way in which they had borne their many hardships and submitted to the severe restrictions which the circumstances of war had brought on them, and rejoiced with them that they had been enabled by their devotion and by the bravery of the soldiers to keep the Queen's flag flying over Ladysmith. And then everybody cheered everybody else, and so, very tired and very happy, we all went home to our belated luncheons.

Walking through the streets it was difficult to see many signs of the bombardment. The tower of the Town Hall was smashed and chipped, several houses showed large holes in their walls, and heaps of broken brickwork lay here and there. But on the whole, the impression produced was one of surprise that the Boers had done so little damage with the sixteen thousand shells they had

Chapter XXVII: After the Siege

fired during the siege. On entering the houses, however, the effect was more apparent. In one the floor was ripped up, in another the daylight gleamed through the corrugated iron roof, and in some houses the inner walls had been completely destroyed, and only heaps of rubbish lay on the floor.

The fortifications which the troops had built, though of a very strong and effective character, were neither imposing nor conspicuous; indeed, being composed of heaps of stone they were visible only as dark lines on the rugged kopjes, and if the fame of the town were to depend on relics of the war it would not long survive the siege. But memories dwell among the tin houses and on the stony hills that will keep the name of Ladysmith fresh and full of meaning in the hearts of our countrymen.

Every trench, every mound has its own tale to tell, some of them sad, but not one shameful. Here and there, scattered through the scrub by the river or on the hills of red stones almost red hot in the sun blaze, rise the wooden crosses which mark the graves of British soldiers.

Near the iron bridge a considerable granite pyramid records the spot where Dick Cunyngham, colonel of the Gordons—what prouder office could a man hold?—fell mortally wounded on the 6th of January.

Another monument is being built on Waggon Hill to commemorate the brave men of the Imperial Light Horse who lost their lives but saved the day. The place is also marked where the noble Ava[1] fell.

But there was one who found, to use his own words, 'a strange sideway out of Ladysmith,' whose memory many English-speaking people will preserve. I do not write of Steevens[2] as a jour-

---

1 Archibald Hamilton-Temple-Blackwood, the Earl of Ava (1863–1900), served as a war correspondent and was mortally wounded at Waggon Hill during the Siege of Ladysmith.
2 George Warrington "G. W." Steevens (1869–1900), the *Daily Mail's* war correspondent who was trapped in Ladysmith. The "strange sideway out of Ladysmith" (by death by disease or starvation) was one of his quotes which appeared in the newspaper printed in the town during the siege, the Ladysmith

nalist, nor as the master of a popular and pleasing style, but as a man. I knew him, though I had met him rarely.

A dinner up the Nile, a chance meeting at an Indian junction, five days on a Mediterranean steamer, two in a Continental express, and a long Sunday at his house near Merton—it was a scanty acquaintance, but sufficient to be quite certain that in all the varied circumstances and conditions to which men are subjected Steevens rang true.

Modest yet proud, wise as well as witty, cynical but above all things sincere, he combined the characters of a charming companion and a good comrade. His conversation and his private letters sparkled like his books and articles. Original expressions, just similitudes, striking phrases, quaint or droll ideas welled in his mind without the slightest effort. He was always at his best. I have never met a man who talked so well, so easily. His wit was the genuine article—absolutely natural and spontaneous.

I once heard him describe an incident in the Nile campaign, and the description amused me so much that I was impatient to hear it again, and when a suitable occasion offered I asked him to tell his tale to the others. But he told it quite differently, and left me wondering which version was the better.

He could not repeat himself if he tried, whereas most of the renowned talkers I have met will go over the old impression with the certainty of a phonograph.

But enough of his words. He was not a soldier, but he walked into the Atbara zareba[3] with the leading company of the Seaforth Highlanders. He wrote a vivid account of the attack, but there was nothing in it about himself.

When the investment of Ladysmith shut the door on soldiers, townspeople, and War Correspondents alike, Steevens set to work to do his share of keeping up the good spirits of the garri-

---

Lyre. He died of enteric fever (typhoid) six weeks before the the relief of the town.

3 A major battle of the campaign in the Sudan to suppress the Mohammedan extremists in 1989.

Chapter XXVII: After the Siege

son and of relieving the monotony of the long days. Through the first three months of the siege no local event was awaited with more interest than the publication of a 'Ladysmith Lyre,' and the weary defenders had many a good laugh at its witticisms.

Sun, stink, and sickness harassed the beleaguered. The bombardment was perpetual, the relief always delayed; hope again and again deferred. But nothing daunted Steevens, depressed his courage, or curbed his wit.

What such a man is worth in gloomy days those may appreciate who have seen the effect of public misfortunes on a modern community. At last he was himself stricken down by enteric fever. When it seemed that the worst was over there came a fatal relapse, and the brightest Intellect yet sacrificed by this war perished; nor among all the stubborn garrison of Ladysmith was there a stouter heart or a more enduring spirit.

Dismal scenes were to be found at the hospital camp by Intombi Spruit. Here, in a town of white tents, under the shadow of Bulwana, were collected upwards of two thousand sick and wounded—a fifth of the entire garrison. They were spared the shells, but exposed to all the privations of the siege.

Officers and men, doctors and patients, presented alike a most melancholy and even ghastly appearance. Men had been wounded, had been cured of their wounds, and had died simply because there was no nourishing food to restore their strength. Others had become convalescent from fever, but had succumbed from depression and lack of medical comforts.

Hundreds required milk and brandy, but there was only water to give them. The weak died: at one time the death rate averaged fifteen a day. Nearly a tenth of the whole garrison died of disease.

A forest of crosses, marking the graves of six hundred men, sprang up behind the camp. It was a painful thing to watch the hungry patients, so haggard and worn that their friends could scarcely recognise them; and after a visit to Intombi I sat and gloated for an hour at the long train of waggons filled with all kinds of necessary comforts which crawled along the roads, and the relief of Ladysmith seemed more than ever worth the heavy price we had paid.

On the evening after Buller's victorious army had entered the town, I went to see Sir George White, and was so fortunate as to find him alone and disengaged.

The General received me in a room the windows of which gave a wide view of the defences. Bulwana, Caesar's Camp, Waggon Hill lay before us, and beneath—for the house stood on high ground—spread the blue roofs of Ladysmith.

From the conversation that followed, and from my own knowledge of events, I shall endeavour to explain so far as is at present possible the course of the campaign in Natal; and I will ask the reader to observe that only the remarks actually quoted should be attributed to the various officers.

Sir George White told me how he had reached Natal less than a week before the declaration of war. He found certain arrangements in progress to meet a swiftly approaching emergency, and he had to choose between upsetting all these plans and entirely reconstructing the scheme of defence, or of accepting what was already done as the groundwork of his operations.

Sir Penn Symons, who had been commanding in the Colony, and who was presumably best qualified to form an opinion on the military necessities, extravagantly underrated the Boer fighting power. Some of his calculations of the force necessary to hold various places seem incredible in the light of recent events.

But everyone was wrong about the Boers, and the more they knew the worse they erred. Symons laughed at the Boer military strength, and laboured to impress his opinions on Sir George White, who having Hamilton's South African experience to fall back on, however, took a much more serious view of the situation, and was particularly disturbed at the advanced position of the troops at Dundee. He wanted to withdraw them.

Symons urged the opposite considerations vehemently. He was a man of great personal force, and his manner carried people with him.

Chapter XXVII: After the Siege

'Besides,' said the General, with a kindling eye and extraordinary emphasis, 'he was a good, brave fighting man, and you know how much that is worth in war.'

In spite of Symons's confidence and enthusiasm White hated to leave troops at Dundee, and Sir Archibald Hunter, his chief of staff, agreed with him. But not to occupy a place is one thing: to abandon it after it has been occupied another.

They decided to ask Sir Walter Hely-Hutchinson what consequences would in his opinion follow a withdrawal. They visited him at ten o'clock at night, and put the question straightly.

Thus appealed to, the Governor declared that in that event 'loyalists' would be disgusted and discouraged; the results as regards the Dutch would be grave, many, if not most, would very likely rise, believing us to be afraid . . . and the effect on the natives, of whom there are some 750,000 in Natal and Zululand, might be disastrous.'

On hearing this opinion expressed by a man of the Governor's ability and local knowledge, Sir Archibald Hunter said that it was a question 'of balancing drawbacks,' and advised that the troops be retained at Glencoe.

So the matter was clinched, 'and,' said Sir George, 'when I made up my mind to let Symons stay I shared and shared alike with him in the matter of troops, giving him three batteries, a regiment, and an infantry brigade, and keeping the same myself.'

For his share in this discussion, the Governor was at one time subjected to a considerable volume of abuse in the public Press, it being charged against him that he had 'interfered' with the military arrangements.

Sir Walter Hely-Hutchinson, with whom I have had many pleasant talks, makes this invariable reply: 'I never said a word to Sir George White until I was asked. When my opinion was called for I gave it according to the best of my judgment.'

In the actual event Dundee had to be abandoned, nor was this a deliberate evacuation arising out of any regular military policy, but a swift retreat without stores or wounded, compelled by the force of the enemy.

It is, therefore, worth while considering how far the Governor's judgment had been vindicated by events. Undoubtedly loyalists throughout the Colony were disgusted, and that they were not discouraged was mainly due to the fact that with the Anglo-Saxon peoples anger at the injury usually overcomes dismay.

The effect on the Dutch was grave, but was considerably modified by the electrical influence of the victory of Elandslaagte, and the spectacle of Boer prisoners marching southward.

The whole of the Klip River country, however, rose, and many prominent Natal Dutch farmers joined the enemy.

The loyalty of the natives alone exceeded the Governor's anticipations, and their belief in the British power and preference for British rule was found to stand more knocking about than those best able to judge expected.

We have reaped a rich reward in this dark season for having consistently pursued a kindly and humane policy towards the Bantu races; and the Boers have paid a heavy penalty for their cruelty and harshness.

On the subject of holding Ladysmith Sir George White was quite clear. 'I never wanted to abandon Ladysmith; I considered it a place of primary importance to hold. It was on Ladysmith that both Republics concentrated their first efforts. Here, where the railways join, the armies of the Free State and the Transvaal were to unite, and the capture of the town was to seal their union.'

It is now certain that Ladysmith was an essential to the carefully thought out Boer plan of campaign. To make quite sure of victory they directed twenty-five thousand of their best men on it under the Commandant-General himself.

Flushed with the spirit of invasion, they scarcely reckoned on a fortnight's resistance; nor in their wildest nightmares did they conceive a four months' siege terminating in the furious inroad of a relieving army.

Chapter XXVII: After the Siege

Exasperated at unexpected opposition—for they underrated us even more than we underrated them—they sacrificed around Ladysmith their chances of taking Pietermaritzburg and raiding all Natal; and it is moreover incontestable that in their resolve to take the town, on which they had set their hearts, they were provoked into close fighting with Sir Redvers Buller's army, and even to make an actual assault on the defences of Ladysmith, and so suffered far heavier losses than could otherwise have been inflicted on so elusive an enemy in such broken country.

'Besides,' said the General, 'I had no choice in the matter. I did not want to leave Ladysmith, but even if I had wanted, it would have been impossible.'

He then explained how not only the moral value, the political significance of Ladysmith, and the great magazines accumulated there rendered it desirable to hold the town, but that the shortness of time, the necessity of evacuating the civil population, and of helping in the Dundee garrison, made its retention actually obligatory.

Passing to the actual siege of the town, Sir George White said that he had decided to make an active defence in order to keep the enemy's attention fixed on his force, and so prevent them from invading South Natal before the reinforcements could arrive.

With that object he had fought the action of October 30, which had turned out so disastrously. After that he fell back on his entrenchments, and the blockade began.

'The experience we had gained of the long-range guns possessed by the enemy,' said Sir George, 'made it necessary for me to occupy a very large area of ground, and I had to extend my lines accordingly. My lines are now nearly fourteen miles in circumference. If I had taken up a smaller position we should have been pounded to death.'

He said that the fact that they had plenty of room alone enabled them to live, for the shell fire was thus spread over a large area, and, as it were, diluted.

Besides this the cattle were enabled to find grazing, but these extended lines were also a source of weakness. At one time on several sections of the defences the garrison could only provide two hundred men to the mile.

'That is scarcely the prescribed proportion. I would like to have occupied Bulwana, in which case we should have been quite comfortable, but I did not dare extend my lines any further. It was better to endure the bombardment than to run the risk of being stormed. Because my lines were so extended I was compelled to keep all the cavalry in Ladysmith.'

Until they began to eat instead of feed the horses, this powerful mounted force, upwards of three thousand strong, had been his mobile, almost his only reserve. Used in conjunction with an elaborate system of telephones the cavalry from their central position could powerfully reinforce any threatened section.

The value of this was proved on January 6. The General thought that the fierce assault delivered by the enemy on that day vindicated his policy in not occupying Bulwana and in keeping his cavalry within the town, on both of which points he had been much criticised.

He spoke with some bitterness of the attacks which had been made on him in the newspapers.

He had always begged that the relieving operations should not be compromised by any hurry on his account, and he said, with earnestness, 'It is not fair to charge me with all the loss of life they have involved.'

He concluded by saying, deliberately: 'I regret Nicholson's Nek; perhaps I was rash then, but it was my only chance of striking a heavy blow. I regret nothing else. It may be that I am an obstinate man to say so, but if I had the last five months to live over again I would not—with that exception—-do otherwise than I have done.'

And then I came away and thought of the cheers of the relieving troops. Never before had I heard soldiers cheer like that. There was not much doubt about the verdict of the army on Sir

Chapter XXVII: After the Siege

George White's conduct of the defence, and it is one which the nation may gracefully accept.

But I am anxious also to discuss the Ladysmith episode from Sir Redvers Buller's point of view.

This officer reached Cape Town on the very day that White was driven back on Ladysmith. His army, which would not arrive for several weeks, was calculated to be strong enough to overcome the utmost resistance the Boer Republics could offer.

To what extent he was responsible for the estimates of the number of troops necessary is not known. It is certain, however, that everyone—Ministers, generals, colonists, and intelligence officers—concurred in making a most remarkable miscalculation.

It reminds me of Jules Verne's story of the men who planned to shift the axis of the earth by the discharge of a great cannon. Everything was arranged. The calculations were exact to the most minute fraction. The world stood aghast at the impending explosion. But the men of science, whose figures were otherwise so accurate, had left out a nought, and their whole plan came to nothing.[4]

So it was with the British. Their original design of a containing division in Natal, and an invading army of three divisions in the Free State, would have been excellent if only they had written army corps instead of division.

Buller found himself confronted with an alarming and critical situation in Natal. Practically the whole force which had been deemed sufficient to protect the Colony was locked up in Ladysmith, and only a few line of communication troops stood between the enemy and the capital or even the seaport.

Plainly, therefore, strong reinforcements—at least a division—must be hurried to Natal without an hour's unnecessary delay. When these troops were subtracted from the forces in the Cape Colony all prospect of pursuing the original plan of invading the Free State was destroyed. It was evident that the war would as-

---

4 *The Purchase of the North Pole* by Jules Verne, published in 1889.

sume dimensions which no one had ever contemplated. The first thing to be done therefore was to grapple with the immediate emergencies, and await the arrival of the necessary troops to carry on the war on an altogether larger scale.

Natal was the most acute situation. But there were others scarcely less serious and critical.

The Cape Colony was quivering with rebellion. The Republican forces were everywhere advancing. Kimberley and Mafeking were isolated. A small British garrison held a dangerous position at Orange River bridge. Nearly all the other bridges had been seized or destroyed by rebels or invaders.

From every quarter came clamourings for troops. Soldiers were wanted with vital need at Stormberg, at Rosmead Junction, at Colesberg, at De Aar, but most of all they were wanted in Natal—Natal, which had been promised protection 'with the whole force of the Empire,' and which was already half overrun and the rest almost defenceless.

So the army corps, which was to have marched irresistibly to Bloemfontein and Pretoria, had to be hurled into the country—each unit as it arrived—wherever the need was greatest where all were great.

Sir Redvers Buller, thus assailed by the unforeseen and pressed on every side, had to make up his mind quickly. He looked to Natal. It was there that the fiercest fighting was in progress and that the strength and vigour of the enemy was apparently most formidable.

He had always regarded the line of the Tugela as the only defensive line which British forces would be strong enough to hold, and had recorded his opinion against placing any troops north of that river.

In spite of this warning Ladysmith had been made a great military depot, and had consequently come to be considered a place of primary importance. It was again a question of balancing drawbacks.

Chapter XXVII: After the Siege

Buller therefore telegraphed to White asking him whether he could entrench and maintain himself pending the arrival of reinforcements. White replied that he was prepared to make a prolonged defence of Ladysmith. To this proposal the General-in-chief assented, observing only 'but the line of the Tugela is very tempting.'

General Buller's plan now seems to have been briefly as follows: First, to establish a *modus vivendi* in the Cape Colony, with sufficient troops to stand strictly on the defensive; secondly, to send a strong force to Natal, and either restore the situation there, or, failing that, extricate Sir George White so that his troops would be again available for the defence of the Southern portion of the Colony; thirdly, with what was left of the army corps—no longer strong enough to invade the Free State—to relieve Kimberley; fourthly, after settling Natal to return with such troops as could be spared and formed with reinforcements from home a fresh army to carry out the original scheme of invading the Free State.

The defect in this plan was that there were not enough troops to carry it out. As we had underestimated the offensive vigour which the enemy was able to develop before the army could reach South Africa, so now we altogether miscalculated his extraordinary strength on the defensive.

But it is impossible to see what else could have been done, and at any rate no one appreciated the magnitude of the difficulties more correctly than Sir Redvers Buller. He knew Northern Natal and understood the advantages that the Boers enjoyed among its mountains and kopjes.

On one occasion he even went so far as to describe the operation he had proposed as a 'forlorn hope,' so dark and gloomy was the situation in South Africa during the first fortnight in November.

It was stated that the General was ordered by the War Office to go to Natal, and went there against his own will and judgment. This, however, was not true; and when I asked him he replied:

'It was the most difficult business of all. I knew what it meant, and that it was doubtful whether we should get through to Ladysmith. I had not the nerve to order a subordinate to do it. I was the big man. I had to go myself.'

What followed, with the exception of the battle of Colenso, our first experience of the Boer behind entrenchments, has been to some extent described in these letters.

Viewed in the light of after knowledge it does not appear that the holding of Ladysmith was an unfortunate act. The flower of the Boer army was occupied and exhausted in futile efforts to take the town and stave off the relieving forces. Four precious months were wasted by the enemy in a vain enterprise.

Fierce and bloody fighting raged for several weeks with heavy loss to both sides, but without shame to either. In the end the British were completely victorious.

Not only did their garrison endure famine, disease, and bombardment with constancy and composure and repel all assaults, but the soldiers of the relief column sustained undismayed repeated disappointments and reverses, and finally triumphed because through thick and thin they were loyal to their commander and more stubborn even than the stubborn Dutch.

In spite of, perhaps because of, some mistakes and many misfortunes the defence and relief of Ladysmith will not make a bad page in British history.

Indeed it seems to me very likely that in future times our countrymen will think that we were most fortunate to find after a prolonged peace leaders of quality and courage, who were moreover honourable gentlemen, to carry our military affairs through all kinds of difficulties to a prosperous issue; and whatever may be said of the generals it is certain that all will praise the enduring courage of the regimental officer and the private soldier.

Index

A

Acton Homes 161, 166, 172, 182
Armoured train
— derailment incident 47
— description 30

B

Baden Powell, Lord 66
Barton, General Geoffrey 140, 147, 148, 157, 219, 220, 223, 228, 232, 244, 246, 248, 249, 252
Bastion Hill 173, 174, 182, 183, 187, 188
Beit, Alfred 69
Belmont 91, 92, 99, 100, 135
Blue Krantz River 125, 219, 221
Boomplatz (Boomplaats) 77
Border Regiment 29, 36, 234, 247
Buller, General Sir Redvers Henry 1, 3, 6, 7, 13, 67, 87, 127, 128, 146, 154, 155, 157–159, 161, 171, 172, 175, 177, 196, 197, 200, 205–212, 217, 218, 220, 225, 227, 228, 231–234, 242, 243, 248, 254, 255, 265–267, 272, 275, 277, 278, 279
Bulwana Hill 37, 68, 98, 145, 225, 255, 265
Burleigh, Bennet 127
Byng, Colonel Julian 148, 158, 173, 183–185, 213

C

Cæsar's Camp 143, 262
Cape Colony 5, 14–16, 77, 96, 127, 136, 277, 278, 279
Cape Town 4, 5, 11, 12, 18, 19, 23, 28, 277
Chamberlain, Joseph 69, 78, 94, 95, 97, 129

Chieveley 31, 45, 130, 139, 140, 146, 147, 149, 157, 176, 191, 210, 212, 217, 219, 220, 228, 231
Childe, Major Charles 173, 183, 187, 188
Churchill, Lord Randolph 60
Churchill, Winston
— accompanies first British troops to relieve Ladysmith 262
— arrives in Pretoria as a prisoner of war 85
— arrives in Lourenço Marques 118
— brother wounded 215
— escapes from captivity 108
— returns in triumph to Durban 121
— reward poster 119
— taken prisoner by the Boers 55
Cingolo 212, 217, 218, 219, 220, 223, 224, 231, 246
Clery, Major General Francis 141, 143, 147, 149, 157, 201–203, 205, 210
Coke, General John 146, 147, 157, 160, 161, 176–178, 202, 219, 244
Colenso 26, 28–33, 35, 37, 40, 44, 60, 61, 125–127, 131, 139, 140, 142–144, 147, 154, 158, 171, 191, 197, 200, 210, 211, 216–218, 225, 227–230, 233, 236, 244, 245, 280
Colesberg 20, 136, 278
Colt Battery 186, 202, 212–215, 246
Courtney, Leonard Henry 15, 16

D

De Aar 18, 20, 22, 23, 278
De Souza, Louis Francisco 92
Doorn Kloof 252, 254
Drakensberg 37, 150
Dublin Fusiliers 29, 30, 36, 45, 50,

52, 88, 90, 93, 100, 126, 173, 190, 191, 216, 234, 235, 239, 256, 266, 267
Dundee 33, 75, 79, 191, 272, 273, 275
Dunottar Castle 3, 6, 13, 18, 28
Durban 13, 118, 120
Durban Light Infantry 33, 45, 47, 100

E

East London 18, 22, 23, 28, 135
Elandslaagte 11, 17, 25, 27, 45, 72, 73–75, 126, 263, 274
Estcourt 23, 26, 28–31, 34, 35, 37, 41, 44, 45, 58–60, 63, 124, 146
Expansive bullets, use of by Boers 243

F

Fort Wylie 210, 233, 244
French, General John 17, 136
Frere 45, 46, 58, 72, 121, 124, 133, 145–147, 149, 157

G

Gatacre, General William 135, 221
Glencoe 11, 12, 16, 17, 29, 36, 273
Gold mines 40, 69, 260
Gomba Valley 228
Gough, Major Hubert 134, 135, 150, 169, 213, 261, 262
Green Hill 218, 220, 225, 227, 228
Gun Hill 141, 159, 193, 217, 218, 219

H

Hamilton, Sir Ian 17, 74, 144, 263, 269, 272
Harcourt, Sir William 15, 16
Hart, Major-general Arthur 147, 157, 161, 163, 173, 190, 201, 216, 219, 220, 228, 233–235, 237, 242, 243, 244, 248
Hely-Hutchinson, Sir Walter 121, 273
Hildyard, General Henry 140, 141, 147, 157, 161, 163, 173, 174, 189, 201, 206, 207, 222, 224, 242, 244, 248
Hlangwani Hill 210, 211, 212, 218, 220, 227, 228, 230–232, 242, 244, 246, 248
Hussar Hill 210–215, 218, 219, 223, 228

I

Imperial Light Horse 27, 29, 36, 148, 149, 163, 165, 166, 170, 222, 262, 266, 269
Imperial Light Infantry 27, 176, 177, 181, 234, 235
Inniskilling Hill 233, 234, 236, 237, 240, 244, 248, 249, 251, 257

J

Jameson Raid 78, 95
Joubert, General Piet 38, 59, 60, 64, 101, 117

K

"Kaffir", explanation of term 19
Karroo 18, 19
Khama, King 14, 204
Kimberley 14, 16, 63, 66, 76, 92, 95, 99, 137, 154, 278, 279
Klip River 68, 262, 274
Komati Poort 116, 118
Kruger, President Paul 4, 38, 64, 233

L

Ladysmith 1, 4, 16, 17, 18, 20, 23, 25, 26, 28–31, 33, 35–37, 41, 42, 44, 58, 59, 63, 66, 68,

Index

71, 72, 99, 125–129, 139, 140, 142–144, 147, 149, 154, 157, 161, 171, 172, 175, 197, 198, 200, 208, 209, ff., 260, 261–264, ff.
Laing's Nek 15, 74, 80
Lockhart, Sir William 12, 45
Long Tom (155mm Creusot cannon) 37, 145, 255
Lord Roberts 5, 229
Lord Rosebery 17
Lourenço Marques 104, 116, 117, 118
Lyttelton, General Neville 147, 157, 159, 161, 172, 176, 178, 201, 202, 204–207, 210, 219, 220, 233, 235, 244

M

Mafeking 12, 14, 16, 63, 66, 94, 278
Majuba 10, 17, 77, 80, 137, 245, 247, 249, 251, 253
Maxim-Nordfelts, "pom pom" 16, 47, 52, 58, 134, 141, 174, 178, 179, 185–187, 192, 203, 204, 206, 228, 246, 252
Milner, Sir Alfred 19, 78
Modderspruit Station 264
Monte Cristo 212, 218–221, 223–231, 242, 246, 248, 249, 252
Mooi River 60
Morning Post 1, 117, 227
Mount Nelson Hotel 18

N

Naauwpoort 18
Natal Carabineers 36, 38, 140, 148, 165, 167, 222, 262
Natal Field Force 17, 29, 126, 127
Nelthorpe 65, 68
Newcastle 26, 33
Nicholson's Nek 93, 177, 276

O

Outlanders (see also "Uitlanders") 27

P

Pepworth's Hill 264
Pietermaritzburg 13, 25, 26, 28, 30, 41, 42, 44, 73, 121, 146, 275
Potgieter's Drift 157, 159

R

Railway Hill 248, 249, 250, 256
Reitz, Francis William 136
Rhodes, Cecil John 66, 69, 78, 89, 95, 96
Rietfontein 11
Royal Dragoons 147, 149, 161, 164, 267

S

Sandbach, Colonel Arthur 155, 220
Schreiner, William Philip 5, 19, 38
Slagters Nek 77
South African Light Horse 2, 134, 140, 141, 147, 155, 159, 165, 167, 173, 182, 183, 187, 190, 202, 212, 213, 215, 219, 224, 234, 239, 246, 255, 261, 266
Spearman's Hill 146, 158–161, 195, 198
Spion Kop 159, 161, 165, 172, 173, 175, 177–179, 181, 182, 191, 193, 194, 196–198, 200, 201, 216, 245, 259
Springfield 149–151, 152, 157, 160, 161, 207, 210, 219, 231
Staats Artillerie (State Artillery), Boer 58
States Model Schools 86, 87, 99, 102, 105, 106, 110, 116
Stormberg 20–23, 104, 136, 221, 278
Symons, Sir Penn 9, 10, 79, 272, 273

283

T

Talana Hill 79, 80, 93
Thorneycroft, Colonel Alexander 140, 148, 165, 167, 176, 177, 180–182, 187, 194, 202, 212, 213, 215, 257, 266
Times of Natal 26
Trichardt's Drift 159, 161–165, 167, 169, 171, 196, 200, 201, 211
Tugela River 33, 42, 65, 126, 128–130, 146, 149–152, 154, 155, 157, 158, 161, 171, 172, 175, 196, 206, 208, 210, 217, 218, 228, 229, 231, 233, 242, 246, 278, 279
Tugela River 42, 128

U

Uitlanders 18, 22, 78

V

Venter's Spruit 157, 171, 182, 196
Volksrust 80, 82, 83
Volksstem newspaper 91, 104, 117
Vryburg 14

W

Warren, Sir Charles 145–147, 157, 161, 162, 165, 172, 173, 176, 179, 180, 193, 194, 196, 210, 219, 228, 253
Weenen 44
White, Sir George 4, 17, 28, 35, 126, 130, 140, 143, 172, 254, 262, 264–268, 272–275, 277, 279
Woodgate, General Edward 146, 147, 157, 161, 164, 173, 176, 177, 194, 201
Wynne, General Sir Arthur 201, 202, 203, 219, 220, 231

Y

Yule, Brigadier-General James 16

Z

Zuid-Afrikaansche Republiek Politie" (South African Republic Police), "ZARP" 85

CPSIA information can be obtained
at www.ICGtesting.com
Printed in the USA
BVHW030458180722
642303BV00008BA/675